The Economics of
Public Issues

D0958373

The Pearson Series in Economics

Abel/Bernanke/Croushore
Macroeconomics*
Bade/Parkin
Foundations of Economics
Berck/Helfand
The Economics of the Environment
Bierman/Fernandez
Game Theory with Economic Applications
Blanchard
Macroeconomics
Blau/Ferber/Winkler
The Economics of Women, Men and Work
Boardman/Greenberg/Vining/Weimer
Cost–Benefit Analysis
Boyer
Principles of Transportation Economics
Branson
Macroeconomic Theory and Policy
Brock/Adams
The Structure of American Industry
Bruce
Public Finance and the American Economy
Carlton/Perloff
Modern Industrial Organization
Case/Fair/Oster
Principles of Economics
Caves/Frankel/Jones
World Trade and Payments: An Introduction
Chapman
Environmental Economics: Theory, Application, and Policy
Cooter/Ulen
Law & Economics
Downs
An Economic Theory of Democracy

Ehrenberg/Smith
Modern Labor Economics
Ekelund/Ressler/Tollison
Economics
Farnham
Economics for Managers
Folland/Goodman/Stano
The Economics of Health and Health Care
Fort
Sports Economics
Froyen
Macroeconomics
Fusfeld
The Age of the Economist
Gerber
International Economics
Gordon
Macroeconomics
Greene
Econometric Analysis
Gregory
Essentials of Economics
Gregory/Stuart
Russian and Soviet Economic Performance and Structure
Hartwick/Olewiler
The Economics of Natural Resource Use
Heilbroner/Milberg
The Making of the Economic Society
Heyne/Boettke/Prychitko
The Economic Way of Thinking
Hoffman/Averett
Women and the Economy: Family, Work, and Pay
Holt
Markets, Games and Strategic Behavior
Hubbard/O'Brien
Economics Money and Banking

*denotes MyEconLab titles. Log onto **www.myeconlab.com** to learn more.

Silberberg
Principles of Microeconomics
Stock/Watson
Introduction to Econometrics
Introduction to Econometrics, Brief Edition
Studenmund
Using Econometrics: A Practical Guide
Tietenberg/Lewis
Environmental and Natural Resource Economics

Environmental Economics and Policy
Todaro/Smith
Economic Development
Waldman
Microeconomics
Waldman/Jensen
Industrial Organization: Theory and Practice
Weil
Economic Growth
Williamson
Macroeconomics

The Economics of
Public Issues

SEVENTEENTH EDITION

Roger LeRoy Miller
Research Professor of Economics
University of Texas-Arlington

Daniel K. Benjamin
Clemson University, South Carolina and
PERC, Bozeman, Montana

Douglass C. North
Washington University
St. Louis, Missouri

Boston Columbus Indianapolis New York San Francisco Upper Saddle River
Amsterdam Cape Town Dubai London Madrid Milan Munich Paris Montreal Toronto
Delhi Mexico City Sao Paulo Sydney Hong Kong Seoul Singapore Taipei Tokyo

Editorial Director: Sally Yagan
Editor in Chief: Donna Battista
Acquisitions Editor: Noel Kamm Seibert
Editorial Project Manager: Carolyn Terbush
Managing Editor: Nancy H. Fenton
Senior Production Project Manager: Kathryn Dinovo
Project Manager: Pat Brown
Operations Specialist: Pat Brown
Executive Marketing Manager: Lori DeShazo
Marketing Assistant: Kim Lovato
Permissions Project Manager: Michael Joyce

Senior Manufacturing Buyer: Carol Melville
Creative Art Director: Jayne Conte
Manager, Visual Research and Permissions: Karen Sanatar
Cover Designer: Jon Boylan
Text Designer: Central Publishing
Production Coordination: Pat Brown
Full Service Project Management: Element LLC
Composition: Central Publishing
Printer/Binder: Interior, Edwards Brothers; Cover, Lehigh-Phoenix Color/Hagerstown

Credits and acknowledgments borrowed from other sources and reproduced, with permission, in this textbook appear on appropriate page within the text.

Copyright © 2012, 2010, 2008, 2006, 2004 Pearson Education, Inc. All rights reserved. Printed in the United States of America. This publication is protected by Copyright and permission should be obtained from the publisher prior to any prohibited reproduction, storage in a retrieval system, or transmission in any form or by any means, electronic, mechanical, photocopying, recording, or likewise. To obtain permission(s) to use material from this work, please submit a written request to Pearson Education, Inc., Permissions Department, One Lake Street, Upper Saddle River, New Jersey 07458 or you may fax your request to 201-236-3290.

Many of the designations by manufacturers and seller to distinguish their products are claimed as trademarks. Where those designations appear in this book, and the publisher was aware of a trademark claim, the designations have been printed in initial caps or all caps.

Library of Congress Cataloging-in-Publication Data
Miller, Roger LeRoy.
  The economics of public issues / Roger LeRoy Miller, Daniel K. Benjamin,
Douglass C. North. — 17th ed.
    p. cm.
  Includes bibliographical references and index.
  ISBN-13: 978-0-13-802113-9 (pbk. : alk. paper)
  ISBN-10: 0-13-802113-9 (alk. paper)
  1. Economics. 2. Industrial policy. 3. Economic policy. I. Benjamin, Daniel K.
II. North, Douglass Cecil. III. Title.
  HB171.M544 2012
  330.973--dc22

                                                        2011011874

10 9 8 7 6 5 4 3 2 1

ISBN-10: 0-13-802113-9
ISBN-13: 978-0-13-802113-9

To Marilyn and Tullio,

Thanks for your support and your advice.

—R.L.M.

To my students over the years,

With gratitude for all they have taught me.

—D.K.B.

Brief Contents

SUGGESTIONS FOR USE

At the request of our readers, we include the following table to help you incorporate the chapters of this book into your syllabus. Depending on the breadth of your course, you may also want to consult the companion paperback, *The Economics of Macro Issues,* 5th edition, which features macroeconomic topics and a similar table in its preface.

Economics Topics	Recommended Chapters in The Economics of Public Issues, 17th Edition
Introduction to Economics	6, 7, 8, 22
Opportunity Costs and Scarcity	1, 2, 8, 19, 24, 25
Demand and Supply	6, 7, 8
Demand and Supply Applications	7, 8, 9, 10, 12, 27
The Public Sector and Public Choice	1, 2, 4, 6, 7, 9, 12, 13, 18, 19, 20, 22 25
Taxes, Transfers, and Public Spending	9, 19, 20, 22, 23, 25, 26
Consumer Behavior	3, 4, 5, 6, 7, 8, 9, 10, 12, 14, 17, 19 20
Elasticity of Demand and Supply	2, 3, 5, 6, 8, 11, 16, 17, 24
Rents, Profits, and the Financial Environment of Business	5, 10, 15, 16, 20, 21, 26, 28
Firm Production and Cost	1, 2, 4, 11, 12, 14, 16, 22, 25, 26, 29
Perfect Competition	22
Monopoly	15, 16, 18
Monopolistic Competition	2, 17
Oligopoly	4, 16, 18
Regulation and Antitrust	1, 4, 18
Unions and the Labor Market	11, 12, 13, 14, 16
Income, Poverty, and Health Care	5, 10, 14, 19, 23, 30
Environmental Economics	2, 8, 24, 25, 26, 27
International Trade	5, 28, 29, 30
International Finance	28, 30

PREFACE

This book is about some issues of our times. Several of these issues are usually thought of as being inherently noneconomic. Others provide classic illustrations of the core of economic science. Many are controversial and thus are likely to evoke noneconomic reactions to what we have to say. In our view, however, the one feature that ties all of the issues together is that they illustrate the power of economics in explaining the world around us. And, we might add, we hope all of them illustrate that economics can be entertaining as well as informative.

NEW TO THIS EDITION

Over the years, we have sought to select issues for this book that—in addition to the attributes noted above—possess a sense of immediacy. We hope you will find the issues we have added for this edition meet this criterion. The new issues include the following:

- The Economics of Oil Spills (why they happen and who should pay)
- Supersize It (the economics of obesity)
- The Underground World (how informal labor markets are raising wealth around the globe)
- Patent Trolls and Seed Monopolies (do patents make us better off?)
- Health Care Reform (big bucks make bad policy)
- The Pension Crisis (our promises are coming home to roost)
- Save that Species (saving a species is easy—with a little bit of economics)

MORE END-OF-CHAPTER QUESTIONS AND ENHANCED LAYOUT

Many users have asked for more discussion questions at the end of chapters. This edition expands the number of such questions by 50 percent, so there are now six questions for each chapter. In addition, the range of difficulty of the questions has been expanded, including more questions about the basics of the material.

The layout of each chapter has been changed as well. Specifically, each chapter now has multiple section headings. This improves readability and it also helps students with their comprehension of the materials by focusing them immediately on the core organizing principles of the chapter.

GLOSSARY AND SELECTED READINGS AND WEB LINKS

This edition also continues two features that seem universally appreciated by students and faculty: a Glossary and a list of Selected Readings, both at the back of the book. The glossary terms are set in bold face in the text the first time they are used, and the terms are arranged alphabetically in the glossary, with a succinct definition for each. The selected readings only scratch the surface of the rich literature we have drawn upon in preparing this book, but the interested reader will be able to use them as a springboard for as much research as she or he wishes to undertake.

A COMPLETE REVISION IN SEVEN PARTS

All of the other chapters in this edition have been partially or completely rewritten, and every chapter is, of course, as up-to-date as we can make it. What you will consistently find is a straightforward application of economic principles as they are taught in virtually all courses in economics, public policy, and the social sciences. This book can be understood by those who have taken a course in economics, are taking a course in economics, or have never taken a course in economics: We have made it self-contained, as well as accessible to a wide range of students.

The chapters are organized into seven parts. Part One examines the foundations of all economic analysis, including the concepts of scarcity, trade-offs, opportunity cost, marginal analysis, and the like. In a sense, the five chapters in this introductory part set the stage for the remaining twenty-five chapters. The second through sixth parts of the book cover the topics such as demand and supply, labor markets, imperfect competition, environmental issues, and the impact of government policies—that are integral to virtually every course in which economics plays a role. At the end of the book, Part Seven examines global affairs, because these matters are an essential part of the public issues of today.

Every part has a several-page introduction that prepares the reader for the material that is included in the following chapters. These part openers summarize and tie together the relevant issues, thus serving as launch pads for the analyses that follow. We hope you will have your students read these part openers before they embark on any of the chapters they precede.

Instructor's Manual

Every instructor will want to access the *Instructor's Manual* that accompanies *The Economics of Public Issues*. It is available online to all adopters of the book. In writing this manual we have tried to incorporate the very best of the teaching aids that we use when we teach from *The Economics of Public Issues*. For each chapter, the features of this manual are:

- A synopsis that cuts to the core of the economic issues involved in the chapter.
- A concise exposition of the "behind-the-scenes" economic foundations of the text discussion. In almost all cases, this exposition is supplemented with one or more diagrams that we have found to be particularly useful as teaching tools.
- Answers to the Discussion Questions posed at the end of the chapter that further develop the basis economic analysis of the chapter, and almost always suggest new avenues of discussion.

The Future

The world of public issues continues to evolve. By the time you read this preface, we will be working on the next edition. If you have any particular subjects you would like included in the future, let us know by writing us in care of Pearson.

Special Thanks and Acknowledgements

Several chapters in this edition draw on the "Tangents" column that Benjamin writes for *PERC Reports*. We are grateful to the Property and Environment Research Center (PERC) for permission to use that material. Special thanks go to Cyril Morong of San Antonio College for his unstinting willingness to propose new topics and new readings for existing topics. In addition, literally dozens of kind users of the last edition of this book, as well as several extremely diligent and thoughtful reviewers, offered suggestions for the current edition. They include:

Thomas Birch, University of New Hampshire-Manchester
Kent M. Ford, SUNY Onondaga Community College

Colleen P. Kirk, Mercy College
Ronnie Liggett, University of Texas-Arlington
Mehrdad Madresehee, Lycoming College
John McArthur, Wofford College
Cyril Morong, San Antonio College
Randall Russell, Yavapai College
Dominick Sampogna, Mercy College
Kristin Stowe, Wingate University

Scarcity precluded us from adopting all of their recommendations, but we believe they will be able to identify the impact they each had on this edition. To them and to our users who wrote to us we offer our sincere thanks and hope that the end result was worthy of their time and concern. We also thank Noel Seibert and Carolyn Terbush for shepherding the project, Sue Jasin for her expert manuscript preparation, and Robbie Benjamin, whose editorial skills once again have improved the final product. All errors remain, of course, solely our own.

R.L.M.
D.K.B.
D.C.N.

PART ONE

The Foundations of Economic Analysis

Introduction

Our world is one of **scarcity;** we want more than we have. The reason is simple. Although we live in a world of limited **resources,** we have unlimited wants. This does not mean we all live and breathe solely to drive the fastest cars or wear the latest clothes. It means that we all want the right to make decisions about how resources are used—even if what we want to do with those resources is to feed starving children in developing nations.

Given the existence of scarcity, we must make choices; we cannot have more of everything, so to get more of some things, we must give up other things. Economists express this simple idea by saying that we face **trade-offs.** For example, a student who wants higher grades generally must devote more time to studying and less time to, say, going to the movies; the trade-off in this instance is between grades and entertainment.

DEATH BY BUREAUCRAT

The concept of a trade-off is one of the (surprisingly few) basic principles you must grasp to understand the economics of public issues. We illustrate the simplicity of these principles with Chapter 1, which examines a behind-the-scenes trade-off made every day on our behalf by the U.S. Food and Drug Administration (FDA). This federal government agency is charged with ensuring that new prescription medicines are both safe and effective. In carrying out its duties, the FDA requires pharmaceutical companies to subject proposed new drugs to extensive testing. Additional testing improves the chances that a drug will be both safe and effective, but it also slows the approval of new drugs, thus depriving some individuals of the ability to use the drugs to treat their illnesses.

1

The drug approval process undoubtedly reduces pain and suffering for some people and even saves the lives of others because it lowers the chances that an unsafe or ineffective drug will reach the market. Yet because the process also slows the rate at which drugs reach the market (and may even prevent some safe and effective drugs from ever being introduced), the pain and suffering of other individuals are increased. Indeed, some people die as a result. This, then, is the terrible trade-off we face in Chapter 1: Who shall live and who shall die?

THE ECONOMICS OF OIL SPILLS

Trade-offs are again the issue in Chapter 2. For example, the BP oil company traded off safety against speed and ended up dumping about 600,000 metric tons of crude oil into the Gulf of Mexico—by far the worst oil spill in American history. It looks like the spill will cost BP something like $36 billion, so although BP thought the decisions it made to speed up the drilling process were going to raise its profits, they turned out to nearly destroy the company. And there will be an important policy trade-off that must be faced. Some people have argued that the BP spill instructs us that we should stop drilling in the Gulf altogether. But doing this would necessitate that we incur additional costs and environmental hazards elsewhere. Indeed, the greatest messages of the BP spill are twofold: Nothing in life is free, and trade-offs simply cannot be avoided.

SUPERSIZE IT

In a world of scarcity, incentives play a key role in understanding behavior. In Chapter 3, we see that even subtle changes in incentives can have profound effects. Obesity is rising in the United States, chiefly as a result of three separate economic forces at work. First, wages paid in sedentary occupations have risen relative to those in physically demanding jobs, inducing people to spend more of their time exercising their brains at work, rather than their muscles. An even more important factor, however, is that the entry of women into the workforce has increased the demand for prepackaged prepared foods—which have been gladly supplied by producers. This has sharply reduced the **full cost** of eating (especially the full cost of snacks), and so increased the amount of food consumed. Finally, a variety of public policy changes have raised the full cost of consuming cigarettes over the last twenty years or so. This in turn has induced people to substitute from cigarettes to food. On balance, the health effects of this last development likely have been positive.

Nevertheless, because expanding waistlines today will almost surely generate adverse health effects in the future, we can expect obesity to become a widely debated public issue in the years to come.

FLYING THE FRIENDLY SKIES

All public issues compel us to face the question of how to make the best choices. Economists argue that doing so requires the use of what we call **marginal analysis.** The term *marginal* in this context means "incremental" or "additional." All choices involve costs and benefits—we give up something for anything that we get. As we engage in more of any activity (eating, studying, or sleeping, for example), the **marginal benefits** of that activity eventually decline: The *additional* benefits associated with an *additional* unit of the activity get lower. In contrast, the **marginal costs** of an activity eventually rise as we engage in more and more of it. The best choices are made when we equate the marginal benefits and marginal costs of activity; that is, we try to determine whether engaging in any more of a given activity would produce additional costs that exceed the additional benefits.

In Chapter 4 we apply the principles of marginal analysis to the issue of airline safety. How safe is it to travel at 600 miles per hour seven miles above the ground? How safe *should* it be? The answers to these and other questions can be explored using marginal analysis. One of the conclusions we reach is that *perfect* safety is simply not in the cards. Every time you step into an airplane (or even the street), there is some risk that your journey will end unhappily. As disconcerting as this might sound at first, we think you will find after reading this chapter that once the costs and benefits are taken into account, you would have it no other way.

THE MYSTERY OF WEALTH

Every choice we make entails a **cost:** In a world of scarcity, something must be given up to obtain anything of value. Costs, combined with the benefits of our choices, comprise the **incentives** that ultimately inform and guide our decisions. That these decisions—and thus the incentives— have real and lasting consequences is nowhere more evident than in Chapter 5. Here we seek to answer a simple but profound question: Why are the citizens of some nations rich while the inhabitants of others are poor? Your initial answer might be "because of differences in the **natural resource endowments** of the nations." It is true that ample endowments of energy, timber, and fertile land all help raise wealth. But it turns out that natural resources are only a very small part of the answer.

Far more important in determining the wealth of the citizenry are the fundamental political and legal **institutions** of a nation. Institutions such as political stability, secure private property rights, and legal systems based on the **rule of law** create the incentives that encourage people to make long-term investments in improving land and in all forms of **physical** and **human capital.** These investments raise the **capital stock,** which in turn provides for more growth long into the future. And the cumulative effects of this growth over time eventually yield much higher standards of living: They make us rich. Thus, incentives, comprising both costs and benefits, turn out to be an integral component of the foundations of economic analysis, as well as the foundations of society.

CHAPTER 1

Death by Bureaucrat

How would you rather die? From a lethal reaction to a drug prescribed by your doctor? Or because your doctor failed to prescribe a drug that would have saved your life? If this choice sounds like one you would rather not make, consider this: Employees of the Food and Drug Administration (FDA) make that decision on behalf of millions of Americans many times each year. More precisely, FDA bureaucrats decide whether or not new medicines (prescription drugs) should be allowed to go on sale in the United States. If the FDA rules against a drug, physicians in America may not legally prescribe it, even if thousands of lives are being saved by the drug each year in other countries.

A Brief History of The FDA

The FDA's authority to make such decisions dates back to the passage of the Food and Drug Safety Act of 1906. That law required that medicines be correctly labeled as to their contents and that they not contain any substances harmful to the health of consumers. Due to this legislation, Dr. Hostatter's Stomach Bitters and Kickapoo Indian Sagwa, along with numerous rum-laden concoctions, cocaine-based potions, and supposed anticancer remedies, disappeared from druggists' shelves. The law was expanded in 1938 with the passage of the Food, Drug, and Cosmetic Act, which forced manufacturers to demonstrate the safety of new drugs before being allowed to offer them for sale. (This law was prompted by the deaths of 107 people who had taken Elixir Sulfanilamide, an antibiotic that contained poisonous diethylene glycol, a chemical cousin of antifreeze.)

The next step in U.S. drug regulation came after a rash of severe birth defects among infants whose mothers during pregnancy had taken a sleep aid known as thalidomide. When these birth defects first became apparent, the drug was already widely used in Europe and Canada, and the FDA was nearing approval for its use in America. In fact, about 2.5 million thalidomide tablets were already in the hands of U.S. physicians as samples. The FDA ordered all of the samples destroyed and prohibited the sale of the drug here. This incident led to the 1962 Kefauver-Harris Amendments to the 1938 Food, Drug, and Cosmetic Act, radically altering the drug-approval process in the United States.

THE IMPACT OF THE 1962 AMENDMENTS

Prior to the 1962 amendments, the FDA was expected to approve a new drug application within 180 days unless the application failed to show that the drug was safe. The 1962 amendments added a "proof of efficacy" requirement and also removed the time constraint on the FDA. The FDA has free rein to determine how much and what type of evidence it will demand before approving a drug for sale and thus may take as long as it pleases before either granting or refusing approval.

The 1962 amendments drastically increased the costs of introducing a new drug and markedly slowed the approval process. Prior to 1962, for example, the average time between filing and approval of a new drug application was seven months; by 1967, it was thirty months; and by the late 1970s, it had risen to eight to ten *years*. The protracted approval process involves costly testing by the drug companies—$800 million or more for each new drug—and delays the receipt of any potential revenue from new drugs. Because this reduced the expected profitability of new drugs, fewer of them have been brought onto the market.

Debate continues over how much FDA regulation is needed to ensure that drugs are both safe and efficacious, but there is little doubt that the 1962 amendments have resulted in a U.S. "drug lag." On average, drugs take far longer to reach the market in the United States than they do in Europe. Admittedly, it takes time to ensure that patients benefit from, rather than are harmed by, new drugs, but regulation-induced drug lag can itself be life-threatening. Dr. George Hitchings, a winner of the Nobel Prize in Medicine, has estimated that the five-year lag in introducing Septra (an antibiotic) to the United States killed 80,000 people in this country. Similarly, the introduction of a class of drugs called beta blockers (used to treat heart attack victims and people with high blood pressure) was delayed nearly a decade in

America relative to Europe. According to several researchers, the lag in the FDA approval of these drugs cost the lives of at least 250,000 Americans.

TERRIBLE TRADE-OFF

In effect, the law requires FDA bureaucrats to make what is truly a terrible trade-off. Lives are saved because unsafe or ineffective drugs are kept off the market, but the regulatory process delays (or even prevents) the introduction of some safe and efficacious drugs, thereby costing lives. Let us now take a more systematic look at this trade-off.

Every time a new drug is introduced, there is a chance that it should not have been—either because it has adverse side effects that outweigh the therapeutic benefits (it is not safe) or because it really does little to help the individuals who take it (it is not effective). When such a drug is introduced, we say that a **Type I error** has been committed. Since 1962, the incidence of Type I error—the thalidomide possibility—has been reduced by the added testing required by the FDA. But other people have been the victims of what is called **Type II error.** Their cost is the pain, suffering, and death that occur because the 1962 amendments have prevented or delayed the introduction of safe, efficacious drugs. Type II error—as with Septra or beta blockers—occurs when a drug *should* be introduced but is held back by FDA regulation.

Over the past twenty or thirty years, outcries over the harm caused by the drug lag have, in some cases, induced the agency to shorten the testing period when the costs of Type I error are small relative to the damages due to Type II error—as in the case of terminally ill patients. One famous example involved azidothymidine (AZT), which emerged as a possible treatment for AIDS. Gay men, among whom AIDS was most prevalent at the time, took the lead in pressuring the FDA to approve the drug quickly, and the FDA responded accordingly, giving it the OK after only eighteen months of testing. Similarly, Taxol, an important new drug used to treat breast cancer, received expedited review by the FDA, in this case because of pressure applied by women in whose families there was a history of breast cancer. The FDA now has a formal program in which it seeks to expedite testing for drugs that seem to offer great promise for alleviating death or suffering. Nevertheless, although the average approval time for new drugs has shortened considerably, it still takes more than ten times as long for a new drug to be approved as it did before the 1962 amendments.

LESSONS FROM THE FDA STORY

What can we learn from the FDA regulation of new drugs that will guide us in thinking about other public issues of our time? There are several key principles:

1. *There is no free lunch.* Every choice, and thus every policy, entails a cost—something must be given up. In a world of **scarcity,** we cannot have more of everything; so to get more of some things, we must give up other things. Although FDA review of drugs saves lives by preventing the introduction of unsafe or ineffective drugs, the cost is billions of dollars of added expenses, plus delayed availability of safe and efficacious drugs, resulting in the deaths of hundreds of thousands of people.

2. *The cost of an action is the alternative that is sacrificed.* Economists often express costs (and benefits) in terms of dollars because this is a simple means of accounting for and measuring them. But that doesn't mean that costs have to be monetary, nor does it mean that economics is incapable of analyzing costs and benefits that are quite human. The costs that led to the 1938 and 1962 amendments were the very visible deaths caused by sulfanilamide and the terrible birth defects due to thalidomide. Subsequent revisions to the FDA process for reviewing drugs, as with AZT and Taxol, have been in response to the adverse effects caused by the regulation-induced drug lag.

3. *The relevant costs and benefits are the marginal (incremental) ones.* The relevant question is not whether safety is good or bad; it is instead how much safety we want—which can only be answered by looking at the added (marginal) benefits of more safety compared to the added (marginal) costs. One possible response to the sulfanilamide poisonings or thalidomide was to have outlawed new drugs altogether. That would guarantee that no more people would be harmed by new drugs. But surely this "solution" would not be sensible, because the marginal cost (due to higher Type II errors) would exceed the marginal benefit (caused by reduced Type I errors).

4. *People respond to incentives.* And this is true whether we are talking about consumers, suppliers, or government bureaucrats. Here the incentive to amend the law in 1938 and 1962 was the very visible death and disfigurement of individuals. The eventual FDA decision to speed up the review process was prompted by intense lobbying by individuals who believed (correctly, as it turned out) that they might be benefited by drugs not yet approved.

5. *Things aren't always as they seem.* Many analyses of the effects of government policies take an approach that doesn't fully recognize the actions that people would otherwise have taken. Thus, official pronouncements about the effects of policies routinely misrepresent their impact—not because there is necessarily any attempt to deceive but because it is often difficult to know what would have happened otherwise. Pharmaceutical manufacturers, for example, have strong incentives to avoid introducing drugs that are unsafe or ineffective because the companies are subject to loss of reputation and to lawsuits. For similar reasons, physicians have strong incentives to avoid prescribing such drugs for their patients. Even without FDA regulation, there would thus be extensive testing of new drugs before their introduction. Hence, it is incorrect to ascribe the generally safe and effective nature of modern drugs entirely to FDA protection. The flip side, however, is that the drug development process is inherently long, complicated, and costly. Even without FDA oversight, some people would die waiting for new drugs because self-interested manufacturers would insist on some testing and cautious physicians would proceed slowly in prescribing new drugs.

The people who work at the FDA (and members of Congress) are publicly castigated when they "allow" a Type I error to occur—especially when it is a drug that kills people. Thus, FDA bureaucrats have a strong incentive to avoid such errors. But when testing delays cause a Type II error, as with Septra, it is almost impossible to point to specific people who died because the drug was delayed. As a result, officials at the FDA are rarely attacked directly for such delays. Because the costs of Type II errors are much more difficult to discern than the costs of Type I errors, many observers believe that there is an inherent bias at the FDA in favor of being "safe rather than sorry"—in other words, excessive testing.

6. *Policies always have unintended consequences, and as a result, their net benefits are almost always less than anticipated.* In the case of government regulations, balancing incremental costs and benefits (see principle 3) fails to make good headlines. Instead, what gets politicians reelected and regulators promoted are *absolute* notions such as safety (and motherhood and apple pie). Thus, if a little safety is good, more must be better, so why not simply mandate that drug testing "guarantee" that everyone is free of risk from dangerous drugs? Eventually, the reality of principle 3 sinks in, but in this case not before the drug lag had killed many people.

As is often true with important public issues, our story has one more interesting twist. Thalidomide is back on the market. In 1998, it was approved by the FDA for use in treating Hansen's disease (leprosy), and in 2006, the FDA gave physicians the OK to use it in treating bone marrow cancer. In each instance, there are strong protections to prevent pregnant women from taking the drug. And so perhaps the very drug that brought us the deadly drug lag will turn out to be a lifesaver for a new generation of patients.

DISCUSSION QUESTIONS

1. Why don't individuals simply force the FDA to do what is best for consumers of prescription drugs?

2. Why don't the employees at the FDA accurately balance the marginal benefits to drug consumers against the marginal costs to those consumers?

3. Does the structure of the drug industry have any bearing on the types of errors that drug firms are likely to make? That is, would a drug industry made up of numerous highly competitive firms be more or less likely to introduce unsafe drugs than an industry consisting of a few large firms?

4. How could the incentives facing the people at the FDA be changed to reduce the incidence of Type II errors? (*Hint:* Is it possible to compare the FDA approval process with the drug-approval process in other nations?)

5. What would be the advantages and disadvantages of a regulatory system in which, rather than having the FDA permit or prohibit new drugs, the FDA merely published its opinions about the safety and efficacy of drugs and then allowed physicians to make their own decisions about whether or not to prescribe the drugs for their patients?

6. Suppose, for simplicity, that Type I and Type II errors resulted in deaths only. Keeping in mind that too little caution produces Type I errors and too much caution produces Type II errors, what would be the best mix of Type I and Type II errors?

CHAPTER 2

The Economics of Oil Spills

At 11:00 A.M. on April 20, 2010, contractors working on British Petroleum's (BP) Deepwater Horizon oil platform met with the platform's BP managers. The well being drilled by the platform was situated in water 5,000 feet deep, some 41 miles off the Louisiana coast line in the Gulf of Mexico. At the time of the meeting, the well had reached a depth of more than 13,000 feet below the sea floor. BP wanted to finish the work on the well because it was much delayed and millions of dollars over budget. The contractors were not happy with some of the cost-saving measures that BP hoped would speed the process, but BP management prevailed at the meeting. By 5:00 P.M. that day, at least some workers on the rig knew that gas was leaking into the well. Gas and oil together are a deadly combination.

Later than evening, in preparation for final work on the project, BP decided to remove from the well the drilling mud used to hold back the high-pressure mixture of gas and oil under the sea floor. This was a critical and deadly decision. At 9:45 P.M., enough mud had been removed that what remained, together with sea water, oil, and natural gas, began shooting out of the oil rig like water from a fire hose. Workers raced to tame the well. When they hit the emergency button to activate a safety device and detach the rig from the well, it was too late. Escaping gas exploded. Eleven workers lost their lives.

The worst oil spill in American history had begun.

WHO IS TO BLAME?

Of course, no one wanted to accept responsibility for the Deepwater Horizon explosion and oil spill. BP blamed its contractors for the disaster. The contractors blamed each other and BP management. Many of those outside and inside government blamed the "cozy relationship" that the federal government's Minerals Management Service had with the oil industry. Finally, others blamed our continuing reliance on fossil fuels to power our cars and our factories.

According to some experts, BP cut too many corners to make up for lost time and cost overruns. For example, the company shortened a procedure designed to detect gas in the well and remove it before it becomes a problem. BP did not quality test the cement around the pipe, cement that serves as another buffer against gas. And BP used a single pipe drilling method, which is less costly than the double pipe method, but also riskier. Moreover, the BP manager who oversaw the final well tests had almost no experience in deepwater drilling.

Of course, spokespersons for BP claimed that it did not cut corners and that both safety and operational reliability were priorities. Undoubtedly, the "blame game" will continue, particularly as the many lawsuits against BP and its contractors weave their way through the federal courts.

WHO SHOULD PAY?

Those whose livelihoods depend on tourism and fishing sustained billions of dollars of damages as a result of the BP oil spill. Beaches were closed on the Gulf Coast, as were large inshore and offshore fishing areas. Unlike the response to the 2008 financial crisis, no one argued that federal taxpayers should compensate those who suffered economic (and psychological) damages because of the incident. Instead, BP quickly agreed when President Obama suggested it create a $20 billion pool of funds that would be doled out to those who had been harmed. In principle, this pool will compensate most of those harmed by the spill for most of the damages they sustained.

Overall, there is little doubt that BP shareholders have paid a huge price for whatever real or not-so-accurate blame was placed on BP. Within three weeks of the Deepwater Horizon explosion, the **market value** of the company had dropped by more than $36 billion—about a 20 percent fall. This decline in market value reflects the $20 billion damage fund noted above, as well as other anticipated costs of the spill—damages not covered by the official damage fund, the value of the oil that could have been pumped from the well, and the likely higher costs of drilling in the future.

At issue here is the creation of **negative incentives** that will induce BP and other oil companies to account fully for the risks surrounding offshore oil drilling. The economically **efficient** amount (and location) of drilling occurs only when the companies must pay for the full costs of their drilling—which include the environmental impacts. The creation of a damage pool such as instituted in the Deepwater Horizon case is one way that such incentives can be brought to bear. But the key point is that to achieve economic efficiency, any user of a resource should bear the full cost of using that resource. If not, the resource will be used too intensively and our overall wealth will be lower. "User pays" is a principle that not only seems fair to most people but also minimizes the chances that resources—including, of course, environmental resources—will be wasted.

WHAT ABOUT LONG-LASTING ENVIRONMENTAL DAMAGES?

One commentator called April 20, 2010, our "environmental 9/11." Although the immediate damage to shorelines and wildlife turned out to be far less than was generally predicted, longer-term issues remain unsettled. For example, we know that escaped oil still sits on the ocean floor in parts of the Gulf of Mexico because of this disaster, and that there is still oil suspended in the deep waters of the Gulf. Because oil has seeped from the floor of the Gulf for millions of years, deepwater bacteria have evolved to feed on the oil. Thus, all of the oil is biodegradable, but we do not know how many years this process will take. Nor do we know what damage might accumulate over this period.

Partly in response to such concerns, President Obama banned all deep water oil drilling in the Gulf of Mexico for six months. Some observers argued that we should also increase subsidies for ethanol production and other alternative forms of energy. The Sierra Club announced that it wanted the permanent phasing out of *all* offshore exploration production.

THOSE NASTY TRADE-OFFS

It is true that if we ban all drilling in the Gulf of Mexico, then in the U.S. portion of the Gulf, there can be no further oil spills. But we cannot ban such oil drilling in *non*-U.S. territorial waters. Brazil, Mexico, and Cuba are already drilling in the Gulf of Mexico and will continue to do so. Therefore, the threat of another oil spill harming the environment near or on our shores cannot be reduced to zero.

About one million barrels per day come from our own offshore oil platforms in the Gulf of Mexico. That constitutes about one-fourth of total domestic oil production. If there were a permanent ban on such oil production, the United States would have to do one of the following:

1. *Increase* onshore *oil production,* perhaps by authorizing exploration in the currently closed Alaska National Wildlife Refuge.

2. *Develop oil shale located in western states.* Currently, such production is uneconomic—the costs exceed the potential revenues. Oil prices would have to rise considerably higher than they are now and stay high for a long time to make oil shale a preferred choice. Also, extraction of oil from oil shale requires huge amounts of water (heated to make steam that is injected into the oil-bearing shale), which would put severe pressure on existing water supplies in the arid western United States.

3. *The United States can import more oil from overseas.* Of course, there is a political argument against this action because we do not want to be "held hostage" to oil-exporting countries. Additionally, more imported oil means more risk of oil spills from oil tankers.

4. *Increase usage of ethanol.* Because most ethanol is made from corn or sugar cane, Midwestern corn farmers and Brazilian sugar cane growers would like this. But the adverse environmental consequences would be considerable. There is already an 8,500-square-mile dead zone in the Gulf caused by farm runoff coming down the Mississippi River. The prime culprit here is nitrogen fertilizer, and the corn used to make ethanol in America is notoriously nitrogen-hungry. So more ethanol means either a bigger Gulf dead zone or damage to Amazonian rain forests that would have to be cut down to make way for more sugarcane.

We could increase the list of alternatives to offshore drilling, but the inference would remain exactly the same. Every alternative to the continued flow of oil from offshore wells in the Gulf of Mexico involves a **trade-off.** Otherwise stated, every alternative action involves an **opportunity cost.** If you are an environmentalist, you might not want to allow oil drilling in now-prohibited parts of Alaska, or a larger Gulf dead zone or smaller Amazonian rain forests. If you are a farmer in the western states, you might not wish to see part of your water supply diverted to help extract oil from shale. And if you are worried about other countries determining our energy fate, you likely are against importing even more oil.

Putting the Deepwater Horizon
Disaster into Perspective

Eventually, the BP well was capped, and thus far no additional oil has leaked from it. It is estimated that the total spill was about 600,000 metric tons of oil. The closest accidental oil disaster of that size occurred off the Mexican coast in 1979 when the Ixtoc I platform leaked about 500,000 metric tons of oil into the Gulf over a nine-month period. During the Persian Gulf War in 1991, retreating Iraqi troops purposely created the largest oil spill in history—pouring 1.2 million metric tons into the Persian Gulf.

Prior to April, 2010, the biggest oil spill in U.S. territorial waters was caused by the *Exxon Valdez,* which leaked 39,000 metric tons of oil in Prince William Sound in 1989. Over time, for every offshore drilling spill, there have been seven major tanker spills and numerous smaller tanker accidents. Overall, during the 70 years for which there are data, tankers have spilled four times more oil than have offshore drilling accidents.

Perhaps more surprisingly, Mother Nature dumps even more oil into our oceans and waters, by way of natural seeps. Such seepage constitutes over 60 percent of oil in North American marine waters according to the National Research Council. Another one-third of the oil going into the oceans around our country comes from the urban runoffs, spills on land, and discharges from marine vessels. Added to this, every year Americans literally pour one million metric tons of oil down their household drains. This leaves less than 5 percent of oil in North American marine waters that is caused by extraction and transportation. The damage potential of the BP spill was heightened by its concentration in time and space—but its long-lasting effects are likely to be small.

The Perils of Seeking Zero
Environmental Risk

Those who worry about our environment—and that includes just about everyone—have sometimes advocated zero environmental risk from oil extraction and transportation activities. Even getting close to zero risk would be extraordinarily costly to society, though.

Consider how much time you spend proofing an important paper you have written for a critical class in college. You might use a spelling and grammar checking program first. Then you might reread your corrected draft. Next, you might put it down for an hour or a day and reread it again. The next time you proof it, you are likely to find very few errors. When do you stop? You stop when the **marginal cost** of doing more would exceed the expected **marginal benefit** (where "marginal" refers to the last or incremental unit).

What is your marginal cost? It is the value you place on the time you would have to spend for an additional proofing. That is your opportunity cost, the value of the best alternative use of your time. This might be studying for another course or it might be the pleasure you get from playing a video game. Your expected marginal benefit is the expected improvement in your grade on the paper and then on your final grade.

The key point, of course, is that you don't spend your entire college career proofreading a single paper. Instead, you take into account the benefits *and* costs of your actions in coming to a sensible decision about the allocation of your time.

THE EFFICIENT AMOUNT OF POLLUTION

Now use this type of reasoning to ascertain the **efficient** amount of oil pollution in the Gulf of Mexico (or anywhere, for that matter). To make it zero clearly cannot be efficient. The **efficient amount of pollution** occurs when marginal benefit equals marginal cost. To ensure that we have *no* oil spills, we would have to ban not only all offshore drilling but also *any* transportation of imported oil into the United States. If we did that, the price of oil products would skyrocket, thereby creating a severe and long-lasting economic crisis for the entire country.

What about the benefits of reducing the risk of oil spills? They would include less destruction to marine life and fewer damages to those who live on the coasts and those who depend on fishing for a livelihood in the same area.

The last major U.S. offshore oil spill occurred more than 40 years ago, off the coast of Santa Barbara, California. The 2009 *Montara* spill in the Timor Sea was the first major platform spill *anywhere* in the world in more than 20 years. History thus suggests that, despite the events of 2010, oil-drilling safety measures have been effective in keeping significant spills few and far between. To be sure, BP cut many corners and appears to have followed risk reduction procedures that met "industry standards," but did not constitute "industry best practices." Given that BP is now paying for its choices, other oil companies, particularly those that operate in the Gulf of Mexico, have up-to-date information about how much it will cost in the future to cut corners on safety. They will certainly invest in risk-reducing activities more than they did before April 20, 2010. And although we will pay for the risk reduction at the pump, we will also likely benefit from having to put up with even fewer spills in the future.

Discussion Questions

1. Why do we use so much oil?

2. How would your life change if there were no offshore drilling and no importation of foreign oil? (*Hint:* The combination of these two changes would reduce the supply of oil in the United States by about 70 percent.)

3. What would be the costs and benefits if the federal government imposed, say, a $3 additional tax on every gallon of gas purchased in the United States?

4. The Deepwater Horizon spill has been called the "Three Mile Island" moment for the oil industry. This is in reference to a core-cooling water leak at a nuclear power plant called Three Mile Island in 1979. Consequent to that disaster, no new nuclear power plants have come online. How has the United States benefited because we have added no new nuclear power plants? What is the trade-off, though, that we have made?

5. Even though you may not consciously calculate the marginal cost and the marginal benefit of studying one more hour for an exam, you still make a choice of whether to study that extra hour or not. Why must you ultimately take into account your opportunity cost for an extra hour of studying (or for any activity, for that matter) if you want to sensibly make choices about how to allocate your scarce time?

6. "The sun is a plentiful source of energy. Therefore, we should be able to harness that energy and slowly wean ourselves from oil imports." What is left out from this statement that has so far prevented solar energy from displacing petroleum products as a source of energy?

CHAPTER **3**

Supersize It

At least one major fast food company has urged customers to "Supersize It." Americans seem to have been taking the message to heart, putting on pounds at a record pace. In the 1960s, the average American man weighed 166 pounds. Today he tips the scales at a bit over 190. Over the same span, the average American woman put on just as much weight, rising to 164 pounds from her previous 140 pounds. The weight gains have been largest among people who were heavier to begin with, so obesity in America has more than doubled over this period. Over 30 percent of Americans now have a body mass index (BMI, a measure of weight relative to height) in excess of 30, the level at which doctors say a person passes from overweight to obese.[1] What explains these developments? Not surprisingly, economic analysis has a lot to say on this question. In fact, some fairly simple changes in demand and supply explain why waistlines in America and elsewhere in the world have been expanding so quickly.

WEIGHT IN THE TWENTIETH CENTURY

Actually, Americans put on weight throughout all of the twentieth century, largely as a result of two factors. First, wages in sedentary occupations (those relying on brains rather than brawn) rose relative

---

1 Using the English measurement system, BMI equals 704.5 multiplied by weight in pounds and then divided by the square of height in inches. BMIs in the range 20–25 are considered healthy. Below 20 is thin, 25–30 is overweight, and 30 and above is obese–the range in which significant adverse health effects (ranging from diabetes to heart disease) begin to show up. Someone who is 5′6″) and weighs 185 pounds or more is officially obese, as is true for someone who stands 6′0″ and weighs 220 pounds or above.

to those in active occupations. People responded by leaving jobs in manufacturing and agriculture and by starting work in service and management jobs. This reduced their calorie expenditures on the job and helped push up average weights. Second, the relative price of food declined during the twentieth century. As predicted by the **law of demand,** this induced people to eat more, increasing their caloric intake and their body weights. Between about 1900 and 1960, the weight of the average male rose 16 pounds, with similar but slightly smaller gains for the average female.

These weight gains during the first part of the twentieth century were probably healthful. Many Americans at the beginning of the twentieth century were actually malnourished, and the added poundage led to better health outcomes for them. The excess weight we added during the last 40 years or so is an entirely different matter. By the 1960s, average BMI in the United States was already at the high end of the healthy range of 20–25, so the extra pounds since then have pushed us into the unhealthy categories of overweight and even obese.

WHY THE WEIGHT GAINS?

How can we explain this surge in poundage? There are three key components. First, as mentioned above, levels of physical activity have declined, although not nearly as much as many popular commentators would have us believe. The big move from active to sedentary employments took place before 1970, so it cannot explain the last 40 years of weight gains. Still, caloric energy expenditures by both men and women in the United States have been falling. Americans are spending less time at work and on household chores, and more time watching TV, looking at computer monitors, and talking on the phone. Overall, per capita caloric energy expenditures have dropped a bit more than 25 percent since the 1960s. This is only a small part of the story, however. Indeed, it can explain only a few of the pounds Americans have added over the past 40 years. The rest comes from higher caloric intake.

By far the most important reason for this added caloric intake appears to be a change in the way food is prepared. Due to major developments in food processing technology, the **time cost** involved in preparing meals has fallen dramatically. This has reduced the **full cost** (money plus time cost) of food, leading to the consumption of significantly more calories. The result has been expanding waistlines.

CHANGES IN FOOD PREPARATION

In the 1960s, food was prepared in the home by family members and eaten there. Since then there have been numerous technological innovations in food processing, including:

- Vacuum packing
- Flash freezing
- Improved preservatives and flavorings
- The microwave

Much food preparation now is done outside the home by manufacturers who specialize in that activity and then sell the packaged, prepared food to the consumer to be eaten at home. Thus, over the past 40 years, the amount of time spent on food preparation and cleanup in the home has fallen in half. In addition, outside the home convenient, tasty prepackaged foods are now merely a few steps away in a vending machine, rather than being 10–20 minutes away in the nearest store. On both counts, the full cost of consuming food has declined, and people are consuming more calories. Moreover, they are doing it not by eating more calories at each meal, but rather by eating more "meals" (actually snacks) during the day. Caloric intake during the traditional meals of breakfast, lunch, and dinner has remained nearly constant at about 1,800 per day for men and 1,400 per day for women. But both sexes have nearly doubled their intake of calories from snacks, and per capita daily intake has risen to 3,800 calories from 3,100.

THOSE EXTRA CALORIES

A few questions remain. First, are the additional calories that Americans are consuming each day—the equivalent of a soft drink or a few cookies—really enough to account for the poundage we have been accumulating? The answer is "yes." An extra 150 calories per day for men of average weight and activity levels will eventually lead to 11 pounds of excess waistline baggage. For women, the same 150 calories per day would eventually add an extra 13 pounds. (The weight gain from these extra calories eventually levels off because as people get heavier they burn more calories just doing the things they usually do.)

The second question is: What started the revolution in food processing that made these extra calories cheaper? Although the answer to this is not completely settled, the most likely source may be found in the workforce decisions of women. Beginning about 40 years ago, women began entering the workforce in unprecedented numbers. Indeed, the **labor force participation rate** of women nearly doubled over this period. Moreover, they have been moving into occupations and professions, such as medicine, law, and the upper ranks of business, in which annual earnings are much higher than in the traditional fields of female employment, such as teaching and nursing. Thus, the **opportunity cost** of women's time has been rising, in turn increasing the demand for labor-saving conveniences, such as prepared foods. The food industry has responded just as economic analysis would predict.

DOES CHEAP FOOD MAKE
US WORSE OFF?

A third question being asked by some people is: Are Americans really better off due to the lower cost of food? Ordinarily, economists would argue that a technological improvement that lowered the costs of a good definitely would improve the lot of consumers. But in the present case, the adverse health effects of the extra calories are starting to become significant. Obesity is implicated in diabetes, heart disease, strokes, depression, and some cancers, and the number of people who are disabled due to obesity-related injuries or other health problems is rising sharply. It is estimated that more than $150 billion per year is now spent on obesity-related health problems, about 10 percent of our total health care spending.

As the poundage has piled up across the country, so too have the sales of diet books, as well as the rates of expensive bariatric surgery (in which the stomach is reduced in size to cut caloric intake and absorption). All in all, some analysts have suggested, maybe the lower cost of food has made people *worse* off, by inducing them to do something that they would rather not do—put on weight. This might be particularly the case for people who are said to have little self-control of the amount they eat. There may be something to this argument, but it's also true that people who live in cold weather climates, such as Montana, the Dakotas, and Minnesota, routinely complain about the weather in the winter. People in such climes also spend far more than the average person on clothes to offset the adverse effects of the cold weather. Surely we would not want to argue that such people are worse off for having chosen to live where they do, rather than in warmer locales. Similarly, in the case of people who are said to lack control over the amount they eat, just who is it that shall decide—and enforce—their caloric intake?

THE ROLE OF SMOKING

There is one final point to our story, one that illustrates that even the best of intentions sometimes yield adverse unintended consequences. Over the same period that Americans have been packing on the pounds, the taxes on cigarettes have risen sharply, even while the number of places where it is lawful to smoke has shrunk significantly. On both counts, the full cost of smoking (price per pack, plus the hassle) has been rising, and one consequence is that smoking has declined in the United States. It is well known that people have a tendency to eat more when they stop smoking, and this very fact seems to be showing up in the national statistics on excess poundage. Where the full costs of smoking have risen the greatest, so too has the incidence of obesity. In effect, people are being induced to substitute eating for smoking. Despite the adverse health effects of the resulting weight gains, the *net* health trade-offs here are likely positive, given the highly lethal effects of smoking. Still, this development reminds us that although people's behavior can easily be understood by examining the incentives they face, sometimes it is difficult to determine ahead of time what the full range of incentives will be.

DISCUSSION QUESTIONS

1. Calculate your own BMI, based on the formula in footnote 1, but keep it Top Secret. For comparison purposes, consider the following data for approximate average height and weight of major college football players, by position:

Position	Height (Inches)	Weight (Pounds)
Quarterback	75	220
Running back	71	215
Wide receiver	73	195

   Is the average player at any of these positions officially obese? What factors other than just weight and height might be important in assessing the "healthy" BMI for an individual?

2. Many insurance companies now impose a surcharge (in effect, a higher premium) for people who use tobacco products. What effect on tobacco usage do you predict such surcharges to have? What

would be the expected effect of an insurance surcharge for people who are obese?

3. Over the past twenty years, many state and local governments across America have (i) sharply raised cigarette taxes and (ii) sharply limited the number of places where people may smoke. Both policy changes have helped reduce the amount of cigarette smoking in the United States. If these same governments decided that they wished to reduce obesity, how might they go about doing so?

4. The technological changes in food preparation seem to have had the greatest effect on the time costs of a "meal," rather than affecting the time cost of consuming extra calories during any given meal. What does economics predict about what we should observe has happened to the number of meals consumed each day, compared to the number of calories consumed per meal?

5. The change in food preparation technologies over the past 30–40 years caused the biggest reduction in time costs for married women. What does economics predict should have happened to the weight of married women relative to other people?

6. During the twentieth century, the cost of the automobile fell drastically, leading to a dramatic rise in the number of miles driven. But all of this driving led to automobile accidents, which now kill more than 30,000 people each year and maim hundreds of thousands more. Is it possible that the fall in the price of the automobile actually made Americans worse off? How much would your answer depend on whether those fatalities were among the people driving the cars as opposed to innocent bystanders, such as pedestrians and children? (*Hint:* Take a look at the chapters in Part Six.)

CHAPTER 4

Flying the Friendly Skies?

Most of us hop into our car with little thought for our personal safety, beyond perhaps the act of putting on seat belts. Yet even though travel on scheduled, commercial airlines is safer than driving to work or to the grocery store, many people approach air travel with a sense of foreboding, if not downright fear.

If we were to think carefully about the wisdom of traveling 600 miles/hour in an aluminum tube 7 miles above the earth, several questions might come to mind: How safe is this? How safe should it be? Because the people who operate airlines are not in it for fun, does their interest in making a buck ignore our interest in making it home in one piece? Is some form of government regulation the only way to ensure safety in the skies?

THE ECONOMICS OF SAFETY

The science of economics begins with one simple principle: We live in a world of **scarcity,** which implies that to get more of any good, we must sacrifice some of other goods. This is just as true of safety as it is of pizzas or haircuts or works of art. Safety confers benefits (we live longer and more enjoyably), but achieving it also entails **costs** (we must give up something to obtain that safety).

As the degree of safety rises, the total benefits of safety rise, but the marginal (or incremental) benefits of additional safety decline. Consider a simple example: Adding exit doors to an airplane increases the number of people who can escape in the event of an emergency evacuation. Nevertheless, each *additional* door adds less in safety benefits than the previous one; if the fourth door enables, say, an extra ten people to escape, the fifth may enable only an extra six to escape. (If this sounds implausible, imagine having a door for each person; the last door added will enable at most one more person to escape.) So we say that the marginal (or incremental) benefit of safety declines as the amount of safety increases.

Let's look now at the other side of the equation: As the amount of safety increases, both the total and the marginal (incremental) costs of providing safety rise. Having a fuel gauge on the plane's instrument panel clearly enhances safety because it reduces the chance that the plane will run out of fuel while in flight.[1] It is always possible that a fuel gauge will malfunction, so having a backup fuel gauge also adds to safety. Because having two gauges is more costly than having just one, the total costs of safety rise as safety increases. It is also clear, however, that while the cost of the second gauge is (at least) as great as the cost of the first, the second gauge has a smaller positive impact on safety. Thus, the cost per unit of additional (incremental) safety is higher for the second fuel gauge than for the first.

How Safe is Safe Enough?

How much safety should we have? For an economist, the answer to such a question is generally expressed in terms of **marginal benefits** and **marginal costs.** The economically *efficient* level of safety occurs when the marginal cost of increasing safety just equals the marginal benefit of that increased safety. Put somewhat differently, if the marginal benefits of adding (or keeping) a safety feature exceed the marginal costs of doing so, the feature is worthwhile. But if the added benefits of a safety device do *not* exceed the added costs, we should refrain from installing the device. Note there are two related issues here: How safe should we *be,* and how should we *achieve* that level of safety?

Both of these issues took on added urgency on the morning of September 11, 2001, when terrorists hijacked and crashed four U.S. commercial jetliners. This episode revealed that air travel was far less safe than previously believed. Immediately, it was clear that we should devote additional resources to airline safety; what was not clear was

---

1 Notice that we say "reduces" rather than "eliminates." In 1978, a United Airlines pilot preoccupied with a malfunctioning landing gear evidently failed to pay sufficient attention to his cockpit gauges. When the plane was forced to crash-land after running out of fuel, eight people died.

how *much* additional resources should be thus devoted and precisely *what* changes should be made. For example, almost everyone agreed that more careful screening of passengers and baggage at airports would produce important safety benefits. But how should we achieve this? Should carry-on bags be prohibited or just examined more carefully? How thoroughly should checked luggage be screened for bombs? Even now, our answers to these questions are evolving as we learn more about the extent of the threat and the costs of alternative responses to it. Nevertheless, throughout the process, economic principles can help us make the most sensible decisions.

In general, the efficient level of safety will not be perfect safety because perfection is simply too costly to achieve. For example, to be absolutely certain that no one is ever killed or injured in an airplane crash, we would have to prevent all travel in airplanes—an unrealistic and impracticable prospect. This means that if we wish to enjoy the advantages of flying, we must be willing to accept *some* risk—a conclusion that each of us implicitly accepts every time we step aboard an airplane.

THE IMPORTANCE OF CIRCUMSTANCES

Changes in circumstances can alter the efficient level of safety. For example, if a technological change reduces the costs of bomb-scanning equipment, the marginal costs of preventing terrorist bomb attacks will be lower. It will be efficient to have more airports install the machines and to have extra machines at large airports to speed the screening process. Air travel will become safer because of the technological change. Similarly, if the marginal benefits of safety rise for some reason—perhaps because the president of the United States is on board—it could be efficient to take more precautions, resulting in safer air travel. Given the factors that determine the benefits and costs of safety, the result of a change in circumstances will be some determinate level of safety that generally will be associated with some risk of death or injury.

Airplanes are complex systems, and an amazing number of components can fail. Over the century that humans have been flying, airplane manufacturers and airlines have studied every one of the malfunctions thus far and have put into place design changes and operating procedures aimed at preventing recurring error. The efforts have paid off. Between 1950 and 2010, for example, the fatal accident rate on U.S. commercial airlines was cut by almost 97 percent.

Does the Government Know Best?

Consumers have the greatest incentive to ensure that air travel is safe, and if information were free, we could assert with some confidence that the actual level of safety supplied by firms was the efficient level of safety. Consumers would simply observe the safety offered by different airlines, the prices they charge, and select the degrees of safety that best suited their preferences and budgets, just as with other goods. But information is not free; it is a **scarce good,** costly to obtain. As a result, passengers may be unaware of the safety record of various airlines or the competence of the pilots and the maintenance procedures of an airline's mechanics. Indeed, even the airlines themselves may be uncertain about the efficient level of safety, perhaps because they have no way of estimating the true threat of terrorist attacks, for example. Such possibilities have been used to argue that the federal government should mandate certain minimum levels of safety, as it does today through the operation of the Federal Aviation Administration (FAA). Let's look at this issue in some detail.

One argument in favor of government safety standards rests on the presumption that, left to their own devices, airlines would provide less safety than passengers want. This might happen, for example, if customers could not tell (at a reasonable cost) whether the equipment, training, and procedures employed by an airline are safe. If passengers cannot cheaply gauge the level of safety, they will not be willing to reward airlines for being safe or punish them for being unsafe. If safety is costly to provide and consumers are unwilling to pay for it because they cannot accurately measure it, airlines will provide too little of it. The conclusion is that government experts, such as the FAA, should set safety standards for the industry.

Do Consumers Know Best?

This conclusion seems plausible, but it ignores two simple points. First, how is the government to know the efficient level of safety? Even if the FAA knows the costs of all possible safety measures, it still does not have enough information to set efficient safety standards because it does not know the value that people place on safety. Without such information, the FAA has no way to assess the benefits of additional safety and hence no means of knowing whether those benefits are greater or less than the added costs.

The second point is that people want to reach their destinations safely. Even if they cannot observe whether an airline hires good pilots or bad pilots, they can see whether that airline's planes land safely or crash. If it is *safety* that is important to consumers—and not the obscure, costly-to-measure *reasons* for that safety—the fact that consumers cannot easily measure metal fatigue in jet engines may be totally irrelevant to the process of achieving the efficient level of safety.

Interestingly, evidence shows that consumers are indeed cognizant of the safety performance of airlines, and that they "punish" airlines that perform in an unsafe manner. Researchers have found that when an airline is at fault in a fatal plane crash, consumers appear to downgrade their safety rating of the airline (i.e., they revise upward their estimates of the likelihood of future fatal crashes). As a result, the offending airline suffers substantial adverse financial consequences over and above the costs of losing the plane and being sued on behalf of the victims. These findings suggest a striking degree of safety awareness on the part of supposedly ignorant consumers.

WHAT ABOUT TERRORISM?

Of course, this discussion leaves open the issue of how to handle safety threats posed by terrorists and other miscreants. For example, much of the information that goes into assessing terrorist threats is classified as secret, and its revelation to airlines or consumers might compromise key sources of the data. Hence, there could be an advantage to having the government try to approximate the efficient safety outcome by mandating certain screening provisions without revealing exactly why they are being chosen. Similarly, because airlines are connected in networks (so that people and baggage move from one airline to another in the course of a trip), achieving the efficient level of safety might require a common set of screening rules for all airlines. Even so, this does not inform us whether the government should impose those rules or the airlines should come to a voluntary joint agreement on them.

We began this chapter with the commonplace observation that airlines are safer than cars. Yet many people still worry for their safety every time they get on an airplane. Are they being irrational? Well, the answer, it seems, is in the eye of the beholder. Measured in terms of fatalities per mile traveled, airplanes are about 15 times safer than cars (and 176 times safer than walking, we might add). But this number masks the fact that 68 percent of aircraft accidents happen on takeoff and landing, and these operations occupy only 6 percent of flight time. It is presumably this fact that quite sensibly makes people nervous whenever they find themselves approaching an airport.

Discussion Questions

1. Is it possible to be too safe? Explain what you mean by "too safe."

2. Suppose it is possible to observe (or measure) four attributes of airlines: (i) the size of their planes (measured in passenger-carrying capacity), (ii) the experience levels of their pilots, (iii) the age of their planes, and (iv) the length of the typical route they fly. Which airlines would be likely to have the fewest fatal accidents? Which would be expected to have the most?

3. Is safety likely to be a "normal" good (i.e., something people want to consume more of as they get richer)? Use your answer to this question to predict likely safety records of airlines based in North America and Europe, compared to those based in South America and Africa. Then go to www.airsafe.com to see if your prediction is confirmed or refuted by the facts.

4. Many automobile manufacturers routinely advertise the safety of their cars, yet airlines generally do not mention safety in their advertising. Can you suggest an explanation for this difference?

5. Many economists would argue that private companies are likely to be more efficient than the government at operating airlines. Yet many economists would also argue that there is a valid reason for government to regulate the safety of those same airlines. Can you explain why the government might be good at ensuring safety, even though it might not be good at operating the airlines?

6. Professional football teams sometimes charter airplanes to take them to their away games. Would you feel safer on a United Airlines plane that had been chartered by the Washington Redskins than on a regularly scheduled United Airlines flight?

CHAPTER 5

The Mystery of Wealth

Why are the citizens of some nations rich while the inhabitants of others are poor? Your initial answer might be "because of differences in the **natural resource endowments** of the nations." It is true that ample endowments of energy, timber, and fertile land all help raise wealth. But natural resources can be only a very small part of the answer, as witnessed by many counterexamples. Switzerland and Luxembourg, for example, are nearly devoid of key natural resources, yet the real incomes of citizens of those lands are among the world's highest. Similarly, Hong Kong, which consists of a few square miles of rock and hillside, is one of the economic miracles of modern times, while in Russia, a land amply endowed with vast quantities of virtually every important resource, most people remain mired in economic misery.

A number of studies have begun to unravel the mystery of **economic growth.** Repeatedly, they have found that it is the fundamental political and legal **institutions** of society that are conducive to growth. Of these, political stability, secure private property rights, and legal systems based on the **rule of law** are among the most important. Such institutions encourage people to make long-term investments in improving land and in all forms of **physical capital** and **human capital.** These investments raise the **capital stock,** which in turn provides for more growth long into the future. And the cumulative effects of this growth over time eventually yield much higher standards of living.

THE IMPORTANCE OF LEGAL SYSTEMS

Consider first the contrasting effects of different legal systems on economic growth. Many legal systems around the world today are based on one of

TABLE 5–1 Differing Legal Systems

Common Law Nations	Civil Law Nations
Australia	Brazil
Canada	Egypt
India	France
Israel	Greece
New Zealand	Italy
United Kingdom	Mexico
United States	Sweden

two models: the English **common law system** and the French **civil law system.** Common law systems reflect a conscious decision in favor of a limited role for government and emphasize the importance of the judiciary in constraining the power of the executive and legislative branches of government. In contrast, civil law systems favor the creation of a strong centralized government in which the legislature and the executive branches have the power to grant preferential treatment to special interests. Table 5–1 shows a sampling of common law and civil law countries.

Research reveals that the security of **property rights** is much stronger in common law systems, such as observed in Britain and its former colonies, including the United States. In nations such as France and its former colonies, the civil law systems are much more likely to yield unpredictable changes in the rules of the game—the structure of **property and contract rights.** This unpredictability makes people reluctant to make long-term fixed investments, a fact that ultimately slows the economic growth of these nations and lowers the standard of living for their citizens.

The reasoning here is simple. If you know that the police will not help you protect your rights to a home or a car, you are less likely to acquire those assets. Similarly, if you cannot easily enforce business or employment contracts that you make, you are less likely to make those contracts—and hence less likely to produce as many goods or services. And if you cannot plan for the future because you don't know what the rules of the game will be in 10 years or perhaps even one year from now, you are less likely to make the kinds of productive long-term investments that take years to pay off. Common law systems seem to do a better job at enforcing contracts and securing property rights and so would be expected to promote economic activity now and economic growth over time.

THE ECONOMIC IMPACT
OF INSTITUTIONS

Research into the economic performance of nations around the world from 1960 to the 1990s found that economic growth was one-third higher in the common law nations, with their strong property rights, than in civil law nations. Over the more than three decades covered, the standard of living—measured by real **per capita income**—increased more than 20 percent in common law nations compared to civil law nations. If such a pattern persisted over the span of a century, it would produce a staggering 80 percent real per capita income difference in favor of nations with secure property rights.

Other research has taken a much broader view, both across time and across institutions, in assessing economic growth. Institutions such as political stability, protection against violence or theft, security of contracts, and freedom from regulatory burdens all contribute to sustained economic growth. Indeed, it is key institutions such as these, rather than natural resource endowments, that explain long-term differences in economic growth and thus present-day differences in levels of real income. To illustrate the powerful effect of institutions, consider the contrast between Mexico, with per capita real income of about $14,000 today, and the United States, with per capita real income of about $50,000. Had Mexico developed with the same political and legal institutions that the United States has enjoyed, per capita income in Mexico would today be equal to that in the United States.

THE ORIGINS OF INSTITUTIONS

Given the great importance of such institutions in determining long-term growth, one might ask another important question: How have countries gotten the political and legal institutions they have today? The answer has to do with disease, of all things. An examination of more than seventy former European colonies reveals that a variety of strategies were pursued. In Australia, New Zealand, and North America, the colonists found geography and climates that were conducive to good health. Permanent settlement was attractive, so colonists created institutions to protect private property and curb the power of the state. But when Europeans arrived in Africa and South America, they encountered tropical diseases, such as malaria and yellow fever, which produced high mortality rates. This discouraged permanent settlement and encouraged a mentality focused on extracting metals, cash crops, and other resources. As a result, there were few **incentives** to promote democratic institutions or stable long-term property rights systems. The differing initial institutions helped shape economic growth over the years and, because of the broad persistence of those institutions, continue to shape the political and legal character and the standard of living in these nations today.

INSTITUTIONAL CHANGE TODAY

Recent events also illustrate that the effects of political and legal institutions can be drastically accelerated—in either direction. Consider China, which in 1979 began to change its institutions in two key ways. First, as we discuss more fully in Chapter 30, China began to experiment with private property rights for a few of its citizens, under narrow circumstances. Second, the Chinese government began to clear away obstacles to foreign investment, making China a more secure place for Western companies to do business. Although the institutional changes have been modest, their combined effects have been substantial. Over the years since, economic growth in China has accelerated, averaging almost 7 percent per year. And if that doesn't sound like much, keep in mind that it has been enough over that period to raise real per capita income in China by a factor of 8.

For an example of the potential *destructive* impact of institutional change, we need to look no further than Zimbabwe. When that country won its independence from Britain in 1980, it was one of the most prosperous nations in Africa. Soon after taking power as Zimbabwe's first (and so far only) president, Robert Mugabe began disassembling that nation's rule of law, tearing apart the institutions that had helped it grow rich. He reduced the security of property rights in land and eventually confiscated those rights altogether. Mugabe has also gradually taken control of the prices of most goods and services in his nation and even controls the price of its national currency, at least the price at which Zimbabweans are allowed to trade it. Moreover, the Mugabe government has confiscated large stocks of food and much of anything of value that might be exported out of or imported into Zimbabwe. In short, anything that is produced or saved has become subject to confiscation, so the incentives to do either are—to put it mildly—reduced.

As a result, between 1980 and 1996, real per capita income in Zimbabwe fell by one-third, and since 1996, it has fallen by an additional third. Eighty percent of the workforce is unemployed, investment is nonexistent, and the annual inflation rate reached an astonishing 231 million percent. (In 2009 Zimbabwe gave up on having its own currency, and now uses American dollars and South African rand.) The fruit of decades of labor and capital investment has been destroyed because the institutions that made that progress possible have been eliminated. It is a lesson we ignore at our peril.

DISCUSSION QUESTIONS

1. Go to a source such as the CIA Factbook or the World Bank and collect per capita income and population data for each of the nations listed in Table 5–1. Compare the average per capita income of the common law countries with the average per capita income of the civil law countries. Based on the discussion in the chapter, identify at least two other factors that you think are important to take into account when assessing whether the differences you observe are likely due to the systems of the countries.

2. Most international attempts to aid people living in low-income nations have come in one of two forms: (i) gifts of consumer goods (such as food) and (ii) assistance in constructing or obtaining capital goods (such as tractors, dams, or roads). Based on what you have learned in this chapter, how likely are such efforts to *permanently* raise the standard of living in such countries? Explain.

3. Both Louisiana and Quebec have systems of local law (state and provincial, respectively) that are heavily influenced by their common French heritage, which includes civil law. What do you predict is true about per capita income in Louisiana compared to the other U.S. states, and per capita income in Quebec compared to the other Canadian provinces? Is this prediction confirmed by the facts (which can be readily ascertained with a few quick Web searches)? Identify at least two other factors that you think are important to take into account when assessing whether the differences you observe are likely due to the influence of civil law institutions.

4. Consider two countries, A and B, which have identical *physical* endowments of a key natural resource. In country A, any profits that are made from extracting that resource are subject to confiscation by the government, while in country B, there is no such risk. How does the risk of expropriation affect the *economic* endowment of the two nations? In which nation are people richer?

5. In light of your answer to question 4, how do you explain the fact that in some countries there is widespread political support for government policies that expropriate resources from some groups for the purpose of handing them out to other groups?

6. If the crucial factor determining a country's low standard of living is the adverse set of legal and cultural institutions it possesses, can you offer suggestions for how the other nations of the world might help in permanently raising that country's standard of living?

PART TWO

Supply and Demand

Introduction

The tools of **demand** and **supply** are the most basic and useful elements of the economist's kit. Indeed, many economists would argue that the **law of demand**—the lower the price of a good, the greater the quantity of that good demanded by purchasers—is the single most powerful proposition in all of economics. Simply stated, the law of demand has the capacity, unmatched by any other proposition in economics, to explain an incredibly diverse range of human behaviors. For example, the law of demand explains why buildings are taller in downtown areas than in outlying suburbs and also why people are willing to sit in the upper deck of football stadiums even though lower-deck seats are clearly superior. The great explanatory power of the law of demand is almost matched by that of the **law of supply,** which states that the higher the price of a good, the greater will be the quantity of that good supplied by producers. The law of supply helps us understand why people receive a premium wage when they work overtime, as well as why parking places at the beach are so much more expensive during the summer months than during the winter.

SEX, BOOZE, AND DRUGS

When the laws of demand and supply are combined, they illuminate the enormous **gains from trade** that arise from voluntary exchange. In Chapter 6, we examine what happens when the government attempts to prohibit the exchanges that give rise to these gains. The consequences are often surprising, always costly, and—sadly—sometimes tragic. We find, for example, that when the federal government made alcoholic beverages illegal during the era known as Prohibition, Americans responded by switching from beer to hard liquor and by getting drunk more often when they drank.

We also show that the government's ongoing efforts to prevent individuals from using drugs such as marijuana and cocaine cause the drive-by shootings that have occurred in many major cities and also encourage drug overdoses among users. Finally, we explain why laws against prostitution help foster the spread of AIDS.

KIDNEYS FOR SALE

Sometimes markets can create gains for humanity in the most unexpected places. One instance involves the transplantation of human organs. Many thousands of people die each year waiting in vain for the donation of a lifesaving organ. As we see in Chapter 7, one key impediment to saving their lives lies in the fact that although we allow voluntary organ donations at a zero price, we prohibit individuals from being paid for a human organ for transplant. It is legal to pay the surgeons who perform the transplants and lawful for hospitals to make a profit on organ transplants performed in their operating rooms. But it is against the law for you to sell a cornea, a kidney, or a lobe of your liver; it is even unlawful for your loved ones to benefit from the harvesting of any of your organs after your death. This reduces the number of human organs available for transplant and thus results in the deaths of many thousands of people. We know from the experience of other nations that paying for organs induces many more donations. Safeguards against abuse (such as involuntary "donations") are also relatively easy to implement. Moreover, paying for organs would add relatively little to the costs of the insurance programs that already pay for virtually all transplants. On balance, it thus appears that allowing payment for transplant organs would benefit the donors and, even more important, save the lives of many thousands of recipients—which is surely a classic illustration of the gains from trade.

ARE WE RUNNING OUT OF WATER?

Despite abundant everyday evidence of the power of prices to stimulate production, ration consumption, and ensure the efficient allocation of scarce goods, sometimes people deny that prices can perform their wonders even for goods like water, so essential to human life. This denial appears to be based on a variety of myths that surround water—notions that the planet is somehow drying up or that water cannot (because it is essential to life) be allocated through markets or that salty ocean water cannot readily be converted into freshwater. As we see in Chapter 8, such ideas simply can't stand up to careful scrutiny. The earth is a closed system: Water can be dirtied, cleaned up, or moved around, but when we use it, we don't destroy it. Moreover, because it *is* so precious to us, water is an *ideal* candidate for the unfettered operation of competitive markets. Any attempts to interfere with open markets for water will reduce our total wealth and will place a disproportionate share of the burden on the people least able to bear it—those at the bottom of the income distribution.

One important conclusion of this chapter is that the water shortages and water crises that periodically afflict various parts of the world are rarely the result of droughts. They are far more often caused by government officials who are unwilling or unable to accept the reality of the laws of demand and supply.

The (Dis)incentives of High Taxes

As we see in Chapter 9, the effective prices faced by demanders and suppliers are importantly influenced by the taxes we impose on activities or goods. The consequences can be large-scale and sometimes counterproductive. When we tax income more heavily, people work less. When we tax goods more heavily, people consume less of those goods. Even so, at low levels of taxes, such responses are often modest, so that a higher **tax rate** can yield more **tax revenue.** But at some point, the disincentive effects of higher taxes can so discourage demanders or suppliers that revenues collected from the tax actually *fall.* When combined with the fact that the disincentive effects of taxes cause a reduction in the overall output produced in society, the result is surely a "lose–lose" outcome by any definition.

Bankrupt Landlords, from Sea to Shining Sea

Our final application of demand and supply analysis comes in Chapter 10. This chapter brings us back to the issue discussed in Chapter 6, the effects of government interference with free markets, in this case in the form of **rent controls**—legal ceilings on the rent that landlords may charge for apartments. Although the effects of rent controls are perhaps less tragic than some of the effects observed in Chapter 6 or 7, they are just as surprising and often as costly. We find, for example, that legal ceilings on rents have increased the extent of homelessness in the United States, have led to a rise in racial discrimination, and have caused the wholesale destruction of hundreds of thousands of dwelling units in our nation's major cities. We cannot escape one simple fact: Politicians may pass legislation, and bureaucrats may do their best to enforce it, but the laws of demand and supply ultimately rule the economy.

CHAPTER 6

Sex, Booze, and Drugs

Before 1914, cocaine was legal in this country; today it is not. Alcoholic beverages are legal in the United States today; from 1920 to 1933, they were not. Prostitution is legal in Nevada today; in the other forty-nine states, it is not.[1] All these goods—sex, booze, and drugs—have at least one thing in common: The consumption of each brings together a willing seller with a willing buyer, creating an act of mutually beneficial exchange (at least in the opinion of the parties involved). Partly because of this property, attempts to proscribe the consumption of these goods have met with less than spectacular success and have yielded some peculiar patterns of production, distribution, and usage. Let's see why.

SUPPLY-SIDE ENFORCEMENT

When the government seeks to prevent voluntary exchange, it must generally decide whether to go after the seller or the buyer. In most cases—and certainly where sex, booze, and drugs are concerned—the government targets sellers because this is where the authorities get the most benefit from their enforcement dollars. A cocaine dealer, even a small retail pusher, often supplies dozens or even hundreds of users each day, as did speakeasies (illegal saloons) during Prohibition; a hooker typically services three to ten "tricks" per day. By incarcerating the supplier, the police can prevent several, or even several hundred, transactions from taking place, which is usually much more cost-effective than going after the buyers one by one. It is not that the police ignore the

---

1 These statements are not entirely correct. Even today, cocaine may be obtained legally by prescription from a physician. Prostitution in Nevada is legal only in counties that have chosen to permit it. Finally, some counties in the United States remain "dry," prohibiting the sale of beer, wine, and distilled spirits.

consumers of illegal goods; indeed, sting operations, in which the police pose as illicit sellers, often make the headlines. Nevertheless, most enforcement efforts focus on the supply side, and so shall we.

Law enforcement activities directed against the suppliers of illegal goods increase the suppliers' operating costs. The risks of fines, jail sentences, and possibly even violence become part of the costs of doing business and must be taken into account by existing and potential suppliers. Some entrepreneurs will leave the business, turning their talents to other activities; others will resort to clandestine (and costly) means to hide their operations from the police; still others will restrict the circle of buyers with whom they are willing to deal to minimize the chances that a customer is a cop. Across the board, the costs of operation are higher, and at any given price, less of the product will be available. There is a reduction in supply, and the result is a higher price for the good.

This increase in price is, in a sense, exactly what the enforcement officials are after, for the consumers of sex, booze, and drugs behave according to the **law of demand:** The higher the price of a good, the lower the amount consumed. So the immediate impact of the enforcement efforts against sellers is to reduce the consumption of the illegal good by buyers. There are, however, some other effects.

Violence Emerges

First, because the good in question is illegal, people who have a **comparative advantage** in conducting illegal activities will be attracted to the business of supplying (and perhaps demanding) the good. Some may have an existing criminal record and are relatively unconcerned about adding to it. Others may have developed skills in evading detection and prosecution while engaged in other criminal activities. Some may simply look at the illegal activity as another means of thumbing their noses at society. The general point is that when an activity is made illegal, people who are good at being criminals are attracted to that activity.

Illegal contracts are usually not enforceable through legal channels (and even if they were, few suppliers of illegal goods would be foolish enough to complain to the police about not being paid for their products). So buyers and sellers of illegal goods must frequently resort to private methods of contract enforcement, which often entails violence.[2] Hence, people who are relatively good at violence are attracted to illegal

---

2 Fundamentally, violence—such as involuntary incarceration—also plays a key role in the government's enforcement of legal contracts. We often do not think of it as violence, of course, because it is usually cushioned by constitutional safeguards and procedural rules.

activities and have greater **incentives** to employ their talents. This is one reason why the murder rate in America rose to record levels during Prohibition and then dropped sharply when liquor was again made legal. It also helps explain why the number of drug-related murders soared during the 1980s and why drive-by shootings became commonplace in many drug-infested cities. The Thompson submachine gun of the 1930s and the MAC-10 machine gun of the 1980s were just low-cost means of contract enforcement.

USAGE CHANGES

The attempts of law enforcement officials to drive sellers of illegal goods out of business have another effect. Based on recent wholesale prices, $50,000 worth of pure heroin weighs about 1 pound; $50,000 worth of marijuana weighs about 50 pounds. As any drug smuggler can tell you, hiding 1 pound of contraband is a lot easier than hiding 50 pounds. Thus, to avoid detection and prosecution, suppliers of the illegal good have an incentive to deal in the more valuable versions of their product, which for drugs and booze mean the more potent versions. Bootleggers during Prohibition concentrated on hard liquor rather than on beer and wine; even today, moonshine typically has roughly twice the alcohol content of legal hard liquor such as bourbon, scotch, or vodka. After narcotics became illegal in this country in 1914, importers switched from the milder opium to its more valuable, more potent, and more addictive derivative, heroin.

The move to the more potent versions of illegal commodities is enhanced by enforcement activities directed against users. Not only do users, like suppliers, find it easier (cheaper) to hide the more potent versions, but there is also a change in relative prices due to user penalties. Typically, the law has lower penalties for using an illegal substance than for distributing it. Within each category (use or sale), however, there is commonly the same penalty regardless of value per unit. For example, during Prohibition, a bottle of wine and a bottle of more expensive, more potent hard liquor were equally illegal. Today, the possession of 1 gram of 90 percent pure cocaine brings the same penalty as the possession of 1 gram of 10 percent pure cocaine. Given the physical quantities, there is a fixed cost (the legal penalty) associated with being caught, regardless of value per unit (and thus potency) of the substance. Hence, the structure of legal penalties raises the relative price of less potent versions, encouraging users to substitute more potent versions—heroin instead of opium, hashish instead of marijuana, and hard liquor instead of beer.

Penalties against users also encourage a change in the nature of usage. Prior to 1914, cocaine was legal in this country and was used openly as a mild stimulant, much as people today use caffeine. (Cocaine was even an ingredient in the original formulation of Coca-Cola.) This type of usage—small, regular doses over long time intervals—becomes relatively more expensive when the substance is made illegal. Extensive usage (small doses spread over time) is more likely to be detected by the authorities than intensive usage (a large dose consumed at once), simply because possession time is longer and the drug must be accessed more frequently. Thus, when a substance is made illegal, there is an incentive for consumers to switch toward usage that is more intensive. Rather than ingesting cocaine orally in the form of a highly diluted liquid solution, as was commonly done before 1914, people switched to snorting or injecting it. During Prohibition, people dispensed with cocktails before dinner each night; instead, on the less frequent occasions when they drank, they more often drank to get drunk. The same phenomenon is observed today. People under the age of 21 consume alcoholic beverages less frequently than people over the age of 21. But when they do drink, they are more likely to drink to get drunk.

INFORMATION COSTS RISE

Not surprisingly, the suppliers of illegal commodities are reluctant to advertise their wares openly; the police are as capable of reading billboards and watching TV as potential customers are. Suppliers are also reluctant to establish easily recognized identities and regular places and hours of business because to do so raises the chance of being caught by the police. Information about the price and quality of products being sold goes underground, often with unfortunate effects for consumers.

With legal goods, consumers have several means of obtaining information. They can learn from friends, advertisements, and personal experience. When goods are legal, they can be trademarked for identification. The trademark cannot legally be copied, and the courts protect it. Given such easily identified brands, consumers can be made aware of the quality and price of each. If their experience does not meet expectations, they can assure themselves of no further contact with the unsatisfactory product by never buying that brand again.

When a general class of products becomes illegal, there are fewer ways to obtain information. Brand names are no longer protected by law, so falsification of well-known brands ensues. When products do not meet expectations, it is more difficult (costly) for consumers to punish suppliers. Frequently, the result is degradation of and uncertainty about product quality. The consequences for consumers of the illegal goods are often unpleasant and sometimes fatal.

DANGEROUS SEX

Consider prostitution. In Nevada counties where prostitution is legal, the prostitutes are required to register with the local authorities, and they generally conduct their business in well-established bordellos. These establishments advertise openly and rely heavily on repeat business. Health officials test the prostitutes weekly for venereal disease and monthly for AIDS. Contrast this with other areas of the country, where prostitution is illegal. Suppliers are generally streetwalkers because a fixed, physical location is too easy for the police to detect and raid. They change locations frequently to reduce harassment by police. Repeat business is reported to be minimal; frequently, customers have never seen the prostitute before and never will again.

The difference in outcomes is striking. In Nevada, the spread of venereal disease by legal prostitutes is estimated to be almost nonexistent; to date, none of the registered prostitutes in Nevada has tested positive for AIDS. By contrast, in some major cities outside Nevada, the incidence of venereal disease among prostitutes is estimated to be near 100 percent. In Miami, one study found that 19 percent of all incarcerated prostitutes tested positive for AIDS; in Newark, New Jersey, 52 percent of the prostitutes tested were infected with the AIDS virus, and about half of the prostitutes in Washington, DC, and New York City are also believed to be carrying the AIDS virus. Because of the lack of reliable information in markets for illegal goods, customers frequently do not know exactly what they are getting; as a result, they sometimes get more than they bargained for.

DEADLY DRUGS AND BAD BOOZE

Consider alcohol and drugs. Today, alcoholic beverages are heavily advertised to establish their brand names and are carried by reputable dealers. Customers can readily punish suppliers for any deviation from the expected potency or quality by withdrawing their business, telling their friends, or even bringing a lawsuit. Similar circumstances prevailed before 1914 in this country for the hundreds of products containing opium or cocaine.

During Prohibition, consumers of alcohol often did not know exactly what they were buying or where to find the supplier the next day if they were dissatisfied. Fly-by-night operators sometimes adulterated liquor with far more lethal methyl alcohol. In tiny concentrations, this made watered-down booze taste like it had more kick, but in only slightly higher concentrations, the methyl alcohol blinded or even killed the unsuspecting consumer. Even in "reputable" speakeasies (those likely to be in business at the same location the next day), bottles bearing the labels of high-priced foreign whiskeys were refilled repeatedly with locally (and illegally) produced rotgut until their labels wore off.

In the 1970s, more than one purchaser of what was reputed to be high-potency Panama Red or Acapulco gold marijuana ended up with low-potency pot heavily loaded with stems, seeds, and maybe even oregano. Buyers of cocaine must worry about not only how much the product has been cut along the distribution chain but also what has been used to cut it. In recent years, the purity of cocaine at the retail level has ranged between 10 and 95 percent; for heroin, the degree of purity has ranged from 5 to 50 percent. Cutting agents can turn out to be any of various sugars, local anesthetics, or amphetamines; on occasion, rat poison has been used. We noted earlier that the legal penalties for the users of illegal goods encourage them to use more potent forms and to use them more intensively. These facts and the uncertain quality and potency of the illegal products yield a deadly combination. During Prohibition, the death rate from acute alcohol poisoning (due to overdose) was more than thirty times higher than today. In 1927 alone, twelve thousand people died from acute alcohol poisoning, and many thousands more were blinded or killed by contaminated booze. Today, about four thousand people per year die as a direct result of consuming either cocaine or heroin. Of that total, it is estimated, roughly 80 percent die from either an overdose caused by an unexpectedly potent product or an adverse reaction to the material used to cut the drug. Clearly, caveat emptor ("let the buyer beware") is a warning to be taken seriously if one is consuming an illegal product.

SUCCESS IS LIMITED

We noted at the beginning of this chapter that one of the effects of making a good illegal is to raise its price. One might well ask, by how much? During the early 1990s, the federal government was spending about $2 billion per year in its efforts to stop the importation of cocaine from Colombia. One study concluded that these efforts had hiked the price of cocaine by 4 percent relative to what it would have been had the federal government done nothing to interdict cocaine imports. The study estimated that the cost of raising the price of cocaine an additional 2 percent would be $1 billion per year. More recently, Nobel Laureate Gary Becker and his colleagues have estimated that America's war on drugs costs at least $100 billion per year. And the results? The prices of heroin and cocaine are at record-low levels.

The government's efforts to halt imports of marijuana have had some success, presumably because that product is easier to detect than cocaine. Nevertheless, suppliers have responded by cultivating marijuana domestically instead of importing it or by bringing it in across the relatively open U.S.-Canadian border rather than from elsewhere. The net effect has been an estimated tenfold increase in potency due to the superior farming techniques available in this country and Canada, as well as the use of genetic bioengineering to improve strains.

A few years ago, most states and the federal government began restricting sales of cold medicines containing pseudoephedrine because that ingredient was widely used for making the illegal stimulant methamphetamine in home laboratories. The restrictions succeeded in sharply curtailing home production of "meth." They also led to a huge increase in imports of a far more potent version of meth from Mexico. Overall, it is estimated that neither consumption of nor addiction to methamphetamine was reduced by the restrictions. But overdoses from the drug rose sharply because of the greater purity of the imports.

Consider also the government's efforts to eliminate the consumption of alcohol during the 1920s and 1930s. They failed so badly that the Eighteenth Amendment, which put Prohibition in place, was the first (and so far the only) constitutional amendment ever to be repealed. As for prostitution, it is reputed to be "the oldest profession" and by all accounts continues to flourish today, even in Newark and Miami.

The government's inability to halt the consumption of sex, booze, or drugs does not mean that those efforts have failed. Indeed, the impact of these efforts is manifested in their consequences, ranging from tainted drugs and alcohol to disease-ridden prostitutes. The message instead is that when the government attempts to prevent mutually beneficial exchange, even its best efforts are unlikely to meet with spectacular success.

DISCUSSION QUESTIONS

1. From an economic perspective, is it possible for laws restricting dangerous or destructive activity to be *too* strict? Explain. (*Hint:* Revisit Chapter 4.)

2. In recent years several states have passed so-called medical marijuana laws. Typically, these laws permit individuals to lawfully purchase marijuana from licensed stores, provided they have letter from their doctor recommending its use. Use the reasoning in this chapter to predict how the characteristics of medical marijuana will differ from illegal marijuana. Focus specifically on price, quality, variety, and consistency (or predictability).

3. The federal government currently taxes alcohol on the basis of the 100-proof gallon. (Alcohol that is 100 proof is 50 percent pure ethyl alcohol; most hard liquor sold is 80 proof, or 40 percent ethyl alcohol, whereas wine is usually about 24 proof, and most beer is 6–10 proof.) How would alcohol consumption patterns change if the government taxed alcohol strictly on the basis of volume rather than also taking its potency into account?

4. During Prohibition, some speakeasy operators paid bribes to ensure that the police did not raid them. Would you expect the quality of the liquor served in such speakeasies to be higher or lower than in those that did not pay bribes? Would you expect to find differences (e.g., with regard to income levels) among the customers patronizing the two types of speakeasies?

5. The markets for prostitution in Nevada and New Jersey have two important differences: (1) prostitutes in New Jersey face higher costs because of government efforts to prosecute them and (2) customers in New Jersey face higher risks of contracting diseases from prostitutes because the illegal nature of the business makes reliable information about product quality much more costly to obtain. Given these facts, in which state would you expect the price of prostitution services to be higher? Which state would have the higher amount of services consumed (adjusted for population differences)? Explain your answer.

6. According to the Surgeon General of the United States, nicotine is the most addictive drug known to humanity, and cigarette smoking kills perhaps 300,000–400,000 people per year in the United States. Why isn't tobacco illegal in America?

CHAPTER 7

Kidneys for Sale

This year, more than eight thousand Americans will die waiting for an organ transplant. They will not die because physicians are unable to transplant organs or because their health insurance does not cover the cost of the transplant. They will die because since 1984, it has been against federal law to pay for human organs.[1] It is lawful to pay a man for his sperm, a woman for her eggs, and members of either gender for their blood. It is even lawful to donate an organ or to receive one as a gift. And it is certainly legal to pay the surgeons who perform the transplants. It is even lawful for hospitals to make a profit on organ transplants performed in their operating rooms. But it is against the law for you to sell a cornea, a kidney, or a lobe of your liver; it is even unlawful for your loved ones to benefit from the harvesting of any of your organs after your death. And thus eight thousand people die every year, waiting in vain for someone to donate an organ to them.

AN OVERVIEW OF ORGAN TRANSPLANTS

The transplantation of human body parts is not new. The first cornea was successfully transplanted in Austria in 1905. The first successful kidney transplant (between identical twins) was conducted in Boston in 1954. Since then, successful transplants of the pancreas, liver, heart, lung, hand, and even face have been performed. Indeed, there are now thirty-seven different organs and types of human tissues that can be transplanted. None of this is cheap. In the United States, a kidney transplant costs about $250,000 on average, a liver transplant

---

1 This legislation was originally introduced by Rep. Al Gore (D., Tenn.), who went on to become vice president of the United States (1993–2001).

runs $520,000, and a heart transplant costs an average of $650,000. But there are services that arrange for international transplants (performed, for example, in India or China) of any of these organs at less than half the price. None of these figures include payment for the organ itself because such payments are illegal in the United States and in most other countries.

These astronomical sums are obviously out of the reach of most people. In fact, however, transplants done in the United States are generally not paid for directly by the recipients. For a person under the age of 65 with health insurance, private insurance pays for the transplant. For anyone 65 or older, the federal Medicare system pays for the transplant. And for people under 65 with neither private insurance nor the wealth to pay by themselves, transplants are paid for by the Medicaid system, which is financed jointly by the federal government and the states. (Neither private insurance plans nor Medicare or Medicaid will pay for international transplants, which are generally chosen only by relatively affluent people who are unwilling to wait— or to die waiting.)

THE CASE OF KIDNEYS

Now, to begin our inquiry into the economics of organ transplants, let's consider the case of kidneys. We start here because the technical features of the transplant process have become relatively routine and because we each are born with two kidneys but can get by quite well with only one. In fact, thanks to the technique known as dialysis, humans can actually survive for years without functioning kidneys. In 2011, over ninety thousand people were awaiting kidney transplants in the United States. That same year, ten thousand Americans received transplants from deceased strangers. Another six thousand received a transplant from a living donor (recall that "extra" kidney we each have), usually a close friend or relative. Tragically, more than five thousand of the people waiting for a kidney either died or were dropped from the list because they had become too sick to qualify for a transplant. Another three thousand died that year waiting for a liver, heart, lung, or other critical organ. Could they be saved, if it were as lawful to pay for kidneys as it is to pay for the surgeons who transplant them? Or would a market for kidneys ultimately become a black market, relying on "donated" organs removed from unwilling victims by unscrupulous brokers motivated by cash rather than kindness? That is precisely the nexus of the debate over whether we should permit people (or the relatives of just-deceased donors) to be remunerated for lifesaving organ donations.

First things first: Surely we cannot object to a market for organs because the act of donating a kidney or the lobe of a liver is potentially hazardous to the donor. After all, we currently permit people to undergo such risks under the current system with *no* monetary compensation. If it is safe enough to allow friends or family to donate without payment, why is it too risky for someone to give up a kidney or part of his or her liver in return for money?

THE CASE OF IRAN

There are, of course, many other contentious issues. To start exploring them, let's look first at a nation where it *is* legal to pay people for human organs: Iran, which just happens to have the highest living-donor rate in the world, at twenty-three donations per million people. Monetary compensation for organs in Iran has been lawful there since 1988, and in the ensuing decade, Iran eliminated the *entire* backlog of kidney transplant patients, something no other nation has achieved.

Under the Iranian system, a person awaiting a kidney must first seek a suitable, willing donor in his or her family. If none is forthcoming, the person must wait up to six months for a suitable deceased donor. At that point, the potential recipient can apply to the national transplant association for a kidney from a willing donor who is paid for the kidney. The donor receives from the government $1,200 plus a year of fully paid health insurance and a payment of $2,300–$4,500 from the recipient (or a charity, if the recipient is poor). Donor and recipient are also free to agree to an additional cash payment, although in most cases, the sums already mentioned are sufficient to get the job done. There are still purely altruistic donors in Iran, as well as cadaveric donations from the recently deceased. But it is the payment for organs that has permitted essentially all who seek kidney donations in Iran to get them, and the Iranian system has done so *without* leading to "back alley" donations or to people who are unable to afford a transplant because of the high cost of the organs themselves. Meanwhile, the system has saved the lives of thousands of Iranians.

THE FEAR OF INVOLUNTARY DONATIONS

Many people worry about a system of payment for human transplant because of the possibility that it would yield *involuntary* donors. That is, if there is a market for organs, some unscrupulous brokers might be tempted by profits to knock people over the head and harvest their organs for sale at the highest price. Yet it is generally agreed that the Iranian system has worked for more than 20 years without a hint of any such activities. Perhaps this should not be too surprising, given the medical techniques that have been developed to ensure that the tissue match between organ and recipient is close enough to make transplant feasible. These and other DNA tests can now quickly ascertain with substantial certainty that "organ A" came from voluntary "donor A" rather than from involuntary "donor B."

Indeed, apart from gruesome works of fiction, most of the horror stories about the hazards of allowing markets for human organs are stories about behavior caused by the *lack* of a market for organs. In China, for example, many "transplant tourists" in the past received organs taken from the bodies of the thousands of prisoners who are executed there every year. China insisted that the prisoners' organs were used only with their "consent," a claim that many human rights groups have disputed. But on one point all agree: There were no payments to the prisoners or their surviving relatives. The organs were simply taken (a practice now supposedly halted).

In both the United States and Britain, there have been highly publicized cases of what amount to "body snatching"—removal of organs and other body parts from the recently deceased. Some of these cases involved body parts used in research, while other body parts were intended for sale at a profit. In each of these cases, removal was done without the prior consent of the deceased or the postmortem consent of relatives. But this amounts to theft; it is singularly horrifying, but we must remember that it is theft. Consider another form of stealing: Every year many thousands of senior citizens are defrauded of their hard-earned retirement funds by unscrupulous individuals who masquerade as "financial advisers." Should we make it illegal for anyone to pay for investment advice—or should we devote our efforts to prosecuting and incarcerating the perpetrators of such crimes?

In Pakistan and the Philippines, there were small-scale markets for transplant organs until recently, although Pakistan has now banned the trade in human organs and transplants for non-Filipinos have been outlawed in that nation. In both countries, there were anecdotes of donors who sold kidneys for $2,000–$3,000 (about a year's worth of per capita income in either nation), but who later came to regret the transaction because of adverse long-term health effects. But this would be a potential issue even with unpaid donors, and in any nation such as the United States, donors in a market for organs would surely receive at least as much medical and psychological counseling as volunteer donors receive now.

THE COSTS OF PAYING FOR ORGANS

Now, what about the added expense of allowing payments for donated organs? Would this break the budgets of Medicare or Medicaid or empty the coffers of the private insurance companies that pay for the bulk of transplants? In the case of kidneys, we have enough information from elsewhere to say the answer is probably not. In Iran, where per capita income is about $12,000 per year, payments to donors smaller than this amount have been sufficient to clear the market for kidneys. In Pakistan and the Philippines, payments equivalent to a year's worth of per capita income were enough to support a substantial transplant tourist market in both countries.

At almost $50,000 per year, average per capita income in the United States is clearly much higher than in any of these nations, suggesting that payments for kidneys would also have to be much larger to induce a substantial increase in the number of donations. But experts have estimated that even if the payment for a kidney were as much as $100,000, private and public insurance systems (which, as we have noted, pay for almost all of the transplants in the United States) could actually *save* money on many transplants because dialysis (at $70,000 per year) and the other treatments associated with chronic kidney disease are so expensive.

It is true that allowing payments for human organs would almost surely increase the number of transplants each year—indeed, this is the very point. Payments would bring forth more organs, and this would in turn reduce deaths among people waiting for transplants. A payment system would have added costs associated with it: There would be more transplant operations (at $250,000 each for kidneys, for example, plus another, say, $100,000 for each of the organs themselves). Suppose that the payments for kidneys enabled an additional five thousand transplants per year (assuming that the U.S. system would be as successful as the Iranian system in eliminating the excess demand for kidneys). That would yield added costs nationwide of about $1.75 billion (five thousand transplants estimated at $350,000 each).

And there is a second cost: Paying for organs would cause a reduction in the number of altruistic donations. How many fewer there would be we cannot know for sure, but let us make two assumptions to be on the safe side. First, we assume that there would be *no* altruistic donations from living donors under a payment system. Second, we assume that the relatives of all deceased donors would insist on payment. Together these assumptions imply there would be an added expense of $100,000 on each of the sixteen thousand kidney transplants performed under the current system. The added cost here would be $1.6 billion per year, which, when added to the $1.75 billion cost of the new transplants, yields a total added annual cost of $3.35 billion for the organ payment system.

THE BENEFITS OF PAYING FOR ORGANS

In return for this sum, we would surely recoup some savings from the dialysis system because at least five thousand people per year would no longer be on dialysis at $70,000 per year—they would instead have a kidney to do that work for them. Moreover, the current three- to four-year delay on kidney transplants would be sharply reduced, generating additional savings. But far more important, we would be saving the lives of five thousand people every year, at a cost per life saved of but $600,000—and this number does not count any of the savings from reduced dialysis treatments.

All these calculations seem a callous way to view a human life. But by the standards of medical care of today, allowing payments for human organs is almost surely a safe and remarkably cheap way to alleviate needless suffering and save thousands of lives every year. And once this is clear, aren't the truly callous people those who would deprive human beings of that opportunity?

DISCUSSION QUESTIONS

1. For the purposes of this question, assume that allowing payment for kidney donations would cause us to spend another $3.5 billion on kidney transplants. (This is slightly above the estimate provided in the text.) Also assume that permitting such payments saves the lives of five thousand patients who would otherwise die waiting for a kidney? How much must we value a human life for it to make economic sense to permit payments for kidneys? How much is that number reduced if each of the five thousand also ends up spending 18 months less on dialysis? Show all of your calculations.

2. Per capita income varies substantially across the country. If there was a free market in which payments for kidneys was permitted within the United States, would you expect there to be different prices in different parts of the country? In which areas of the countries would you expect the most organs to be offered for donation? Keeping in mind that insurance, either private or public, pays for essentially all transplants, would these same areas also be the chief "exporting" areas? Explain.

3. Why might the owners of the private insurance companies that pay for most organ transplants be in favor of a system that prohibits paying for a donated organ? Should the taxpayers of the United States, who ultimately cover the cost of Medicare and Medicaid transplants, similarly be opposed to paying for donated organs?

4. If payment for organs drives up the financial costs of transplants, is it possible that private insurance companies, and even Medicare and Medicaid, might tighten their standards for transplants so as to reduce the number of transplants each year? If they do, who would gain and who would lose compared to the current system?

5. The average waiting time on transplant lists is three to four years for kidneys (although this is expected to rise sharply, due to the rising incidence of diabetes, a major cause of kidney damage). Many of these people waiting must undergo dialysis, at a cost of $70,000 per year, paid for by private insurance, Medicare, or Medicaid. Suppose that if payment for organs were permitted, the transplant waiting time was shortened by three years, and that for the average patient, the result was 18 months less on dialysis. At what price for a kidney would a system of paying for organs be a "break-even" proposition for insurers? Show all calculations and explain your reasoning.

6. The United States currently has an "opt-in" system for organ donations from the deceased: People must explicitly choose postmortem donation ahead of time (as when they obtain their driver's licenses). Many other nations have "opt-out" systems: A desire to donate postmortem is presumed to exist unless an individual explicitly chooses ahead of time *not* to permit donation. How—if at all—would a shift to an opt-out system likely change the supply of cadaveric (postmortem) donations?

CHAPTER 8

Are We Running Out of Water?

If you believe the headlines, humans are about to die of thirst. A few samples should be enough to convince you:

"A World of Thirst" (*U.S. News & World Report*)

"Water Shortages May Lead to War" (*Financial Times*)

"Drying Up" (*The Economist*)

"Water Shortages Could Leave World in Dire Straits" (*USA Today*)

The world, it seems, is running out of water.

But how can this be true? After all, about 71 percent of the earth's surface is covered in water. Lake Michigan alone contains more water than the world's population uses in two years. Even more to the point, the earth is a closed system. Using water does not destroy water. Whether we drink it, flush it, irrigate with it, or even let it evaporate, it comes back to us eventually, just as clean and pure as the raindrops of a spring shower. In fact, every three weeks, enough rain falls to satisfy the water uses of the entire world's population for a year. So what, exactly, is the problem?

THE ULTIMATE RENEWABLE RESOURCE

Water is the ultimate renewable resource: The act of using it begins the process that returns it to us. But—and this is the crux—water is also *scarce*. That is, having the amount of clean water we want, where we want it, when we want it there is not free. We must sacrifice other resources to accomplish this. And as the level of economic activity grows, the demand for water grows, and so the costs of consuming water also grow.

In this sense, water is no different from any other **scarce good.** If we want more of it, we must sacrifice more of other things to achieve that goal. But what makes water seem different is that unlike, say, broccoli, if we do entirely without it, disastrous things happen in a relatively short period of time. If water gets sufficiently scarce, people may start doing some pretty unpleasant things to each other to ensure that they, rather than their neighbors or enemies, are the ones who end up with it. But before we see if this is really something we should worry about, we had better start by learning a little more about water.

WATER, WATER EVERYWHERE

Of the enormous amount of water on the earth's surface, about 97.2 percent is ocean water, which is too saline under normal circumstances to drink or use for irrigation. Another 2.15 percent is polar ice, which is certainly not a very convenient source. Of the remaining 0.65 percent, about 0.62 percent is underground in aquifers and similar geological structures. This groundwater takes hundreds of years to recharge and so is not really a sustainable source of freshwater over the relevant time span. That leaves us with rain.

Fortunately, it rains a lot, and despite the headlines, on a *worldwide* basis, the amount of rainfall doesn't vary much from year to year. About two-thirds of the rain falls on the world's oceans, where almost no one lives. But even so, and even taking into account evaporation and the fact that much of the rain over land quickly runs off into the oceans before it can be captured, there is still a lot of usable rainfall every year. Indeed, there is enough every day to yield 5,700 liters per person—about six times as much as the average person actually consumes in all uses.

Of course, Mother Nature is not particularly evenhanded in the distribution of this usable rainfall. For example, China gets only 5 percent of it, despite having 20 percent of the world's population. Brazil, Canada, and Russia, which together have 6 percent of the world's population, receive 29 percent of the usable rainfall. And although the United States does pretty well on average, picking up 5 percent of the rain and having about 5 percent of the world's population, there are plenty of differences within our borders. Massive amounts of rain fall in southeastern Alaska and on the mountain slopes of Hawaii, while very little falls in Southern California. But the fact that people routinely choose to locate themselves in places where it does not rain highlights one of the fundamental points of this chapter: Water is an **economic good**, and the distribution and consumption of water are fundamentally economic problems, ones that can be solved in markets, just as other economic problems (such as the provision of food, shelter, and clothing) are solved in markets. To focus clearly on this point, let's examine some of the myths that have grown up around water in recent years:

Myth 1: The planet is drying up. As we have suggested earlier, there is nothing to worry about here. The cheapest (and completely sustainable) source of clean freshwater is rainfall, and roughly 113,000 cubic kilometers (3 quadrillion gallons) of the stuff falls every year on land areas around the world, year in and year out. Although small amounts of this are temporarily stored in plants and animals while they are alive, all of it eventually either recharges groundwater or evaporates, forms clouds, and precipitates—all 113,000 cubic kilometers, year after year. Sometimes, more is in Brazil and less in Sudan, and sometimes more of it inconveniently runs off in floods. But because the earth is a closed system, all of that water stays with us.

Myth 2: We can save water by flushing less and using less in agriculture. Remember the closed system? That applies to toilets and alfalfa, too. Flushing the toilet does not send the water to the moon. It just sends it through the sewer system to a water treatment plant and eventually into aquifers under the ground or back down on our heads in the form of raindrops. So-called low-flow toilets (and showers) have no effect on the amount of water in existence. (Because they may slightly reduce the amount of water running through water and sewer systems, they may conserve a bit on the amount of resources used in these systems. But there are offsets. Such devices are routinely more costly to produce than regular toilets or shower heads, and they occupy people's time—because of double flushes and longer showers. On balance, besides not "saving" water, there is thus no evidence that such devices conserve resources at all.)

Even agriculture, notorious for consuming an enormous amount of (usually subsidized) water around the world, does not destroy the stuff. Most of the water used by agriculture evaporates or runs off into rivers or soaks into underground aquifers. A small amount is temporarily stored in the crops, but this, soon enough, is consumed by animals or humans and simply returns to the same system that delivers 113,000 cubic kilometers of water onto our heads every year. There is no doubt that all of this use of water in agriculture is costly because it could be used elsewhere. Moreover, agricultural use of water is generally subsidized by taxpayers. Making farmers pay full market value for water would reduce agricultural use and raise our collective wealth by improving the allocation of resources. But it would not alter the amount of water available.

Having said this, agricultural use of water does present two important economic issues. First, as we just noted, government policies around the world routinely cause water for agriculture to be heavily subsidized. Farmers often pay as little as $10 to $20 per acre-foot (about 325,000 gallons) for water that costs anywhere from $500 to $1,000 per acre to provide to them. Because of this huge subsidy, farmers are no doubt richer, but the losses to society are much greater, meaning that our overall wealth is lower. (For an explanation of why we get such subsidies despite this, see Chapters 22 and 26.)

Second, we not only subsidize water use for agriculture, but also routinely forbid farmers to sell or lease their water to other users, especially nonagricultural users. This is a particular problem in the relatively arid American West, where farmers effectively own most of the rights to surface and groundwater but must "use it or lose it"—if they don't put it to beneficial use on their crops, they lose their rights to it. But often this water would be much more productively "used" if it were left in the streams to help support the spawning and other essential life activities of downstream species, such as trout or salmon. Laws are slowly changing to recognize environmental uses as being "beneficial" uses, but existing restrictions on the use of water still yield lower overall wealth for us.

Myth 3: Water is different from other goods. Many people seem to think that because it is essential to life, water is somehow different from other goods—or at least that it should be treated differently in some very specific ways. Let's first get rid of the notion that water doesn't obey the laws of demand and supply. In fact, although the demand for water in some uses is relatively inelastic, usage of water in *all* uses responds as predicted by the law of demand—when the price of water goes up, people use less of it. Similarly, although getting water from where it is to where people would like it to be is costly, the law of supply still holds true—when the price of water rises, suppliers of water provide more of it to consumers. Sometimes this process is as simple as diverting a stream or capturing rainfall. Sometimes it is as complicated as using reverse osmosis to convert seawater into freshwater. But even if the production technique is as esoteric as recycling urine into fresh, drinkable water (as is done on the international space station), the fact remains that when water becomes more valuable, people are incredibly ingenious in finding ways to make sure it is available.

Myth 4: Price controls on water protect low-income consumers. Some people claim that water should *not* be treated like other goods, specifically arguing that both the price of water received by suppliers and the price paid by consumers should be kept down by government decree. This, it is said, will protect people, especially those who are poor, from high water prices and will prevent suppliers from earning "excessive" profits. After all, some 1.1 billion people around the world currently do not have ready access to clean water, which makes an inviting target for anyone who might become a monopoly supplier to substantial numbers of these people.

It is true that governments can reduce the profits of the suppliers of water (or anything else) by limiting the prices they charge. But in reality, this does not protect consumers, particularly not the poorest consumers. Price controls on water *reduce* the amount supplied and, especially for the poor, generally make consumers worse off. They end up with less water than if prices were allowed to reach equilibrium levels, and they are forced to undergo nonprice rationing schemes (ranging from limited hours of service to getting no clean water at all). In fact, if we examine places around the world where the poor have little or no access to clean water, we find that government efforts to "protect" people from potential suppliers of water are in fact a key source of this lack of access. In Brazil, for example, government limits on private water rates forced a major international water project company to cease operations there, reducing the supply of clean water. In India, the widespread insistence by many local governments that water be provided free of charge has effectively stalled most efforts to improve water distribution in that country. And in China, government price controls have discouraged water utilities from developing new water supplies and from upgrading water distribution systems. As we see in detail in Chapter 10, government controls on prices make goods *more* scarce, not less, and it is generally the disadvantaged members of society who suffer the most as a result.

Myth 5: The ocean is too salty to drink. As a practical matter, prolonged consumption of saltwater by species not specifically adapted for it is highly deleterious. But the technology for desalination of seawater is advancing rapidly, and the cost of desalination is falling just as rapidly—more than 95 percent over the past 20 years. In relatively arid parts of the earth (including Southern California) desalination has become price-competitive with other sources of supply, and large-scale desalination plants are in operation around the world.

The process yields highly concentrated brine as a by-product. To avoid damage to ocean species that are sensitive to excess salinity, this brine must be dealt with carefully (dispersed widely) when it is returned to the sea. Nevertheless, this is simply a matter of routine care. Moreover, if local conditions make wide dispersal impractical or expensive, the brine can be evaporated, and the resulting solid materials then either used or disposed of in ordinary landfills. The upshot is that with continued technological progress in desalination, water from the ocean will likely become cheaper than collecting rainfall in large portions of the world. Far from running out of water, people everywhere will then find themselves able to secure it as easily as, well, turning on the tap.

DISCUSSION QUESTIONS

1. How much water do people "need"? Is your answer the same if you have to pay their water bills?

2. Evaluate the following: "Although taxpayers foot the bill for federal water sold to farmers at subsidized prices, they also eat the crops grown with that water. Because the crops are cheaper due to the subsidized water, taxpayers get back exactly what they put in, and so there is no waste from having subsidized water for farmers." Would you give the author of this quote an A or an F in economics? Explain.

3. During the droughts that periodically plague California, farmers in that state are able to purchase subsidized water to irrigate their crops, at the same time that many California homeowners have to pay large fines if they water their lawns. Can you suggest an explanation for this difference in the treatment of two different groups of citizens in the state of California?

4. If allocating water through nonprice means generally harms society, can you suggest why governments often do this?

5. Consider two otherwise identical communities; call them P and N. Suppose that in P, all homes, apartments, and businesses have meters that record the usage of water. In addition, the users of the water must pay more when they use more water. Thus, water is priced like most other goods. In community N, there are no meters and the local supplier of water charges everyone in the community a fixed amount per person, per month for their water service. Thus, using another gallon costs the user nothing additional. In which community will per capita water use be higher? Explain, using the relevant principles of economics.

6. Referring back to the facts of the previous question: Suppose you knew that in one community water is supplied by a privately owned company, while in the other community water is supplied by the local government. In which community do you predict that water is supplied by the privately owned company? Explain.

CHAPTER 9

The (Dis)incentives of Higher Taxes

Politicians always seem to be looking for additional ways to raise tax revenues. And most often, politicians talk (and even act) as though their taxing decisions have no effect on the quantity supplied or the quantity demanded of whatever good or service they wish to tax. Indeed, there is a saying among economists that politicians believe all demand curves and supply curves are **perfectly inelastic.** In such a world, higher taxes would have no effect on either quantity demanded or quantity supplied. What a wonderful world that would be—for politicians.

THE LUXURY TAX

In the real world, however, changes in taxes cause changes in **relative prices,** and individuals in their roles as consumers, savers, investors, and workers react to these relative price changes. Consider a truly telling example: the luxury tax enacted by Congress in 1991. Members of Congress were looking for additional revenues to reduce the federal budget deficit. What better way to raise these hoped-for revenues than with new taxes on the purchases of high-priced luxury items, such as big boats, expensive cars, furs, planes, and jewelry. After all, rich people don't really care how much they pay, right? That is why we call them rich. So Congress passed a 10 percent luxury surcharge tax on boats priced over $100,000, cars over $30,000, aircraft over $250,000, and furs and jewelry over $10,000.

The federal government estimated that it would rake in $9 billion in extra revenues over the following five-year period. Yet just a few years later, the luxury tax was quietly eliminated. Why? Because the actual take for the federal government was almost *nothing.*

Rich people, strange as it may seem, react to relative price changes, too. For high-priced new boats, for example, they had alternatives. Some bought used luxury boats instead of new ones. Others decided not to trade in their older luxury boats for new ones. Still others bought their new boats in other countries and never brought them back to the United States to be taxed. The moral of the story for politicians is that the laws of supply and demand apply to everyone, rich and poor, young and old, whatever their description might be.

STATIC VERSUS DYNAMIC ANALYSIS

The discrepancy between the fantasyland of politics and the reality of human behavior can be traced in part to the fact that politicians routinely engage in **static analysis.** They assume that people's behavior is static (unchanging), no matter how the constraints they face—such as higher taxes—might change. If the politicians who had pushed for the luxury tax had used **dynamic analysis,** they would have correctly anticipated that consumers (even rich ones) were going to change their buying decisions when faced with the new taxes.

Dynamic analysis takes into account the fact that the impact of the tax *rate* on tax *revenue* actually collected depends crucially on the **elasticity** of the relevant demand or supply curves. That is, even a high *rate* (measured in tax per item, or as a percentage of the value of the item) can yield relatively little *revenue* (total dollars collected) if consumers are highly responsive to the tax-inclusive price of the good. For example, in the case of the luxury tax, the **elasticity of demand** for new, high-end boats was relatively high: When the tax per boat went up, the quantity demanded fell so far that tax collections were negligible.

INCOME TAXES AND LABOR SUPPLY

Now let's shift from the demand side of this taxing issue to the supply side. Does quantity supplied react to changing relative prices? Yes, but you might not know it from listening to politicians. The first modern federal personal income tax was imposed in 1916. The highest rate was 15 percent. Eventually, the top federal personal marginal income tax rate reached an astounding 91 percent, during the years 1951–1964. This marginal tax rate was cut to 70 percent in 1965. In 1980, it was lowered to 50 percent. For much of the 1980s and since, the highest federal marginal income tax rate has ranged from 31 percent to about 40 percent.

Often politicians (and even some members of the general public) believe that the income tax rates paid by America's richest individuals do not matter to them because they are so rich that even after paying taxes, they are still very rich. The underlying "theory" behind such a belief is that the supply of labor is completely unresponsive to the net after-tax price received by the providers of labor. Stated another way, if you were to draw the **supply curve** of labor, it would be a nearly vertical line for each individual at some fixed number of work hours per year. Supposedly, then, the **elasticity of supply** of labor is low.

To be sure, you might know somebody who loves work so much that she or he will work with the same intensity and for the same number of hours per year no matter what the income tax rate is. But changes occur at the margin in economics (meaning in the real world). If there are *some* individuals who respond to higher federal marginal tax rates by working less, then the overall supply curve of labor is going to be upward-sloping even for the ultrarich—just like all other supply curves for goods and services.

THE EVIDENCE IS CLEAR

The data seem to confirm our economic predictions. In 1980, the top marginal income tax rate was 70 percent. The highest 1 percent of income-earning Americans paid 19 percent of all federal personal income taxes in that year. In 2007, when the top tax rate was 35 percent, the richest 1 percent paid more than double that share. How can this be explained? The answer is relatively straightforward: Lower marginal income tax rates create an incentive for people to work more and harder because the rewards of doing so are greater. Also, in their role as risk-taking entrepreneurs, individuals are almost always going to be willing to take bigger risks if they know that success will yield greater net after-tax increases in their incomes.

Data from Europe suggest that exactly the same incentives are at work across a broad spectrum of income earners. Researchers have found that a tax increase of just over 12 percentage points induces the average adult in Europe to reduce work effort by over 120 hours per year—the equivalent of almost four weeks' work. Such a tax change also causes a sharp reduction in the number of people who work at all and causes many others to join the underground economy. Overall, then, higher tax rates cause lower output and higher unemployment and also induce marked increases in efforts devoted to tax evasion.

INCENTIVES APPLY TO EVERYONE

It is also true that what we have been talking about applies even among people who are at the very bottom of the income distribution. In many countries today, and in many circumstances in the United States, poorer individuals receive benefits from the government. These benefits can be in the form of food stamps, subsidized housing, subsidized health care or health insurance, and direct cash payments (often referred to as "welfare"). Those who receive such government benefits typically pay no income taxes on these benefits. In the case of the United States, they may even receive an **Earned Income Tax Credit,** which is a type of **negative tax** or **tax credit.**

If such individuals were to accept a job (or a higher-paying job, if they are already employed), two things will normally occur. The first is that they will lose some or all of their government benefits. The second is that they may have to start paying federal (and perhaps state) personal income taxes. They understand that the loss of a benefit is the equivalent of being taxed more. And when they also have to pay explicit taxes, they know that the result is effectively double taxation.

A Lesson from Ireland

Just as at the top end of the income ladder, the quantity of labor supplied by people at the lower end is affected by changes in the marginal income tax rates they face. If taking a good job and getting off the welfare rolls means losing benefits plus paying income taxes, the person on welfare has less incentive to accept a job. A good case in point is Ireland, which for most of the past twenty years was the fastest-growing economy in Europe. Twenty-five years ago, its economy was a disaster, one of the poorest among European countries. One of the problems was that individuals on welfare faced an effective (implicit) marginal income tax rate of about 120 percent if they got off the dole and went back to work. Obviously, they weren't directly taxed at 120 percent, but with the actual income tax that did apply, combined with the loss in welfare benefits, the *implicit* marginal tax rate was indeed 120 percent. Stated differently, their available spendable income would drop by about 20 percent if they went back to work! Needless to say, large numbers of poorer Irish stayed on the welfare roles until the program was completely overhauled.

Interestingly enough, this overhaul of the incentives facing low-income individuals was accompanied by an overhaul of the tax rates (and thus incentives) facing high-income corporations, with much the same results. In the 1990s, the Irish slashed the corporate profits tax to 12.5 percent, the lowest in Europe and only about one-third as high as the U.S. rate of 35 percent. Beginning in 2004, the Irish government also began offering a 20 percent tax credit for company spending on research and development, offering high-tech firms an opportunity to cut their taxes by starting up and expanding operations in Ireland. Almost immediately, Ireland became a magnet for new investment and for successful companies that didn't want to hand over one-third or more of their profits to the tax collector.

The combination of lower corporate tax rates and tax breaks on research and development induced hundreds of multinational corporations to begin operations in Ireland. They brought with them hundreds of thousands of new jobs (and this to a nation of only four million residents), and Ireland quickly became number one among the European Union's fifteen original members in being home to companies that conduct research and development. And tax revenues of the Irish government? Well, despite the drastic cut in tax rates, tax revenues actually soared to levels never seen before. Indeed, measured as a share of gross domestic product, Ireland soon collected 50 percent more tax revenues out of corporate profits than America did, despite Ireland's lower tax rate.

The lesson of our story is simple. It is true that "nothing in life is certain but death and taxes." But it is equally true that higher tax rates don't always mean higher tax revenues. And that is a lesson that politicians can ignore only at their own peril.

DISCUSSION QUESTIONS

1. Suppose the government spends more this year than it collects in taxes, borrowing the difference. Assuming that the government will repay its debts, what does this imply about what must happen to taxes in the *future*? How might people adjust their behavior to account for this predicted change in taxes?

2. Consider three scenarios. In each, your neighbor offers to pay $500 if you will clear brush out of his backyard this week.

   Scenario 1: If you decline the offer, you can collect $200 in unemployment benefits this week. If you accept the offer, you get to keep the entire $500, without having to pay taxes on it.

   Scenario 2: If you decline the offer, you can collect $100 in unemployment benefits this week. If you accept the offer, you must pay $100 in income taxes out of your earnings from work.

   Scenario 3: If you decline the offer, you collect no unemployment benefits. If you accept the offer, you must pay $200 in income taxes out of your earnings from work.

   What is the net monetary gain from working in each of these three scenarios? How, if at all, do your incentives change between scenarios? Explain, briefly.

3. If you found yourself in the 91 percent federal personal income tax bracket in 1951, how great would have been your incentive to find legal loopholes to reduce your federal tax liabilities? If you found yourself in the lowest federal personal income tax bracket of, say, 15 percent, would your incentive to find loopholes to reduce your tax bill be the same? Explain.

4. Explain how the incentive effects of each of the following hypothetical taxes would cause people to change their behavior. Be sure to explain what people are likely to do *less* of and what they are likely to do *more* of in response to each tax:

   (a) A $1,000,000-per-story tax on all office buildings more than two stories tall

   (b) A $2,000-per-car tax on all red (and only red) cars

   (c) A $100-per-book tax on all *new* college textbooks

5. Suppose that federal marginal personal income tax rates will rise significantly over the next 10 years. Explain the ways in which individuals at all levels of income can react over time, not just immediately after taxes are raised. How will the size of the response differ, say, a year after the rise in tax rates compared to a week after the increase? Is it possible that some people will actually change their behavior *before* the higher tax rates go into effect? Explain.

6. How does a country's tax structure affect who decides to immigrate into the nation or emigrate out of the nation? Contrast, for example, nations A and B. Assume that nation A applies a 20 percent tax on every dollar of income earned by an individual. Nation B applies a 10 percent tax on the first $40,000 per year of income and a 40 percent tax on all income above $40,000 per year earned by an individual. Start by computing the tax bill in each country that must be paid by a person earning $40,000 per year and the tax bill that must be paid by a person earning $100,000 per year. Then consider the more general issue: If the language, culture, and climate of the two nations are similar, and if a person can choose to live on one side or the other of a river separating the two nations, who is more likely to choose to live in A and who is more likely to choose to live in B? To what extent does your reasoning apply if an ocean, rather than a river, separates the two countries? Does it apply if the language, culture, or climate in the two nations differs? Explain.

CHAPTER 10

Bankrupt Landlords, from Sea to Shining Sea

Take a tour of Santa Monica, a beachfront enclave of Los Angeles, and you will find a city of bizarre contrasts. Pick a street at random, and you may find run-down rental units sitting in disrepair next to homes costing $800,000. Try another street, and you may see abandoned apartment buildings adjacent to luxury car dealerships and trendy shops that sell high-fashion clothing to Hollywood stars. Sound strange? Not in Santa Monica—known locally as the People's Republic of Santa Monica—where stringent rent-control laws once routinely forced property owners to leave their buildings empty and decaying rather than even bothering to sell them.

Three thousand miles to the east, rent-control laws in New York City—known locally as the Big Apple—have forced landlords to abandon housing units because the laws imposed on owners huge financial losses. Largely as a result of such abandonments, the city government of New York owns thousands of derelict housing units—empty, except for rats and small-time cocaine dealers. Meanwhile, because the controls also discourage new construction, the city faces a housing gap of 200,000 rental units—apartments that could easily be filled at current controlled rental rates if the units were in habitable condition.

From coast to coast, stories like these are commonplace in the two hundred or so American cities and towns that practice some form of **rent control**—a system in which the local government tells building owners how much they can charge for rent. Time and again, the stories are the same: poorly maintained rental units, abandoned apartment buildings, tenants trapped by housing gridlock in apartments no longer suitable for them, bureaucracies bloated with rent-control enforcers, and even homeless families that can find no one who will rent to them. Time and again, the reason for the stories is the same: legal limits on the rent that people may pay for a place to live.

A BRIEF HISTORY OF RENT CONTROLS

Our story begins in 1943, when the federal government imposed rent control as a temporary wartime measure. Although the federal program ended a few years after the war, New York City continued the controls on its own. Under New York's controls, a landlord generally could not raise rents on apartments as long as the tenants continued to renew their leases. Rent controls in Santa Monica are more recent. They were spurred by the inflation of the 1970s, which, combined with California's rapid population growth, pushed housing prices and rents to record levels. In 1979, the city of Santa Monica (where 80 percent of the residents were renters) ordered rents rolled back to the levels of the year before and stipulated that future rents could go up by only two-thirds as much as any increase in the overall price level. In both New York and Santa Monica, the objective of rent controls has been to keep rents below the levels that would be observed in freely competitive markets. Achieving this goal required that both cities impose extensive regulations to prevent landlord and tenant from evading the controls—regulations that are costly to enforce and that distort the normal operation of the market.

It is worth noting that the rent-control systems in New York and Santa Monica are slowly yielding to decontrol. For a number of years, some apartments in New York have been subject only to "rent stabilization" regulations, which are somewhat less stringent than absolute rent controls. In addition, New York apartments renting for over $2,000 per month are deregulated when a lease ends. In Santa Monica, the state of California mandated that as of 1999, rent for newly vacant apartments could increase. Even so, in both cities, much of the rental market is dominated by rent controls. Accordingly, in this chapter we focus on the consequences of those controls.

THE ADVERSE EFFECTS OF RENT CONTROLS

In general, the unfettered movement of rental prices in a freely competitive housing market performs three vital functions: (1) it allocates existing scarce housing among competing claimants; (2) it promotes the efficient maintenance of existing housing and stimulates the production of new housing, where appropriate; and (3) it rations usage of housing by demanders, thereby preventing waste of scarce housing. Rent control prevents rental prices from effectively performing these functions. Let's see how.

Rent control discourages the construction of new rental units.
Developers and mortgage lenders are reluctant to get involved in building new rental properties because controls artificially depress the most important long-run determinant of profitability—rents. Thus, in one

recent year, eleven thousand new housing units were built in Dallas, a city with a 16 percent rental vacancy rate but no rent-control statute. In that same year, only two thousand units were built in San Francisco, a city with a 1.6 percent vacancy rate but stringent rent-control laws. In New York City, the only rental units being built are either exempt from controls or heavily subsidized by the government. Private construction of new apartments in Santa Monica also dried up under controls, even though new office space and commercial developments—both exempt from rent control—were built at a record pace.

Rent control leads to the deterioration of the existing supply of rental housing. When rental prices are held below free market levels, property owners cannot recover through higher rents the costs of maintenance, repairs, and capital improvements. Thus, such activities are sharply curtailed. Eventually, taxes, utilities, and the expenses of the most rudimentary repairs—such as replacing broken windows—exceed the depressed rental receipts; as a result, the buildings are abandoned. In New York, some owners have resorted to arson, hoping to collect the insurance on their empty rent-controlled buildings before the city claims them for back taxes. Under rent controls in Santa Monica, the city insisted that owners wishing to convert empty apartment buildings to other uses had to build new rental units to replace the units they no longer rented. At a cost of up to $50,000 per apartment, it is little wonder that few owners were willing to bear the burden, choosing instead to leave the buildings empty and graffiti-scarred.

Rent control impedes the process of rationing scarce housing. One consequence of this is that tenant mobility is sharply restricted. Even when a family's demand for living space changes—due, for example, to a new baby or a teenager's departure for college—there can be substantial costs in giving up a rent-controlled unit. In New York City, landlords often charge "key money" (a large up-front cash payment) before a new tenant is allowed to move in. The high cost of moving means that large families often stay in cramped quarters while small families or even single persons reside in large apartments. In New York, this phenomenon of nonmobility came to be known as *housing gridlock.* It is estimated that more than 20 percent of renters in New York City live in apartments that are bigger or smaller than they would otherwise occupy. In Santa Monica, many homeowners rented out portions of their houses in response to soaring prices in the 1970s and then found themselves trapped by their tenants, whom they could not evict even if they wanted to sell their homes and move to a retirement community.

EFFORTS TO EVADE CONTROLS

Not surprisingly, the distortions produced by rent control lead to efforts by both landlords and tenants to evade the rules. This in turn leads to the growth of cumbersome and expensive government bureaucracies whose job is to enforce the controls. In New York, where rents can be raised when tenancy changes hands, landlords have an incentive to make life unpleasant for tenants or to evict them on the slightest pretense. The city has responded by making evictions extremely costly for landlords. Even if a tenant blatantly and repeatedly violates the terms of a lease, the tenant cannot be evicted if the violations are corrected within a "reasonable" time period. If the violations are not corrected—despite several trips to court by the owners and their attorneys—eviction requires a tedious and expensive judicial proceeding. For their part, tenants routinely try to sublet all or part of their rent-controlled apartments at prices substantially above the rent they pay the owner. Because both the city and the landlords try to prohibit subletting, the parties often end up in the city's housing courts, an entire judicial system developed chiefly to deal with disputes over rent-controlled apartments.

Strict controls on monthly rents force landlords to use other means to discriminate among prospective tenants. Simply to ensure that the rent check comes every month, many landlords rent only to well-heeled professionals. As one commentator put it, "There is no disputing that Santa Monica became younger, whiter, and richer under rent control." The same pattern occurred under the rent-control laws of Berkeley, California, and Cambridge, Massachusetts.

BUREAUCRACIES FLOURISH

There is little doubt the bureaucracies that evolve to administer rent-control laws are cumbersome and expensive. Between 1988 and 1993, New York City spent $5.1 billion rehabilitating housing confiscated from private landlords. Even so, derelict buildings continued piling up at a record rate. The overflow and appeals from the city's housing courts clog the rest of New York's judicial system, impeding the prosecution of violent criminals and drug dealers. In Santa Monica, the Rent Control Board began with an annual budget of $745,000 and a staff of twenty people. By the early 1990s, the staff had tripled in size, and the budget was pushing $5 million. Who picked up the tab? The landlords did, of course, with an annual special assessment of $200 per unit levied on them. And even though the 1999 state-mandated changes in the law meant that apartment rents in Santa Monica can be increased when a new tenant moves in, the new rent is then controlled by the city for the duration of the tenancy. Indeed, the Rent Control Board conveniently maintains a Web site where one can go to learn the maximum allowable rent on any of the tens of thousands of rent-controlled residences in Santa Monica.

THE LOSERS FROM RENT CONTROLS

Ironically, the big losers from rent control—in addition to landlords— are often low-income individuals, especially single mothers. Indeed, many observers believe that one significant cause of homelessness in cities such as New York and Los Angeles is rent control. Poor individuals often cannot assure the discriminating landlord that their rent will be paid on time—or paid at all—each month. Because controlled rents are generally well below free market levels, there is little incentive for apartment owners to take a chance on low-income individuals as tenants. This is especially true if the prospective tenant's chief source of income is a welfare check. Indeed, a significant number of the tenants appearing in New York's housing courts have been low-income mothers who, due to emergency expenses or delayed welfare checks, have missed rent payments. Often their appeals end in evictions and residence in temporary public shelters or on the streets. Prior to the state-mandated easing of controls, some apartment owners in Santa Monica who used to rent one- and two-room units to welfare recipients and other low-income individuals simply abandoned their buildings, leaving them vacant rather than trying to collect artificially depressed rents that failed to cover operating costs. The disgusted owner of one empty and decaying eighteen-unit building had a friend spray-paint his feelings on the wall: "I want to tear this mess down, but Big Brother won't let me." Perhaps because the owner had escaped from a concentration camp in search of freedom in the United States, the friend added a personalized touch: a drawing of a large hammer and sickle, symbol of the former Soviet Union.

DAMAGE AROUND THE WORLD

It is worth noting that the ravages of rent controls are not confined to the United States. In Mumbai, India, rents are still set at the levels that prevailed back in 1940. A two-bedroom apartment near the center of the city may have a controlled rent of as little as $8.50 per month. (Nearby, free market rents for an apartment of the same size can be as much as $3,000 per month.) Not surprisingly, landlords have let their rent-controlled buildings decay, and collapsing apartments have become a regular feature of life in this city of twelve million people. Over the past 10 years, about ninety people have been killed in the collapse of more than fifty rent-controlled buildings. The city government estimates that perhaps one hundred more apartment buildings are on the verge of collapse.

Even Communist nations are not exempt from rent controls. In a heavily publicized news conference several years ago, the foreign minister of Vietnam, Nguyen Co Thach, declared that a "romantic conception of socialism" had destroyed his country's economy after the Vietnam War. Thach stated that rent control had artificially encouraged demand and discouraged supply and that all of the housing in Hanoi had fallen into disrepair as a result. Thach concluded by noting, "The Americans couldn't destroy Hanoi, but we have destroyed our city by very low rents. We realized it was stupid and that we must change policy."

Apparently, this same thinking was what induced the state of California to compel changes in Santa Monica's rent-control ordinance. The result of that policy change was an almost immediate jump in rents on newly vacant apartments, as well as a noticeable rise in the vacancy rate—exactly the results we would expect. Interestingly enough, however, prospective new tenants were less enthusiastic about the newly available apartments than many landlords had expected. The reason? Twenty years of rent controls had produced many years of reduced upkeep and hence apartments that were less than pristine. As one renter noted, "The trouble is, most of this area … [is] basically falling apart." And another complained, "I don't want to move into a place that's depressing, with old brown carpet that smells like chicken soup." Higher rents are changing both the ambience and the aroma of Santa Monica apartments—but only at the same rate that the market is allowed to perform its functions.

DISCUSSION QUESTIONS

1. Why do you think governments frequently attempt to control apartment rents but not house prices?

2. What determines the size of the key-money payments that landlords demand (and tenants offer) for the right to rent a controlled apartment?

3. Who, other than the owners of rental units, loses as a result of rent controls? Who gains from rent controls? What effect would the

imposition of rent controls have on the market price of an existing single-family house? What effect would rent controls have on the value of vacant land?

4. Why do the owners of rental units reduce their maintenance expenditures on the units when rent controls are imposed? Does their decision have anything to do with whether they can afford those expenditures?

5. Because rent controls reduce the rental price below the market clearing price, the quantity of rental units on the market must decline. What does this imply *must* happen to the full cost of renting an apartment including "key money," harassment by the landlord, and so forth? Explain.

6. How does the percentage of voters who are renters (as opposed to owners) affect the incentives for politicians to propose rent controls? Does this incentive depend on the likelihood that renters are less likely to vote in local elections than are owners of apartments and houses? Why do you suppose renters are less likely to vote in local elections? Explain.

PART THREE

Labor Markets

Introduction

Almost everyone participates in the labor market, and most of us do so for most of our lives. In one sense, labor (or **human capital,** as it is sometimes called by economists) is no different from any other **economic good.** After all, labor is a **scarce good,** and so the basic tools used by economists can be applied to understanding the markets for it. Nevertheless, special care is sometimes required to understand what is going on in labor markets because not all aspects of these markets are what they seem to be.

(Why) Are Women Paid Less?

As you will see in Chapter 11, since the middle of the twentieth century, there has been a revolution in the labor market as women have entered in unprecedented numbers. Yet even though women now regularly work in jobs formerly closed to them, the data still suggest that they are being paid less than men. Much of this seeming discrimination in pay is attributable to the occupational choices made by women: They work in less hazardous environments and take jobs that offer greater flexibility and fewer hours of work per week. Safe, flexible employment that demands fewer hours of work per week is desirable; once we correct for these job attributes, the real differences in pay between men and women are much smaller than they appear to be at first glance. Nevertheless, the question remains: Do women select such jobs because that is really their preferred choice, or are they forced into such work because discrimination by male business owners and managers gives women no real alternatives? This is an issue that only further study will resolve.

THE EFFECTS OF THE MINIMUM WAGE

The issue of discrimination also arises when we examine what happens when the government interferes with the operation of labor markets. We examine this in Chapter 12. As we shall see time and again in this book, the effects of government actions are not always what they seem, nor are they usually what their proponents claim for them. The chief losers from the **minimum wage**— disadvantaged minority teenagers—are often the very people who can least afford those losses, while those who claim to support the law on altruistic grounds are in fact likely to be the biggest winners. The message of this chapter may well be this simple piece of advice: When someone claims to be doing something *for* you, it is wise to ask what that person is doing *to* you.

IMMIGRATION, SUPERSTARS, AND POVERTY

The plight of the disadvantaged is the central focus of Chapter 13. Over the past forty or fifty years, people at the bottom of the income distribution in America have experienced a rising standard of living. In more recent years, however, this rise seems to have slowed relative to the improving standard of living at the very top of the income distribution. Here we learn that several factors are likely at work, including the rising premium on education, technological changes that have helped top performers ("superstars") earn even more, and high rates of immigration that have depressed wages near the bottom of the income distribution. Sadly, it also appears that some (though not all) government programs directed at improving life for the least fortunate have had the reverse effect. Once again, we see that when it comes to important public issues, things are rarely what they appear to be.

THE UNDERGROUND ECONOMY

Chapter 14 examines what many people consider to be the seamy underside of labor markets—namely, the underground economy. The participants of this shadowy economy can be found all over the world. They speak different languages, use different currencies, and have different skill levels. But they all deal in cash only and usually pay no taxes, regardless of their earnings. They all work "off the books." Some are there because local tax rates payable in the regular economy are too high for them to bear. Some have been driven there because onerous labor market regulations prevent them from finding steady employment with a regular salary and fringe benefits. But however they get there, what makes them stay is that their lives are better there than in any relevant alternative. So, despite the fact that *we* might not like to be doing what they do for the pay they receive, their participation in such markets raises their wealth and the wealth of those with whom they trade. Thus, once again we see that mutually beneficial exchange can work its wonders even in the unlikeliest of locations.

CHAPTER 11

(Why) Are Women Paid Less?

Since the middle of the twentieth century, there has been a revolution in the job market. Women have entered the paid workforce in unprecedented numbers. In 1950, for example, only about one-third of working-age women were in the paid workforce; today, some 60 percent are. And because the male **labor force participation rate** has fallen from 89 percent to 74 percent over this period, women now account for almost half of the paid workforce in America. There has also been an overwhelming change in the nature of paid work done by women. Fifty years ago, professional careers for women outside of nursing or teaching were unusual. Today, women comprise roughly half of the newly minted attorneys and physicians starting work each year. Over the same fifty-year period, there has been a transformation of wages, too. In 1950, median earnings of women were only two-thirds those of men. Today, women earn 80 percent of what men are paid.

Reread that last sentence. On average, for every dollar a man earns, a woman gets paid 80 cents. Can this possibly be true? Consider this fact: Nearly 70 percent of employers' costs are accounted for by labor. An employer who hired only women at 80 cents on the dollar could cut labor costs by 20 percent relative to an employer who hired only men. This would yield added profits of about 14 percent of sales—which would *triple* the **profit** earned by the typical firm. If women are paid 20 percent less than men, how could any employer possibly afford to hire anyone *but* women?

IS IT DISCRIMINATION?

At this point you may be saying to yourself, "Surely, there are differences between men and women other than their sex that can help account for this 'gender gap' in earnings." And you would be correct. Earnings are a reflection of experience, education, marital status, and age, for example. But even when economists control for all of these individual characteristics, using nationwide data, such as from the U.S. Census Bureau or the Bureau of Labor Statistics, unexplained differences between the pay of men and women persist. Men with the same measured individual characteristics are paid at least 10 percent more than women, and some studies find a difference twice that size.

The widespread opinion of many observers is that the unexplained gap between the pay of men and women is chiefly the result of discrimination against women. The reasoning is simple. Most business owners and senior managers are men, and given a choice between hiring a man or a woman, the "old-boy network" operates in favor of the man. According to this view, women can get the job only if they agree to accept lower wages.

Consider this fact, however: For more than 40 years, it has been illegal to discriminate in the workforce on the basis of race or gender. Two major federal agencies, the Equal Employment Opportunity Commission and the Office of Federal Contract Compliance, are wholly or largely devoted to ensuring that this antidiscrimination mandate is enforced. As interpreted by the courts, the law now says that if the statistical *appearance* of lower wages for women (or minorities) is present in a workplace, the employer is *presumed* to be guilty of discrimination and must prove otherwise. No one thinks that federal agencies do a perfect job at enforcing the law here or elsewhere, but it is hard to believe that a persistent 20 percent pay difference could escape the notice of even the most nearsighted federal bureaucrat.

A hint of what might be going on begins to emerge when economists study the payroll records of individual firms, using actual employee information that is specific and detailed regarding location of the firm, type of work, employee responsibilities, and other factors. These analyses reveal that the so-called wage gap between men and women is much smaller—typically no more than 5 percent—and often there is no gap at all. The sharp contrast between firm-level data and economy-wide data suggests that something may be at work here besides (or in addition to) outright gender discrimination.

THE IMPORTANCE OF CHILDREN

That something is actually three things. First, women's pay is extremely sensitive to whether or not they have children. In Britain, for example, where this issue has been studied intensively, the average pay earned by a woman begins to fall shortly before the birth of her first child and continues to drop until the child becomes a teenager. Although earnings begin to revive once the first child passes the age of 20 or so, they never fully recover. The earnings drop associated with motherhood is close to one-third, and only one-third of that drop is regained after the nest is empty. American data suggest that the same pattern is present on this side of the Atlantic.

The parenthood pay declines suffered by women stem from a variety of sources: Some are put on the "mommy track," with reduced responsibilities and hours of work; others move to different employers around the time their first child is born, taking jobs that offer more flexible work schedules but offer correspondingly lower pay as well. Overall, a woman with average skills who has a child at age 24 can expect to receive nearly $1 million less compensation over her career, compared to one who remains childless. It is worth emphasizing that no similar effect is observed with men. In fact, there is some evidence that men with children are actually paid *more* than men without children. These findings strongly suggest a fact that will come as no surprise to most people: Despite the widespread entry of women into the labor force, they retain the primary responsibility for child care at home, and their careers suffer as a result.

OCCUPATIONAL SELECTION

The second factor at work in explaining male–female wage differences is occupational selection. Compared to women, men tend to be concentrated in paid employment that is dangerous or unpleasant. Commercial fishing, construction, law enforcement, firefighting, truck driving, and mining, to name but a few, are occupations that are much more dangerous than average and are dominated by men. As a result, men represent 92 percent of all occupational deaths. Hazardous jobs offer what is known as a **compensating differential,** extra pay for assuming the differential risk of death or injury on the job. In equilibrium, these extra wages do no more than offset the extra hazards. So even though measured earnings *look* high relative to the educational and other requirements of the jobs, appearances are deceiving. After adjusting for risk, the value of that pay is really no greater than that for less hazardous employment—but the appearance of higher pay contributes to the measured gender gap.

HOURS OF WORK

The third key factor influencing pay is hours of work. Men are more than twice as likely as women to work in excess of 50 hours per week in paid employment. Overall, the average paid workweek for men is about 15 percent longer than it is for women. Men are also more likely than women to be in full-time, rather than part-time, paid employment, and the wage differences here can be huge. Working an average of 44 hours per week versus 34 hours per week, for example, yields more than twice the pay, regardless of gender. This substantial gender gap in hours of paid work is due in part to the "mommy track" phenomenon, but the question that remains is: Does this constitute discrimination on the part of employers, or is it the result of choices by women?

Although we cannot answer that question definitively, there is reason to believe that some differences in occupational choice (and thus in pay) are due to discrimination. For example, the highest-paying blue-collar jobs are typically union jobs, and industrial and crafts unions have had a long history of opposition to women as members. Or consider medicine. Women are becoming much more numerous in specialties such as dermatology and radiology, where schedules tend to be more flexible, hours of work can be limited, and part-time practice is feasible. But many physicians would argue that the noticeable underrepresentation of women in the high-paying surgical specialties is partly the result of discrimination against women, rather than reflecting the occupational choices preferred by women. If this argument is correct, then even if women in a given specialty are paid the same as men in that specialty, the exclusion of women from high-paying slots will lower their average wages and make them worse off.

The extent of gender discrimination in the workplace is unlikely to be definitively settled anytime soon. Measured earnings differences, even those that account for experience, education, and other factors, clearly overstate the true pay gap between equally qualified men and women. Just as surely, however, given the heavier parenting demands typically made on women, even when they receive equal pay, it is not for equal work.

DISCUSSION QUESTIONS

1. Suppose an employer offers a base wage of $20 per hour for the first 40 hours of work each week and overtime pay of $30 per hour for any hours beyond 40 per week; the employer allows workers to choose their own hours of work. Suppose employee A chooses to work 36 hours per week and employee B chooses to work 42 hours per week. Compute the average weekly earnings for employees A and B, and compute the "earnings gap" (in percentage terms) between them. In your view, does this observed earnings gap constitute discrimination? Justify your conclusion.

2. A recent British study found that married men earned more than unmarried men—but only if their wives did not have full-time paid employment. Suggest an explanation for this finding. (*Hint:* In which case is a man more likely to share in the household responsibilities, including child care?)

3. Women who own their own businesses earn net profits that are only half as large as the net profits earned by men who own their own businesses. First, consider why women would be willing to accept lower profits. Could this reflect poorer options for women as employees? Alternatively, could it reflect other attributes of self-employment that women might find more advantageous than men do? Then think about why women earn lower profits. Is this evidence of discrimination? If so, by whom? If not, what else might account for the lower profits?

4. Why do you think we have laws that prohibit discrimination in pay based on gender or race but permit employers to discriminate in pay based on education or experience?

5. Suppose you own a company. If you hire ten men, each of them at $70,000 per year, your firm will be able to sell $1,000,000 in output this year, and you will be able to earn $50,000 in profits, an amount that is normal for a firm of your size in your industry. (Your firm's other costs, such as for rent and advertising, will be $250,000 this year.) Now assume that you could hire ten women for $56,000 each, instead of hiring the men. What would your total profits be if you hired the women and they were just as productive as the more expensive men? Show all calculations.

6. Refer back to the last question. Based on the discussion in the chapter, what would you want to know about these women to satisfy yourself that they will be at least as productive as the men? List the key factors and explain briefly.

CHAPTER 12

The Effects of the Minimum Wage

Ask workers if they would like a raise, and the answer is likely to be a resounding yes. But ask them if they would like to be fired or have their hours of work reduced, and they would probably tell you no. The effects of the minimum wage are centered on exactly these points.

Proponents of the **minimum wage**—the lowest hourly wage firms may legally pay their workers—argue that low-income workers are underpaid and therefore unable to support themselves or their families. The minimum wage, they say, raises earnings at the bottom of the wage distribution, with little disruption to workers or businesses. Opponents claim that most low-wage workers are low-skilled youths without families to support. The minimum wage, they say, merely enriches a few teenagers at the far greater expense of many others, who can't get jobs. Most important, opponents argue, many individuals at the bottom of the economic ladder lack the skills needed for employers to hire them at the federal minimum. Willing to work but unable to find jobs, these people never learn the basic job skills needed to move up the economic ladder to higher-paying jobs. The issues are clear—but what are the facts?

BACKGROUND

The federal minimum wage was instituted in 1938 as a provision of the Fair Labor Standards Act. It was originally set at 25 cents per hour, about 40 percent of the average manufacturing wage at the time. Over the next forty years, the legal minimum was raised periodically, roughly in accord with the movement of market wages throughout the economy. Typically, its level has averaged between 40 and 50 percent of average manufacturing wages. In response to the high inflation of the late 1970s, the minimum wage was hiked seven times between 1974 and 1981, reaching $3.35 per hour—about 42 percent of manufacturing wages. President Ronald Reagan vowed to keep a lid on the minimum wage, and by the time he left office, the minimum's unchanged level left it at 31 percent of average wages. Legislation passed in 1989 raised the minimum to $3.80 in 1990 and $4.25 in 1991. Five years later, Congress raised it in two steps to $5.15 per hour. Over the period 2007–2009, the minimum was hiked in three steps to its current level of $7.25 per hour.

About half a million workers earn the minimum wage; another 1.5 million or so are paid even less because the law doesn't cover them. Supporters of the minimum wage claim that it prevents exploitation of employees and helps people earn enough to support their families and themselves. Even so, at $7.25 per hour, a full-time worker earns only about two-thirds of what the government considers enough to keep a family of four out of poverty. In fact, to get a family of four with one wage earner up to the poverty line, the minimum wage would have to be above $11.00 per hour.

Yet opponents of the minimum wage argue that such calculations are irrelevant. For example, two-thirds of the workers earning the minimum wage are single, and they earn enough to put them 30 percent above the poverty cutoff. Moreover, about half of these single workers are teenagers, most of whom have no financial obligations, except perhaps clothing and automobile-related expenditures. Thus, opponents argue that the minimum wage chiefly benefits upper middle class teens who are least in need of assistance at the same time that it costs the jobs of thousands of disadvantaged minority youths.

RECENT EVIDENCE

The debate over the minimum wage intensified a few years ago when research suggested that a change in the New Jersey minimum wage had no adverse short-run impact on employment. Further research by other scholars focusing on Canada reveals more clearly what actually happens when the minimum wage is hiked. In Canada, there are important differences in minimum wages both over time and across different provinces. These differences enabled researchers to distinguish between the short- and long-run effects of changes in minimum wages. The short-run effects are indeed negligible, as implied by the New Jersey study. But the Canadian research shows that in the long run, the adverse effects of a higher minimum wage are quite substantial. In the short run, it is true that firms do not cut their workforce by much in response to a higher minimum. But over time, the higher costs due to a higher minimum wage force smaller firms out of business, and it is here that the drop in employment shows up clearly.

The Canadian results are consistent with the overwhelming bulk of the U.S. evidence on this issue, which points to a negative impact of the minimum wage on employment. After all, the number of workers demanded, like the quantity demanded for all goods, responds to price: The higher the price, the lower the number desired. There remains, however, debate over how many jobs are lost due to the minimum wage. For example, when the minimum wage was raised from $3.35 to $4.25, credible estimates of the number of potential job losses ranged to 400,000. When the minimum was hiked to $5.15, researchers suggested that at least 200,000 jobs were at stake. More recently, economists have estimated that the latest increase in the federal minimum wage to $7.25 from $6.55 caused 300,000 people to lose their jobs. With a workforce of over 155 million persons, numbers like these may not sound very large. But most of the people who don't have jobs as a result of the minimum wage are teenagers; they comprise less than five percent of the workforce but bear almost all the burden of foregone employment alternatives.

THE BIG LOSERS

Significantly, the youths most likely to lose work due to the minimum wage are disadvantaged teenagers, chiefly minorities. On average, these teens enter the workforce with the fewest job skills and the greatest need for on-the-job training. Until and unless these disadvantaged teenagers can acquire these skills, they are the most likely to be unemployed as a result of the minimum wage—and thus least likely to have the opportunity to move up the economic ladder. With a teen unemployment rate triple the overall rate and unemployment among black youngsters of 40 percent and more, critics argue that the minimum wage is a major impediment to long-term labor market success for minority youth.

Indeed, the minimum wage has an aspect that its supporters are not inclined to discuss: It can make employers more likely to discriminate on the basis of gender or race. When wages are set by market forces, employers who would discriminate face a reduced, and thus more expensive, pool of workers. But when the government mandates an above-market wage, the result is a surplus of low-skilled workers. It thus becomes easier and cheaper to discriminate. As former U.S. Treasury secretary Lawrence Summers noted, the minimum wage "removes the economic penalty to the employer. He can choose the one who's white with blond hair."

Critics of the minimum wage also note that it makes firms less willing to train workers lacking basic skills. Instead, companies may choose to hire only experienced workers whose abilities justify the higher wage. Firms are also likely to become less generous with fringe benefits in an effort to hold down labor costs. The prospect of more discrimination, less job training for low-skilled workers, and fewer fringe benefits for entry-level workers leaves many observers uncomfortable. As the economist Jacob Mincer noted, the minimum wage means "a loss of opportunity" for the hard-core unemployed.

LIVING WAGES?

Despite these adverse effects of the minimum wage, many state and local governments believe that people with jobs should be paid a wage on which they can "afford to live." In fact, some states and localities mandate that minimum wages (sometimes called "living wages") be even higher, at levels ranging up to almost $10 an hour in Santa Fe, New Mexico, and San Francisco, California. (Both amounts are adjusted up to reflect inflation each year.) In some cases, as in Baltimore, Maryland, the local minimum wage applies only to workers at firms that do business with the relevant government entity. But in the case of the Santa Fe and San Francisco minimum wages and all state-determined minimums, the law applies to all but a few firms that are declared exempt because of their very small size or their industry (such as agriculture).

When politicians decide to raise the minimum wage, it is only after heated battles often lasting months. Given the stakes involved—an improved standard of living for some and a loss of job opportunities for others—it is not surprising that discussions of the minimum wage soon turn to controversy. As one former high-level U.S. Department of Labor official said, "When it comes to the minimum wage, there are no easy positions to take. Either you are in favor of more jobs, less discrimination, and more on-the-job training, or you support better wages for workers. Whatever stance you choose, you are bound to get clobbered by the opposition." When Congress and the president face this issue, one or both usually feel the same way.

DISCUSSION QUESTIONS

1. Are teenagers better off when a higher minimum wage enables some to earn higher wages but causes others to lose their jobs?

2. Are there methods other than a higher minimum wage that could raise the incomes of low-wage workers without reducing employment among minority youngsters?

3. Why do you think organized labor groups, such as unions, are supporters of a higher minimum wage, even though all their members earn much more than the minimum wage?

4. Is it possible that a higher minimum wage could ever *increase* employment?

5. Even without a minimum wage, the unemployment rate would almost surely be higher among teenagers than among adults. Suggest at least two reasons why this is so.

6. Why is it teenagers (rather than members of any other age group) who are most likely to lose their jobs (or get turned down for employment) when the minimum wage is raised?

CHAPTER 13

Immigration, Superstars, and Poverty

In 1960, the poorest 20 percent of households in the United States received a bit over 4 percent of total income. Today, after nearly five decades of government efforts to relieve poverty, the bottom 20 percent receive a bit less than 4 percent of total income. About forty million Americans lived in poverty in 1960. About forty million U.S. citizens *still* live in poverty, despite the expenditure of hundreds of billions of dollars in aid for the poor. In the richest country in the world, poverty seems remarkably resilient.

START WITH THE FACTS

If we are to understand why, we must begin by getting the facts straight. First, even though the absolute number of Americans living in poverty has not diminished over the past fifty years, population growth has brought a sizable reduction in the *proportion* of impoverished Americans. As conventionally measured, more than 22 percent of Americans lived in poverty in 1960. Today, as we emerge from one of the worse recessions in our history, about 14 percent of the population is below the poverty line.

Second, traditional methods of measuring poverty may be misleading because they focus solely on the *cash income* of individuals. In effect, government statisticians compute a "minimum adequate budget" for families of various sizes—the "poverty line"—and then determine how many people have a cash income below this line. Yet major components of the federal government's antipoverty efforts come in the form of **in-kind transfers** (transfers of goods and services rather than cash) such as Medicare, Medicaid, subsidized housing, food stamps, and school lunches. When the dollar value of these in-kind transfers is included in measures of *total* income, the standard of living of persons at lower income levels has improved substantially over the years.

There is disagreement over how much of these in-kind transfers should be included in measures of the total income of recipients.[1] Nevertheless, most observers agree that these transfers, plus the **Earned Income Tax Credit** (which gives special tax rebates to low-income individuals), are major sources of income for people at the bottom of the income distribution. Adjusting for these transfers and taxes, it seems likely that over the past fifty years, the proportion of Americans living below the poverty line has been cut roughly in half. Just as important, the standard of living for the poorest 20 percent of the population has more than doubled since 1960. In short, the number of poor individuals in this country has declined significantly, and those who remain poor are generally better off than the poor of fifty years ago.

INCOME MOBILITY

Whatever measure of income we use, it is crucial to remember that most Americans exhibit a great deal of **income mobility**—they have a tendency to move around in the income distribution over time. The most important source of income mobility is the "life-cycle" pattern of earnings: New entrants to the workforce tend to have lower incomes at first, but most workers can enjoy rising incomes as they gain experience on the job. Typically, annual earnings reach a maximum at about age fifty-five. Because peak earnings occur well beyond the **median age** of the population (now about thirty-seven), a "snapshot" of the current distribution of earnings will find most individuals on the way up toward a higher position in the income distribution. People who have low earnings now are likely, on average, to have higher earnings in the future.

Another major source of income mobility stems from the operation of Lady Luck. At any point in time, the income of high-income people is likely to be abnormally high (relative to what they can expect on average) due to recent good luck—they may have just won the lottery

---

[1] There are two reasons for this disagreement. First, a given dollar amount of in-kind transfers is generally less valuable than the same dollar amount of cash income because cash offers the recipient a greater amount of choice in his or her consumption pattern. Second, medical care is an important in-kind transfer to the poor. Inclusion of all Medicaid expenditures for the poor would imply that the sicker the poor got, the richer they would be. Presumably, a correct measure of the income added by Medicaid would include only those medical expenses that the poor would have to incur if they were *not* poor and thus had to pay for the medical care (or medical insurance) out of their own pockets.

or received a long-awaited bonus. Conversely, the income of people who currently have low incomes is likely to be abnormally low due to recent bad luck, for example, because they are laid up after an automobile accident or have become temporarily unemployed. Over time, the effects of Lady Luck tend to average out across the population. Accordingly, people with high incomes today will tend to have lower incomes in the future, while people with low incomes today will tend to have higher future incomes; this means that many people living below the poverty line are there temporarily rather than permanently.

The effects of the forces that produce income mobility are strikingly revealed in studies examining the incomes of individuals over time. During the 1970s and 1980s, for example, among the people who were in the top 20 percent (quintile) of income earners at the beginning of the decade, less than half were in the top quintile by the end of the decade. Similarly, among the people who were in the bottom quintile at the beginning of the decade, almost half had moved out of that bracket by the end of the decade. Despite news stories that suggest otherwise, income mobility remains robust. From 1996 to 2005 (the decade most recently studied), more than half of the people who were in the bottom 20 percent income bracket in 1996 had moved out of that bracket by 2005.

INCOMES AT THE TOP

Nevertheless, there are several forces that have either increased income inequality in the United States or given the appearance of such an increase, so it is best to be clear on the nature of these. Consider first that a rising proportion of the population is *far* above the poverty line. In 1969, for example, about 4 percent of all people in America had earnings six times greater than the poverty level. Today, about 6 percent of Americans have earnings that high (above $150,000 for a family of four). Much of this jump in incomes at the top of the income distribution has come at the very top. Thirty years ago, for example, people in the top 10 percent of earners in America pulled in about 31 percent of total income; today they garner 37 percent. And most of this jump is in even more rarified company. The top 1 percent of earners used to account for 9 percent of total income; today they take in 16 percent of income. Thus, although inflation-adjusted incomes are rising across the board, they appear to be rising the fastest at the very top. This pattern, which first became apparent during the 1990s, is one that economists are seeking to explain. Much work remains to be done, but a few answers are emerging.

First, some key demographic changes are occurring. America is aging, and an older population tends to have more income inequality than a young population because older people have had more time to experience rising or falling fortunes. Americans are also getting better educated, and this tends to increase income inequality. People with little education have incomes that tend to cluster together, while the incomes of well-educated people spread out: Some choose to convert their human capital into much higher incomes, while others convert it into added leisure time. Taken together, these two demographic changes (aging and education) can account for more than 75 percent of the *appearance* of greater income inequality.

Second, a substantial part of the rapid income growth at the top has really been a matter of accounting fiction, rather than reality. Until the late 1980s, there were substantial tax advantages for the very wealthy to have a large portion of their incomes counted as corporate rather than personal income; in effect, a big chunk of income for the wealthy used to be hidden, not from the tax authorities, but from the policymakers who worry about the distribution of income. Subsequent changes in the tax laws have since encouraged people to report this income as personal rather than corporate income: Their incomes haven't really changed; it just looks to policymakers like they have.

Nevertheless, it is clear that there are more people in the rarified upper reaches of the income distribution, in part due to the so-called superstar effect. Technological changes have vastly expanded the size of the economic market that top performers can serve. Because of cell phones, videoconferencing, and e-mail, for example, top business managers can effectively direct far larger enterprises than used to be the case. Sports and entertainment stars can now use cable TV and the Internet to reach audiences of tens (or hundreds) of millions, far more than the tens of thousands who can attend a live performance. And these additional customers are each willing to pay for these services, so the incomes of those at the very top have multiplied correspondingly.

INCOMES AT THE BOTTOM

So much for incomes at the top; what about those at the bottom? Well, between 1990 and 2005, there was a huge influx of immigrants to the United States. New immigrants typically earn far less than long-term residents. When large numbers of them are added to the mix of people whose incomes are being measured, *average* income can fall, even when the incomes of all individuals are rising. Thus, immigration has created downward pressure on *measured* incomes at the bottom of the distribution. But new immigrants have also added to competitive pressures in labor markets for less-skilled individuals. On balance, it appears that immigration has probably lowered the wages of high school dropouts in America some 4–8 percent. And although this seems small, remember that it is occurring among people whose incomes are already low. Both of these effects are likely to lessen, perhaps even reverse, due to the recession of 2007–2009. Deteriorating economic conditions in America caused many recent immigrants to return to their homelands.

Public policy has also taken its toll on the incomes of people at the bottom. The war on drugs, for example, has saddled literally millions of individuals with criminal records, and the impact has been disproportionately greatest on African Americans, whose incomes were lower to begin with. For example, since 1990, more than two million African American males have served time in jail on serious (felony) drug charges. Once they return to the workforce, they find that their felony records exclude them from most jobs—and not just jobs in the middle or at the top. Often convicted felons cannot find positions that pay more than $8 per hour. The result is that the incomes of such individuals are sharply diminished, which means more poverty.

The expansion of Social Security Disability Insurance (SSDI) has also likely contributed to income stagnation at the bottom. Originally established in 1956 as a program to help individuals under age sixty-five who are truly disabled, SSDI has become the federal government's fastest-growing transfer program. It now accounts for about $110 billion in federal spending per year. It allows even those who are not truly disabled to receive payments from the government when they do not work. Since 1990, the number of people receiving disability payments from the Social Security Administration has almost tripled to about eight million. This is not surprising when you consider that the real value of the monthly benefits a person can collect has gone up 60 percent in the last thirty-five years, and eligibility requirements have been eased. The federal government spends more on disability payments than it does on food stamps or unemployment benefits.

What does this mean? Simply that people who might have worked through chronic pain and temporary injuries—particularly those without extensive training and education—now choose to receive a government disability benefit instead. The average Social Security disability payment is over $1,000 per month, tax-free. For many at the lower echelon of the job ladder, $1,000 per month seems pretty good. For the truly disabled, SSDI and related federal disability programs have definitely made life better. But experts believe that many disability recipients are now being drawn out of higher-paying jobs by the tax-free status of disability pay, combined with the fact that it enables them to spend more time with family and friends. This development also means that measures of income inequality have risen because even though disability recipients are clearly better off as a result of the program, their incomes as measured by government statisticians are markedly lower.

A NOTE OF OPTIMISM

There is one definite bright spot on the poverty policy front: the "welfare reform" program undertaken in 1996. Previously, low-income families had been eligible to receive—for an unlimited duration— federal payments called Aid to Families with Dependent Children. The program was converted in 1996 to Temporary Assistance to Needy Families. Limits were placed on the length of time individuals could receive payments, and all recipients were given additional **incentives** and assistance to enhance their job skills and enter or reenter the labor force. The full impact of this policy change is still being studied, but it now appears that it has modestly raised incomes among individuals at the bottom of the income distribution.

Although the resilience of poverty in America is discouraging to the poor and to analysts who study their plight, it is useful to consider these issues in an international context. In other industrialized nations, such as Japan and most countries in Europe, people at the bottom of the income distribution sometimes (but not always) fare better than the poor in America. Although the poor typically receive a somewhat larger *share* of national income than in America, the national income in which they are sharing is lower. Thus, compared to America, the poorest 10 percent of the population has a higher average income in Japan and Germany but a lower average income in the United Kingdom and Italy.

In developing nations—which is to say, for the vast majority of people around the world—poverty has a completely different meaning than it does in America. In Africa and much of Asia, for example, it is commonplace for people at the bottom of the income distribution to be living on the equivalent of $400 per *year* or less—in contrast to the $10,000–$15,000 per year they would earn in America. As we noted in Chapter 5, this staggering difference in living standards is due to the vast differences in legal and economic **institutions** that are observed around the world. In America, as in many other industrialized nations, these institutions both give people the incentives to put their talents to work and protect them from having their assets expropriated by the government. Thus, the best antipoverty program anyone has ever seen is the creation of an institutional environment in which human beings are able to make maximum use of the talents with which they are endowed.

DISCUSSION QUESTIONS

1. Why do most modern societies try to reduce poverty? Why don't they do so by simply passing a law that requires that everybody have the same income?

2. How do the "rules of the game" help determine who will be poor and who will not? (*Hint:* How did the Civil Rights Act of 1964, which forbade discrimination on the basis of race, likely affect the incomes of African Americans compared to the incomes of white Americans?) Explain your answer.

3. Which of the following possible in-kind transfers do you think raises the true income of recipients the most: free golf lessons, free transportation on public buses, or free food? Why?

4. Consider three alternative ways of helping poor people get better housing: government-subsidized housing that costs $6,000 per year, a housing **voucher** worth $6,000 per year toward rent on an apartment or a house, or $6,000 per year in cash. Which would you prefer if you were poor? On what grounds might you make your decision?

5. Why don't official counts of who is below the poverty include in people's incomes the value of the in-kind transfers they receive?

6. The current poverty line for a family of four is a bit over $22,000. If we lowered that threshold to, say, $15,000, what would happen to the number of poor people in the United States? Does that mean that we are better (or worse) off? Explain.

CHAPTER 14

The Underground World

Consider the following types of jobs:

- "Gypsy" taxi drivers in some U.S. cities
- Rickshaw drivers in Kolkata, India
- Street vendors in Kiev, Ukraine
- Sidewalk tortilla sellers in Mexico City, Mexico

While the people involved in these jobs speak different languages, use different currencies, and have different skill levels, they all have one thing in common—they are part of the **underground economy.** They deal in cash only and usually pay no taxes, regardless of their earnings. They all work "off the books." There are no official statistics about them, only rough estimates provided by the International Labour Organization (ILO), a few government agencies, and economists interested in this topic.

Before we examine data concerning the size of the underground economy, let's first examine why anyone would want to participate in this "shadow," or "informal," economy.

The Economics of Activity That Is Illegal

Certainly, if you are engaged in the illegal drug trade anywhere in the world, you cannot be part of the **official, reported economy.** You have to use cash and also be careful that your illegal transactions cannot be traced by government authorities, including tax collectors. Otherwise, you'll soon be headed for jail.

Of course, there is no way to know exactly how much underground activity is centered in the illegal drug trade. Estimates of the worldwide total vary from $300 billion per year to well over a $1 trillion per year. As long as certain drugs remain illegal, there will always be those willing to take the risks necessary to engage in those activities.

Not all illegal activities involve drugs, to be sure. The purchase and sale of human organs, for example, is part of the underground economy around the world. Paying for someone else's kidney in the United States is an illegal activity, as it is in most countries (see Chapter 8 for more details). Nevertheless, some of those who are on the waiting list for kidney transplants sometimes turn to "matchmakers" who will find a perfectly healthy person who is willing to donate an organ—for a cash price. The incentives are great for the more than 90,000 residents in the United States on waiting lists for a kidney transplant. About 5,000 of those people will die each year while waiting for a transplant. If a person on kidney dialysis cannot persuade a friend or relative to donate a kidney, a market does exist. The price for the organ—usually acquired from a donor who lives in another country—will likely range from $5,000 to $25,000 (and up). All in cash, all unreported, and all part of the underground economy.

TAXES DO MAKE A DIFFERENCE

Lets face it, if your **marginal income tax rate** were only, say, 15 percent, how much effort would you spend to avoid reporting income? Probably not very much, given that each dollar of unreported income would only save you 15 cents in taxes. In contrast, at a marginal income tax rate of, say, 40 percent, you might be tempted to seek plenty of ways to earn unreported income. In other words, you might wish to become part of the underground economy, at least for some portion of your annual income.

We thus infer that in every country in the world, the greater the marginal income tax rate, the larger will be the share of total annual economic activity that will be unreported and therefore untaxed. This conclusion merely reflects the fact that everyone responds to incentives **on the margin.** Now, this does not mean that high marginal tax rates cause the entire workforce to seek off-the-books income. Rather, the higher the marginal income tax rates are, the greater will be the proportion of individuals who will seek to earn unreported income.

A comparison of Europe and the United States suggests that our conclusion about the importance of taxes is correct. European nations, on average, have imposed higher marginal tax rates on their citizens than has the United States. Estimates of the size of the underground economy are that it is twice as large in Europe as a share of the economy as it is in the United States. About 10 percent of total economic activity in the United States appears to be underground, but the number is over 20 percent for Europe.

There is one thing we can be confident of for the United States. If marginal income tax rates rise compared to what they were during the period 2003–2010, the relative size of the underground economy will grow. This is just one reason why when government officials make their calculations of increased tax revenues due to a new higher tax rates, they are consistently wrong. They fail to take into account the movement into the underground economy that is induced by higher marginal tax rates, and thus overestimate the amount of increased tax revenues from the higher rates.

THE IMPACT OF LABOR MARKET REGULATIONS

In many European countries, particularly France, Germany, and Italy, firing a poorly performing worker is extremely difficult, and in some cases impossible. The amount of paperwork and legal proceedings that an employer has to undertake to get rid of a worker is sometimes beyond belief—at least for Americans. There is even a special judicial system in France for people who are fired. Employers lose these legal battles more than 75 percent of the time.

How do employers react to such an environment? Some, particularly smaller businesses, seek out workers who agree to cash payments and no employment contracts. Thus, unemployed workers may face the option of accepting a cash-only job with no job security instead of remaining unemployed. Moreover, in all countries in which **unemployment benefits** last for many months or even many years, the unemployed are more willing to participate in the underground economy because if they work "off the books" for cash, they can continue to receive unemployment benefits.

In 2010 the U.S. Congress increased the length of eligibility for unemployment benefits to almost two years. In response, some of the people receiving those extended benefits began to seriously seek "off-the-books" jobs, just as their counterparts have long done in Europe. What is a way of life for the unemployed in France, Italy, and Spain has started to become more widespread in America.

Other recent legislation has added to the incentives to become part of the underground economy in the United States. We speak here of the federal health-care legislation passed in 2010, which will, over the next few years, create additional regulations and costs to businesses that offer health insurance to their workers. As a result, some of those businesses will only be willing to hire additional workers if those new workers remain off the books, and thus ineligible for high-cost, employer-provided health insurance. This will increase the number of people seeking government-subsidized health insurance, and thus help raise the costs of the health-care legislation far above the official estimates of those costs. (See Chapter 19 for more details.)

THE ESTIMATED SIZE OF THE UNDERGROUND ECONOMY

On a worldwide basis, about one-third of annual world income goes unreported. As noted earlier, estimates for the United States center on about 10 percent, while it is estimated that around 20 percent of income in Europe is underground and thus goes unreported. Many southern European countries, such as Italy, have underground sectors that account for at least 30 percent of all economic activity.

When we consider developing countries and those with highly corrupt governments, the underground economy may be as great as 70 percent of all economic activity. As Venezuela went from a democracy to an oligarchy with massive amounts of corruption, the size of its underground economy in that country probably tripled, although there is no way to be sure of the exact number.

Wherever we look around the world, however, it appears that taxes, regulations, and government corruption all help stimulate expansion of the underground economy. This is because such obstacles to voluntary trade are more easily circumvented when work is "off the books."

A TALE OF TWO CITIES

In 1959 the completion of the St. Lawrence Seaway provided a short-cut around the port at Buffalo, New York. The city's economy began a gradual deterioration as fewer and fewer ships stopped there. The city's population declined by over 50 percent as residents sought opportunities elsewhere. Buffalo became a shell of its former self.

Now consider another city in another country that suffered a similar downturn. At the start of the 1980s, there were more than 60 textile mills in Ahmedabad, India, employing over 150,000 people. The textile workers received benefits and pension packages in addition to steady wages. Although total compensation in the mills was low relative to pay in the United States, it was above the average for India. But beginning in the middle of the 1980s, Ahmedabad saw its major factories reduce their output and finally shutter. China, Vietnam, and other developing countries could produce the same textiles at lower costs. Only ten mills survived in Ahmedabad, and more than 100,000 workers lost their textile jobs.

When industrial decline hit Buffalo, the economic, geographic, and social mobility of the United States was high enough that most of the displaced workers found jobs elsewhere, often far away from Buffalo. When they departed, they left behind empty houses and a decaying urban center. In India, mobility is far less than in the United States. Hence, one might expect to find that Ahmedabad became plagued by high unemployment when the mills shuttered, perhaps even beset with civil unrest. In fact, Ahmedabad is thriving—all because of the underground economy.

Those former textile workers left their previous industry, but they didn't leave town. Instead, they joined the city's underground economy. The city now has over 70,000 self-employed street vendors and almost 50,000 self-employed trash collectors and recyclers—well, you get the picture. Ahmedabad's informal economy has kept the city alive. It has prevented urban decay and high levels of unemployment. To be sure, the self-employed in this informal underground economy do not have the nicest jobs, nor are they paid wonderful salaries. The local municipal commissioner, I.P. Gautam, admits that per capita income is less than it used to be, "but you get your bread and butter." Indeed, Ahmedabad's underground economy is how that city survived the worldwide recession of 2007–2009.

LESSONS FOR THE FUTURE

The conclusion we draw from this tale of two cities is not that the people who lost jobs in Buffalo should have become self-employed street vendors. Instead, we infer that, particularly in developing countries, a thriving underground economy can help generate **wealth** that would not exist without it. Even in developed countries, more wealth is created through underground activities than would be generated in their absence.

If developed countries' governments continue to impose higher marginal personal income tax rates and more costly regulation of labor markets, the inevitable result will be that more work will be done off the books. Although not reported (or taxed), such work is nevertheless still wealth-creating. And for the people who engage in it, it beats their other options.

We are not suggesting that avoiding taxes by working in the underground economy is laudable. But consider the alternative. Without the option of the underground economy, some (perhaps many) of those workers pushed out of the formal economy would be pushed into more unemployment and even lower wages. Of course, there are disadvantages of the informal economy. Underground workers have fewer rights and almost no recourse to the courts when maltreated by employers. Moreover, they routinely have no fringe benefits and little job security. Nevertheless, regardless of the language spoken or the currency used, for many people around the globe, the underground world beats all other relevant alternatives.

DISCUSSION QUESTIONS

1. What is the relevance of marginal income tax rates when seeking to understand the extent of a country's underground economy?

2. How do employers respond to labor laws that make it difficult or costly to fire incompetent workers? Do such laws actually yield higher employment levels?

3. Is there a difference between becoming part of the underground economy because the activities in which you are dealing are illegal and simply trying to reduce the share of income that you pay in taxes? If so, what is that difference?

4. Why would you predict that a much larger share of total economic activity due to the underground economy will exist when a country's government is very corrupt? What type of activities would you expect would be part of the underground economy?

5. Is it possible that you might prefer to be paid "on the books," while your employer would prefer paying "you off the books"? If so, how would such a disagreement be settled between you?

6. When you voluntarily exchange your labor services with someone else who pays you "on the books," can you be made worse off compared to not working at all? What if you are paid "off the books"?

PART FOUR

Market Structures

Introduction

The competitive model employed in our discussion of **demand** and **supply** assumes that firms on both sides of the market satisfy the conditions of **pure competition.** For sellers of goods, this means the **demand curve** they face is **perfectly elastic:** Suppliers must take the market price as given because any attempt by them to raise their price above the market price will result in the loss of *all* of their sales. Similarly, purchasers in the competitive model face a **supply curve** that is also perfectly elastic. The market price is given, and any attempt by them to purchase at less than that price will be unsuccessful—no one will sell to them.

The conditions of pure competition imply that buyers and sellers have no effect individually on market prices. Even a casual glance at the world suggests that the conditions of pure competition are not always met. Sometimes, as is the case for major corporations, the firms are large enough relative to the market that significant changes in their purchase or sale decisions will have an effect on prices. In other cases, buyers or sellers are "unique," in that no other buyer or seller offers exactly what they do. (Classic examples include the superstars of sports and entertainment, who will sell less of their services if they raise their prices but will still sell some.) Sometimes firms that would otherwise be pure competitors join to form a **cartel,** acting as a single decision-making unit whose collective output decisions affect the market price.

When a seller's decisions affect the price of a good, economists usually call the firm a **monopoly.** Literally, this means "single seller," but what is actually meant is that the firm faces a downward-sloping demand curve for its output, so that its decisions affect the price at which its output is sold. When a buyer's decisions affect the market price, we term the firm a **monopsony,** or "single buyer." This means that the firm faces a positively sloped supply curve, so that its purchasing decisions affect the price at which it buys goods. (Some economists use the term **price searcher** to mean any firm, buyer or seller, whose decisions affect market prices and who must therefore search for—or decide on—the price that maximizes the firm's profits. Following this terminology, a pure competitor would be called a **price taker,** for such a firm takes the market price as given.)

PATENT TROLLS AND SEED MONOPOLIES

The starting point for our examination of market structures is Chapter 15. One lawful source of monopoly in the United States is a patent. This is a set of exclusive rights granted by the federal government to an inventor for a limited period in return for public disclosure of the invention. Patents ensure inventors that they can lawfully protect, and thus profit from, the commercial value of their ideas. And because the inventor must reveal the details of the invention to the public, other people have the opportunity to be inspired by it and perhaps create useful products. But because the patent owner has a monopoly on the invention, the owner can charge a monopoly price for the product, which may be well above the price of the item if it were supplied by many competing firms. This fact creates the trade-off of patents, and thus the policy tension regarding them. People especially worry about monopoly pricing with patents when several, or several hundred, of them are combined in the hands of a patent aggregator (or "patent troll" as they are sometimes called). The common view is that patent trolls just collect money for doing nothing but being monopolists. In fact, however, by bringing many patents together under the same roof, they may be able to vastly increase the productivity of the patents compared to the situation in which ownership of the patents is widespread. And besides, the monopoly pricing potential of a patent arises only to the extent to which it markedly outperforms competing ideas. If workers, ranging from fruit pickers to baseball stars, are paid for the value of what they produce, why shouldn't inventors be paid in accord with the value of what *they* produce?

CONTRACTS, COMBINATIONS, AND CONSPIRACIES

As you will see in Chapter 16, the rigors (and low profits) of competition are such that firms often try to devise ways to avoid competing. One of the most popular is the cartel, which is simply a collective agreement by many or all firms in an industry to reduce total output so that the price of the product—and thus the profits of the cartel's members—can be increased. Cartels are generally illegal in the United States, but the National Collegiate Athletic Association (NCAA) is a cartel that is both legal and flourishing. Cartels are more commonly observed in international markets. Here we examine three international cartels, in the markets for oil, diamonds, and caviar. In each case, we find that although the **incentives** to form cartels are great, even greater are the incentives to cheat on the cartels almost as soon as they are formed. The overriding message of this chapter is that despite their enormous profit potential, competitive pressures make cartels inherently unstable and thus generally short-lived.

COFFEE, TEA, OR TUITION-FREE?

Whatever the degree of competition, firms are always seeking ways to raise profits. Often this means developing new products and striving to offer superior service. But sometimes, as you will see in Chapter 17, it simply means adjusting prices on existing products. The practice of charging prices that differ among customers in ways not due to differences in the marginal costs of supplying them is called **price discrimination.** Although technically illegal in the United States, it is routinely observed in markets ranging from airline travel to college financial aid. In the case of air travel, you are almost certainly the beneficiary of price discrimination, paying a lower price than you would if price discrimination were completely eliminated. But don't feel too smug: By the time you start traveling for business rather than pleasure, you are likely to be on the wrong end of the price discrimination, paying plenty so that the college kid in the seat next to you can enjoy spring break in a sunny clime.

KEEPING THE COMPETITION OUT

As Chapter 18 demonstrates, enlisting the government to hamstring or exclude competitors is probably the most reliable means of ensuring that you are protected from the rigors of competition. Perhaps for this reason, the array of markets in which the government stifles competition is nothing short of remarkable. Here we examine just a handful, ranging from taxicabs to hair braiding, but the list could have gone on and on. In each case, the method is the same: Usually under the guise of "consumer protection," the government prevents entry by some firms into a market, thereby reducing supply in that market. The effect is much the same as that produced by a fully enforced cartel. Firms thus protected by the government enjoy both a higher price for their product and a larger **market share.** The consumers, supposedly "protected" by their government, are usually the big losers due to higher product prices and reduced selection among suppliers.

CHAPTER 15

Patent Trolls and Seed Monopolies

Nathan Myhrvold is a patent troll. Monsanto Corporation is a seed monopoly. Or so their critics claim. Myhrvold, formerly the chief technical officer at Microsoft, founded Intellectual Ventures, which creates and invests in inventions. Monsanto, which got its start by creating the artificial sweetener saccharin, is now the world's leader in creating genetically modified (GM) seeds for agriculture. Whatever their history, however, both Myhrvold's company and Monsanto regularly make headlines because of the many patents they each own.

THE NATURE OF PATENTS

A **patent** is a set of exclusive rights granted by a national government to an inventor for a limited period in return for a public disclosure of the invention.[1] The notion of a patent dates back at least 2,500 years to the Greek city of Sybaris. Patents have been a part of the history of the United States since our nation's inception. Article 1, section 8, clause 8 of the U.S. Constitution specifically authorizes Congress to issue exclusive rights to new ideas, and the Patent Act of 1790 laid out the first rules for doing so in this country. (Thomas Jefferson, in his role as Secretary of State from 1790 to 1793, was our first Patent Commissioner.) Originally, patents in the United States were issued for 14 years. In the nineteenth century this was raised to 17 years, and in 1994 it was upped to 20 years. During the period of the patent, the inventor has exclusive rights to the commercial use of the patented item, but the inventor must publicly disclose all of the details of the patented item.

---

1 **Copyrights** and **trademarks** are similar to patents. The former grant exclusive rights to authors or creators of books (such as this one), songs, or other original works. The latter protect distinctive signs or indicators used by businesses to identify their products or services to consumers. (A famous example is McDonald's "Golden Arches.")

Devising new ideas is an uncertain, costly business. For people to undertake this risky investment, they must have some reasonable expectation of a reward if they are successful. A patent increases the chance of reward by granting the inventor a **monopoly** on the use of his or her new idea. For the duration of the patent, its owner has the exclusive rights to the patented process, design, or good. Anyone else who wants to use the design or process or manufacture the product must compensate the patent's owner.

THE COSTS AND BENEFITS OF PATENTS

The advantages of patents are twofold. First, they ensure inventors (such as the famous Thomas Edison) that they can lawfully protect, and thus profit, from the commercial value of their ideas. Second, because the inventor is required to publicly reveal all elements of his or her idea, other people have the opportunity to be inspired by it and perhaps create other useful products. On both counts, patents tend to foster invention (the creation of new ideas) and innovation (the successful commercial application of new ideas).

But patents may come at a cost. Because the patent owner has a monopoly on the patented item, the owner can charge a monopoly price for the item, which may be well above the price that would be observed if the product were supplied by many competing firms. Hence, the output of the patented item is less than if it were supplied competitively. This in turn implies that the total **gains from trade** associated with the product are lower than they would be if anyone were free to sell it.

This, then, is the **trade-off** of having patents. We get more inventions because the profits are higher for inventors. But we enjoy smaller gains from trade on each individual invention because of the monopoly pricing of them. As a matter of logic, it seems possible that offering patent protection might either raise or lower the total gains from trade arising from inventions.

PATENTS AS PROPERTY RIGHTS

There is another way to think of patents, however. Imagine you own a piece of land that is hilly and covered with scrub trees, weeds, and rocks. In its current condition, it is useful for almost nothing. Now imagine that you clear the weeds, trees, and rocks from the site, and rent a bulldozer to level out the worst of the hilly areas, so that now the property is something on which a residence or business might easily be constructed.

Given that you own the land, you can sell or lease it for "whatever the market will bear." You would likely be surprised if anyone objected to your "monopoly" over this piece of land—and quite upset if someone argued that you should not be allowed to profit from all of your hard work on the property.

Well, a patent can be viewed as nothing more than a **property right** that entitles the inventor to profit from the hard work and expense that he or she puts into creating the invention. It is true that you (the hypothetical landowner) and the inventor each have a "monopoly" over the item you own. But neither of you will be able to charge a price much above the competitive level unless the item in question is appreciably different from or superior to other items in the market. And even in this case, nothing prevents other people from continuing to do what they were doing before the land was cleared or the invention was created. Hence, it is difficult to see what damage to society can come from granting patent rights.

In contrast, as we saw in Chapter 5, it is easy to understand the damage that is done when property rights (such as patents) are either nonexistent or are costly to enforce or transfer. In particular, economic growth is diminished, and in the long run we are poorer as a result. In the absence of patent protection, the damage arises because there is less investment in the creation of new ideas.

ALTERNATIVES TO PATENTS

Patents have not always existed, and they do not exist in all nations today. Yet in their absence, there is still innovation. How does this occur? There are two important ways that inventors can profit from their ideas, even without patent protection.

The first method is simply by getting a product to the market first. Even if competitors are free to copy a product, it will still take them time to do. Until they do so, the inventor will have a monopoly on the item, and hence be able to charge a monopoly price and thereby profit. This method is an important source of profits for fashion designers, whose new creations each year are quickly copied by imitators—but often not before the designers have profited handsomely by being the first to market.

A second and more long-lived way to profit in the absence of a patent is by keeping the essence of an invention secret. **Trade secrets** have long been an important means of protecting **intellectual property.** A famous example of this is the formula for Coca-Cola. When he first concocted the beverage back in 1886, John Pemberton did not seek to patent it and, as far as anyone knows, the formula may not even be something that *could* be patented. But Pemberton and all successive owners of the formula have managed to keep it secret, and thus despite the lack of patent protection the profits have kept rolling in.

Of course, both of these alternatives to patents have significant drawbacks. Being first to market often yields significant profits for a short period of time, perhaps only weeks or months. Long-term profitability in such a setting requires that the innovator keep coming up with one new—and profitable—idea after another, time after time. Few people are able to maintain such a pace of creative endeavor over long periods. As the Coca-Cola example suggests, it is sometimes possible for trade secrets to help avoid this problem, but they present their own problem. If the formula for Coca-Cola is ever revealed, there is nothing to prevent another company from imitating the original, grabbing business by cutting prices, and eliminating Coca-Cola's profits.

PATENT TROLLS

Let's now return to the cast of characters that started our story. As the term "patent troll" is commonly used, it is taken to mean an individual or firm that enforces its patents in a manner that is seen as unduly aggressive or opportunistic. Often the trolls don't actually manufacture anything. They just hold portfolios of patents and collect payments from firms that want to use them—or that simply don't want to be sued by the troll for supposed patent infringement.

But it is difficult to see the difference between a patent troll and, say, computer giants HP and IBM. Both of these companies earn hundreds of millions of dollars from their patents every year, and both of them aggressively enforce their patents. Moreover, in today's world of sophisticated computer and communication systems, it is hard to imagine a setting in which companies didn't cooperate one way or another in their use of patents. Modern electronic devices typically rely on dozens of patented ideas that may have been created by just as many inventors. Each of the patents individually might be almost worthless, yet when combined in a single product may yield something of great value.

Bringing together the owners of many different patents and getting them to agree to act in a common purpose can be a costly, sensitive business. Whether or not they manufacture anything, there is thus a potentially important economic role for companies such as Nathan Myhrvold's firm. Such "patent aggregators" (as they are also known) bring together portfolios of patents and negotiate agreements between patent holders whose inventions are worth far more when combined with other patents than when separate.

SEED MONOPOLIES

What then of our seed monopoly? Monsanto, which for many years focused its business on industrial chemicals, now directs much of its attention to creating genetically modified (GM) seeds. The company's original interest in this line of work came about because of a potent weed killer called Roundup, which the company began selling in 1976. Because Roundup can also kill the plants it is designed to protect against weeds, farmers were limited in when and how they could use the herbicide. Monsanto thus began developing and patenting GM seeds for crops, such as soy beans, which would be resistant to the Roundup. This strategy succeeded so well that sales of "Roundup Ready" seeds now account for 40 percent of the company's revenues.

Just as importantly, the company learned a great deal about the process of genetic modification, and began looking for other ways to apply it. One result was patented GM corn that is resistant to most of the insects that normally attack it. The superiority of Monsanto's genetic innovations is such that Monsanto's patented genes are now being inserted into roughly 95 percent of all soybeans and 80 percent of all corn sold in the United States.

With market share numbers like these, it is no surprise that Monsanto has been pricing its seeds accordingly. Indeed, over the past decade, the company has raised the average price of its seeds by about 80 percent in inflation-adjusted terms. Some farmers have said they wished Monsanto charged less for their seeds. No surprise there. But the biggest complainers about Monsanto, it turns out, are Monsanto's *competitors,* who argue that the company is engaged in "unfair competition."

Let's consider the implications of such competitor complaints. If Monsanto seeds were, say, 50 percent superior to those of other firms and it raised its prices by 80 percent, then farmers would indeed be harmed by Monsanto's patent monopoly. But competitors would benefit because Monsanto would effectively be pricing itself out of the market. Now imagine that Monsanto seeds are, say, 100 percent better than those of competitors and it chooses to raise its prices by "only" 80 percent. In this case, competitors will indeed be harmed (Monsanto is outcompeting them on quality-adjusted price), but only because Monsanto is *benefiting* the farmers who buy its seed. Our inference from this is that the loud complaints from Monsanto's competitors are the surest sign yet that Monsanto's seed monopoly is actually making farmers better off, not worse off.

LOOK OUT FOR MOTHER NATURE

In an ironic twist, Monsanto's Roundup Ready crops are so successful that they have become the dominant variety for many crops. This has helped Monsanto's Roundup remain the most heavily used herbicide in the United States. But the heavy use of Roundup has provoked natural selection in favor of weeds that are relatively resistant to the herbicide. In the long run, this resistance may destroy the value of Monsanto's monopoly of both Roundup and Roundup Ready seeds. And while there is no evidence yet that insects are adapting to Monsanto's insect-repelling corn, don't count Mother Nature out here just yet, either.

DISCUSSION QUESTIONS

1. Suppose property rights to new buildings were limited to 20 years. How would this affect the incentive to invest in new buildings?

2. What is it about innovations that make them more likely to be subject to monopoly pricing than are, say, new buildings?

3. It is possible to produce GM "terminator seeds" that yield healthy crops that are sterile. The crops are perfectly suitable for consumption, but farmers cannot use the seeds from the crops to grow another generation of crops. What is the potential advantage to Monsanto in using "terminator seeds"?

4. Referring back to question 3, what is the potential *disadvantage* to Monsanto from using terminator seeds?

5. If patents are best thought of as strengthening property rights, what are the other legal and institutional characteristics you would expect to see in nations with strong patent laws? (*Hint:* Refer back to Chapter 5.)

6. New pharmaceutical drugs are protected by patents. When the patents expire, other firms are free to produce chemically identical versions of the brand name, formerly patented drug. These are referred to as "generic" versions of the drug. What do you predict will be the price of these generic drugs, compared to the price of the branded drug while it was on patent? What do you predict will happen to the price of the branded drug when its patent ends and the production of generic drugs begins? Explain.

CHAPTER 16

Contracts, Combinations, and Conspiracies

The Sherman Act of 1890 outlaws any "contract, combination, ... or conspiracy, in restraint of trade or commerce" in the United States. Translated from the legalese, this means that firms in America cannot lawfully join with competitors to form a **cartel** to raise prices above the competitive level.[1] Because successful cartels have the potential for great **profits,** there are strong **incentives** to form them. Usually, however, if the government discourages them, or even if it does not actively encourage them, cartels are difficult to keep together. This is because a cartel must meet four requirements if it is to be successful:

1. *Share.* It must control a large share of actual and potential output, so that other producers of the good it sells will not be able to depress prices by expanding output significantly.

2. *Substitutes.* Consumers must regard alternatives to the cartel's product as relatively poor substitutes, and these substitutes must be few in number and relatively inelastic in supply. Such factors all reduce the **elasticity of demand** facing the cartel, helping it raise prices.

3. *Stability.* There must be few outside factors that tend to disturb **cost** or **demand** conditions in the industry, so that the cartel does not continually have to make new price and output decisions in response to changing conditions.

4. *Solidarity.* It must be relatively easy for the cartel to maintain solidarity by identifying and punishing members who cheat on the cartel agreement with price cuts.

---

1 Despite this, many American agricultural producers are legally permitted to collectively agree to raise their prices on products ranging from almonds to oranges. They do so under the umbrella of "marketing orders," which are effectively cartels approved and enforced by the U.S. Department of Agriculture.

All successful cartels have been able to meet these requirements to some extent. Conversely, a breakdown in one or more of these factors has been the downfall of each one that has failed. Most successful cartels are international. They are either effectively beyond (or exempt from) national laws forbidding them or encouraged by or made up of governments themselves.

THE OIL CARTEL

One of the most famous and most successful cartels has been the Organization of Petroleum Exporting Countries (OPEC). Formed in 1960, its members have included many major oil-producing countries, such as Algeria, Indonesia, Iran, Iraq, Kuwait, Libya, Nigeria, Saudi Arabia, and Venezuela. OPEC had little impact on the price of oil until the outbreak of the Middle East war in 1973 provided the impetus for cohesive action. Saudi Arabia, Kuwait, and several other Arab nations sharply reduced their production of oil; because the **demand curve** for oil is downward-sloping, this reduction in supply pushed oil prices—and thus the profits of OPEC members—up sharply. On January 1, 1973, one could buy Saudi Arabian crude oil for about $10 per barrel (in 2009 dollars). Within one year, the price of crude had risen to $32 per barrel; by the next year, to $41, and by the end of the decade, to $80 per barrel with no end in sight.

Several forces combined to send oil prices in the opposite direction by the mid-1980s. At least partly in response to the high prices charged by OPEC, worldwide output of oil from other sources began to grow, led by rising production on Alaska's North Slope and by aggressive marketing of the oil flowing out of the Norwegian and British fields located in the North Sea. Eventually, this additional production significantly reduced the **market share** controlled by OPEC members and thus helped reduce their stranglehold on price.

The most important problem for OPEC, however, as for so many cartels, has been cheating on the cartel agreement by its members. Whenever there are numerous firms or countries in a cartel arrangement, there will always be some that are unhappy with the situation, perhaps because they think they are not getting enough of the profits. They cheat by charging a slightly lower price than the one stipulated by the cartel, a move that will result in a very large increase in the cheater's revenues (and thus profits). The potential for cheating is a constant threat to a cartel's existence, and when enough of a cartel's members try to cheat, the cartel breaks up.

In the case of OPEC, war between the member nations of Iran and Iraq during the 1980s precipitated a major outbreak of cheating as those two nations expanded production beyond their **quotas,** using the extra sales to finance large military expenditures. Expressed in 2009 dollars, the price of crude oil plunged to less than $20 per barrel in 1986, when cheating on output quotas spread throughout the cartel. Saudi Arabia, the world's largest producer of crude, finally restored order when it threatened to double its output if other OPEC members did not adhere to their quotas. Crude oil prices hovered around $25–$30 per barrel from then until early 2004, when they started a sharp climb due to rising world demand. After peaking at over $140 per barrel in 2008, prices subsequently dropped back below $100 in response to worldwide recession.

The Diamond Cartel

The difficulties faced by cartels are also illustrated in the diamond market, where DeBeers, the famous diamond company, once controlled as much as 80 percent of the world supply but now can claim only a 40 percent market share. DeBeers itself produces about 25 percent of the world's diamond output and controls the marketing of another 15 percent through a cartel called the Diamond Trading Company (DTC). Under the direction of DeBeers, the DTC has long restricted the sale of rough-cut diamonds to keep their prices at levels that maximize the profits of its members. After many years of profitable success, however, the diamond cartel hit rough times in the 1980s and 1990s. Cartel profits spurred searches for new sources of supply, and major discoveries were made in Australia and Canada. Moreover, Russia, which accounts for about one-fourth of world output, defected from the DTC cartel to market its diamonds through the Lev Leviev Group, the top DTC competitor. The combined effect of increased supplies and cartel defections pushed the inflation-adjusted price of top-quality diamonds down by 50 percent. Since 2000, the rapid growth of demand in China has helped drive prices back up to near-record levels.

The Caviar Cartel

The Russians have had troubles with their own historically successful cartel, the one that controls—or controlled—the supply of fine caviar. The principal source of some of the world's best caviar is the Volga River delta, where Kazakhstan and Russia (both former members of the Soviet Union) share a border at the northern end of the Caspian Sea. Both the temperature and the salinity of the water in the delta make it the ideal spawning ground for sturgeon, the long-nosed prehistoric fish whose eggs have for centuries been prized as the world's finest caviar. Originally, the Russian royal families ran the show, eating what they wanted of the harvest and then controlling the remaining supplies to their advantage.

When the Russian Revolution disposed of the Romanov dynasty in 1917, the new Communist regime quickly saw the potential profits to be had from cornering the market on caviar. Hence, for the next seventy-five years or so, a Soviet state–dominated cartel controlled the nation's caviar business from top to bottom. Although the Soviet sturgeon were considerate enough to produce an annual catch of some 2,000 tons of caviar, the Communist cartel allowed only 150 tons out of the country. As a result, a state-supplied kilogram (2.2 pounds) of top-grade black caviar costing $5 or less on the Moscow black market commanded $1,000 or more in New York.

The demise of the Soviet Union spawned trouble, however, for **competition** reared its ugly head. As it turns out, the largest sturgeon fisheries fell under the jurisdictions of two different autonomous republics—Russia and Kazakhstan—each of which wanted to own and operate its own lucrative caviar business. Moreover, a variety of individuals, including enterprising Caspian Sea fishermen from these republics, staked private claims and in some cases set up their own **export** channels (behavior officially termed "black market piracy"). The effect of this capitalist behavior was a 20 percent drop in the official caviar export price during the first year of autonomy, plus an escalation of competition since then.

Caviar consumers were pleased at this turn of events, but old-line suppliers were not so happy. "We don't need this kind of competition," complained one. "All of these small rivals mean that prices will fall and the market will be ripped apart. This is a delicacy—we need to keep it elite." Recent years have seen a sharp upswing in world caviar prices, although not because Russia and Kazakhstan have managed to get competition under control. Instead, it turns out that pollution from leftover Soviet industry in the area has sharply reduced the region's sturgeon population. The resulting decline in the amount of harvestable caviar drove costs and prices up and profits even lower. Adding insult to injury, firms in America (whose costs are not affected by the Soviet pollution) have entered the caviar market in response to the higher prices, intensifying the price–cost squeeze that the former Soviet republics are suffering. And so just as Soviet citizens found that communism wasn't all that it was cracked up to be, it appears some of them are now learning that capitalism may be more than they bargained for—but perhaps no less than Karl Marx warned them about.

THE COLLEGE SPORTS CARTEL

Oddly enough, despite the Sherman Act and other tough antitrust laws, one of the longest-running cartels can be found right here in the United States. The National Collegiate Athletic Association (NCAA), which operates under a special exemption from the antitrust laws, sets the rules not only for how intercollegiate sports competition takes place but also for how athletes are recruited and paid. And under NCAA rules, college athletes are not paid much. Indeed, as a practical matter, compensation for collegiate athletes is limited to the cost of room, board, books, and tuition at their university or college, an amount that typically ranges from $30,000 to $60,000 per year. This might sound like pretty good pay to you, and indeed, for a field hockey player or college wrestler, it probably is. But for the so-called revenue sports of college athletics, most notably football and basketball, such sums amount to a pittance compared to what these athletes would bring on the open market. (This, of course, is exactly the point: Universities are joined together in the NCAA in part simply to keep down the costs of college athletics.) In the case of football, this issue has been studied quite intensively, so we actually have a good idea of what top college players are worth. Over a four-year college career, a player who ends up getting drafted by a professional team is underpaid by over $2 million. And while lesser players are underpaid by lesser amounts, numbers like these make it clear that despite encouraging open competition on college playing fields, when it comes to competition in the marketplace, the NCAA is guilty of unsportsmanlike conduct.

DISCUSSION QUESTIONS

1. Why are all cartels inherently unstable?

2. Would it be easier to form a cartel in a market with many producers or one with few producers?

3. What happens to the producers of caviar made from other types of fish eggs (such as salmon, whitefish, and trout) when the price of the finest sturgeon caviar changes? Would these firms ever have an incentive to help the governments of Russia and Kazakhstan reestablish the caviar cartel?

4. If the members of your class were to attempt to form a study-reduction cartel in which everyone agreed to study less, which individuals would have the most to gain from the cartel? Which ones would have the greatest incentive to cheat on the cartel?

5. The economy of India (with a population of one billion) has begun to industrialize, and per capita income there is rising. What impact will this growth have on the demand for oil and diamonds—and thus on their prices? Explain.

6. Suppose there is a decline in marginal costs for one member of a cartel. What impact will this have on the incentive of that firm to cheat on the cartel agreement? Explain.

CHAPTER 17

Coffee, Tea, or Tuition-Free?

A few years ago, the Internet retailing giant Amazon.com received some unwanted publicity when it was revealed that the company was charging different prices for movies sold to different customers. Amazon insisted that the price differences were random and amounted to an effort to simply test the market. But some customers complained that Amazon was using the practice to tailor prices to customer characteristics, charging more to people who were likely to be willing to pay more. The flap over Amazon's "market test" soon died out, but as time passes, Internet firms and other companies are finding it almost impossible to resist regularly charging different prices to different customers. The reason is simple: By tracking people's buying habits, firms can get a pretty good idea of how to engage in **price discrimination** among their customers and thus increase their **profits.**

Shouldn't price discrimination be illegal? Actually, it *is* illegal, at least under some circumstances. Nevertheless, it is routinely practiced by businesses of all descriptions—and perhaps even by the college you attend. Interestingly, although price discrimination definitely benefits the firms (or colleges) that engage in it, you may benefit, too. Let's see how.

THE BASICS OF PRICE DISCRIMINATION

First things first: Price discrimination is defined as the existence of price differences across customers for the same good that are not due to differences in the **marginal costs** of supplying the customers. Thus, price discrimination can occur when marginal costs are the same across customers but prices are different or when prices are the same despite differences in marginal costs. An example of the former occurs when pharmacies or movie theaters charge lower prices to "senior citizens" than to other customers. An example of the latter can be found at "all-you-can-eat" buffets, where the price is the same for all diners, even though some eat much more food than others.

Three conditions must exist for a firm to engage in price discrimination. First, the firm must be, at least to some extent, a **price searcher**—it must be able to raise price above marginal cost without losing all of its sales to rivals. Second, there must be identifiable differences across customers in their willingness (or ability) to pay different prices for the same good. Third, the firm must be able to prevent customers who pay lower prices from reselling the good to customers who otherwise would be charged higher prices—or else customers eligible for the lowest price will buy on behalf of all customers.

The objective of price discrimination is, of course, higher profits for the firm that engages in it. To see how this might work, consider a firm selling to two identifiable groups of customers, say, retirees and working people. Also suppose that the retirees have lower income and so perhaps have a higher **price elasticity of demand** for the good—that is, they tend to be more sensitive to changes in price. In this case, it may be possible for the firm to reallocate sales among customer groups, lowering prices slightly to retirees and raising them somewhat to working people, thereby getting more revenue at the same costs, and so earning higher profits. Of course, to be able to accomplish this, the firm must be able to distinguish between the two groups. (This ability is often approximated by offering the lower prices only to persons who can prove they are older and thus more likely to be retired.) Moreover, the firm must be able to prevent resale from low-price buyers to other customers; in the case of prescription medicines, pharmacies are aided by federal and state laws that forbid such resale, while in the case of movie theaters, the person getting the lower price generally must attend the movie personally to get the lower price. (This helps explain why movie rental companies such as Netflix are less likely than movie theaters to offer senior citizen discounts: It would be too easy for seniors to rent movies on behalf of younger people who wish to avoid the higher prices applicable to them.)

Price Discrimination by Airlines

If you have ever traveled on an airplane, you are likely to have been a beneficiary of price discrimination (although your parents—or their employers—may have been victims of such discrimination if they fly on short-notice business trips). Prior to 1978, the fares charged by airlines in the United States were regulated by the federal government, so all airlines offered the same government-approved fares; discounts were rare beyond late-night ("red-eye") or weekend flights.[1] Once deregulation occurred, airlines quickly discovered that there were large differences in the price elasticity of demand across customers. Business travelers typically had a lower price elasticity of demand and hence were willing to pay higher fares than leisure travelers. Fares charged to business travelers are now higher than they used to be, even though leisure fares are significantly lower than they were in the days of government regulation.

The precision and effectiveness with which the airlines engage in price discrimination have been rising steadily over time, thanks to a process known as "yield management." Combining sophisticated statistical techniques and massive historical databases, together with computerized up-to-the-minute bookings, the airlines can predict with almost pinpoint accuracy how many business customers will want seats on a given flight and how much they'll be willing to pay. As a result, says one industry insider, "high fares get higher and low fares get lower."

The process begins months before a flight ever departs, as the airline divides the seats on a plane into as many as seven or more different fare classes, or categories. Initial fares on a flight are established for each of the categories, and the yield management computers begin the process of monitoring the reservations, comparing them to historical patterns. If advance bookings are slow, the airline will move seats to low-fare categories. But if business travelers buy higher-priced, unrestricted tickets sooner than expected, the yield management computer removes seats from discount categories and holds them for last-minute business passengers that are predicted to show up.

A host of techniques are used to optimize the blend between filling the seats on a plane and getting the highest possible fare for each seat. In the weeks leading up to a flight, the level of fares assigned to each category may be adjusted up or down based on the latest moves by competitors, and as the flight date approaches, lower-priced categories are likely to be closed out altogether. Moreover, some people seeking reservations may be told a given flight is "sold out" even though passengers using that flight as a connector to another of the airline's routes may find ample seating—for a price, of course. The result of all this fine-tuning is that passengers on the same flight from, say, Chicago to Phoenix may pay round-trip fares that vary by a factor of 5—ranging, say, from $280 for the lowest-priced seats to $1,400 for the top fares.

---

1 Those fares were also considerably higher on average than they are today because the federal government agency responsible for regulating the airlines also prevented them from competing on the basis of price.

PRICE DISCRIMINATION BY COLLEGES

Interestingly, the same yield management techniques refined by the airlines are now being used by universities when they decide on financial aid packages offered to students. After all, given the nominal tuition at a university, a more generous financial aid offer can be thought of as a lower price, and students, like everyone else, behave according to the **law of demand.** Universities have found, for example, that they can offer less generous aid packages to students who apply for early admission because such students are more eager to attend; as one financial aid consultant notes, "Those who have the most interest in the school are going to be less price sensitive." In a similar vein, some colleges have found that people who come for campus interviews are more interested in attending; the response has been to offer slightly less generous aid packages to such students, even though the colleges routinely recommend that students come for interviews.

In addition to these regular features of price discrimination in financial aid offers, universities also monitor their enrollment figures each year, just as the airlines watch bookings by fare category. If a school is getting, say, too many premed students and not enough in the humanities, financial aid offers will be adjusted accordingly, with bigger than usual aid offers being made to the students the school is trying to attract. Schools that are noted for excellence in one area but are trying to maintain a balanced mix of majors have become particularly adept at the financial aid game. As the enrollment vice president for Carnegie Mellon University notes, without sophisticated adjustments to the blend of aid packages offered, "I'd have an institution full of engineers and computer scientists and I wouldn't have anybody in arts and design." Carnegie Mellon also recognizes the importance of competition in determining the prices it charges: After admitted students are notified of their aid offers in the spring, they are invited to fax the school any better offers they receive from other colleges. The university generally meets competing offers received by desirable students.

PRICE DISCRIMINATION BY DRUG COMPANIES

Price discrimination can even be practiced on a worldwide scale. Most major pharmaceutical companies price discriminate based on the nationality of the people buying their drugs. Partly because incomes in other nations are lower than in the United States, people in other nations have higher elasticities of demand than American citizens. Consequently, pharmaceutical companies sell prescription drugs elsewhere at lower prices than they do in the United States. But one of these other nations is Canada, and American senior citizens have found that by getting on a bus (or even just visiting the Web site of a Canadian pharmacy), they can save a bundle on their prescriptions.[2] Although this practice is technically illegal, neither the United States nor Canada has stopped it. In fact, by the time you read this, Congress may have legalized the importation of prescription drugs from other nations.

Price discrimination certainly profits the firms that practice it, but there is an entirely different question—one that cannot be answered by economics—as to whether it is fair. Most student travelers who can stay over a Saturday night or make reservations a month in advance probably don't mind the lower fares made possible by price discrimination. But business travelers are far from pleased with the high fares they must pay to get where they want, when they want, usually on short notice. "They've got you, and they know it," says one executive. The flip side, of course, is that without the extra revenue generated by price discrimination, some companies or colleges would be hard-pressed to survive. Indeed, when asked about the equity of fine-tuning aid packages to willingness to attend rather than ability to pay, one financial aid official noted he had little choice in the matter: "I could make it very fair—and be out of business."

DISCUSSION QUESTIONS

1. First-class passengers generally pay higher fares than coach passengers, even when they take advantage of advance-purchase discounts. Is this price discrimination? (*Hint:* Seats in first class are generally leather rather than fabric and are about 50 percent wider than coach seats. Also, there are more flight attendants per passenger in the first-class section.)

2. Is it price discrimination when a professional football team charges, say, $150 per ticket for 50-yard-line tickets in the lower deck and $50 per ticket for upper-deck tickets overlooking the end zone?

3. What factors other than income are likely to affect willingness to pay? How will differences in these factors among its customers affect the likelihood that a firm will engage in price discrimination?

---

2 Another reason for lower prices in Canada is that it has a nationalized health-care system, meaning that the government buys drugs on behalf of all Canadians. This practice makes the Canadian government a **monopsonist** (literally, "single buyer"), with the power to force drug prices down below what they otherwise would be.

4. Consider the following data from three different firms (1, 2, and 3) each selling to two different customers (A and B). Shown are the price (P) per unit charged each customer and the marginal cost (MC) of producing each unit for the customer. (Thus, for example, Firm 1 has different marginal costs between customers and charges different prices.)

	Customer A	Customer B
Firm 1		
Price ($)	100	150
Marginal cost ($)	100	150
Firm 2		
Price ($)	200	200
Marginal cost ($)	100	150
Firm 3		
Price ($)	150	200
Marginal cost ($)	100	100

Which firms are engaged in price discrimination? Explain. Extra credit: For each firm, rank-order the elasticity of demand for the two customers.

5. Suppose a firm starts off with selling a uniform product to two different customers at the same price per unit for each. Now it decides to engage in price discrimination by raising the price to one customer and lowering the price to the other customer. Why doesn't the profit lost due to lowering the price for one customer eliminate all of the higher profits achieved by raising the price to the other customer?

6. Suppose a local beverage shop charges $6 for a six-pack of your favorite beverage, and charges $15 for a case (containing four six-packs) of that same beverage? Is this price discrimination?

CHAPTER 18

Keeping the
Competition Out

Most competitors hate **competition.** And who can blame them? After all, if a firm can keep the competition out, **profits** are sure to rise. How high they will rise obviously varies by industry, but the lowly taxicab market gives some indication of what is at stake.

TAXICAB MEDALLIONS

In New York City, the number of taxicabs is limited by law—limited, in fact, to one cab for every six hundred people, in a town where many people don't own cars. To legally operate a taxi in New York, one must own a taxi medallion, a city-issued metal shield affixed to the cab's hood. Although the number of taxi medallions in New York is fixed by law, you are free to buy one from a current owner, assuming that you can come up with the prevailing market price, about $600,000. That price, we should note, does not include the taxi itself, although it does entitle you to the right to work a seventy-hour week, subject to robbery, rude customers, and the erratic driving habits of other cabbies. And lest you think New York taxi drivers are crazy to pay such sums, keep this in mind: Because the city keeps the competition out, the taxi business is so lucrative that the medallions can be used as collateral to borrow at favorable interest rates, and any cabbie who wants to leave the business can immediately find a buyer for his or her medallion, usually at a price that will bring even more profit. In fact, the long-run **rate of return** on New York taxi medallions compares favorably with the long-run rate of return on stocks listed on the New York Stock Exchange.

Keeping the competition out works quite simply. Reducing the number of firms in an industry decreases the **supply** of the good, thus driving up its price. Firms that remain thus enjoy both a higher price for their product and a larger **market share.** Consumers lose, however, suffering not only from higher prices but also from fewer alternative sources of supply from which to choose. Another group of losers are the firms that are excluded. They are forced to go into lower-paying pursuits for which they are not as well suited. The higher profits enjoyed by the firms that are protected from competition thus come at the expense of consumers and excluded competitors. The net result is also an overall loss to society as a whole because the limit on competition reduces the total extent of mutually beneficial exchange.

Note that we said that the number of taxi medallions in New York is limited by the government. This is typical. Even though many government agencies (for example, the Federal Trade Commission and the Department of Justice at the federal level) are supposed to promote competition, getting the government involved is usually the most effective way to *stifle* competition. Consider telephones. It used to be that both long-distance and local telephone markets were regulated by the federal government. In 1984, the long-distance market was deregulated, and AT&T had to begin competing with MCI and Sprint for customers. The result was a 40 percent drop in inflation-adjusted long-distance rates. Local telephone service continued to be regulated by the Federal Communications Commission (FCC), however, and over the same period of time, local phone rates *rose* 40 percent in real terms—chiefly because the FCC kept competition out of the local phone service market.

OCCUPATIONAL LICENSING

Keeping the competition out seems to be growing in popularity across America. As the economy has moved from manufacturing to services, the number of people working in licensed professions has risen sharply. Thirty years ago, there were about 80 occupations for which one or more state governments required a license. Today, there are roughly 1,100 occupations, ranging from secretaries in Georgia to wallpaper hangers in California, which require a license in at least one state. About 29 percent of the U.S. labor force, about forty-five million individuals, now belongs to a licensed profession. Officially, of course, this is all done to protect the consumer from unscrupulous or incompetent practitioners. In fact, such licensing requirements serve chiefly—if not solely—to keep the competition out and raise the earnings of those who manage to get licensed.

Many of the decision makers who work for the government agencies that limit competition are lawyers, so it is not surprising that competition among lawyers is limited. For example, in every state but one (California), the number of law schools is capped by state law, thereby restricting entry into the profession and driving up earnings. Real estate agents are also well represented among the members of state legislatures, and so it may come as no surprise that they, too, have been successful in keeping the competition out. In addition to having to pass examinations to be licensed, real estate agents are prohibited—at their own request—from engaging in all sorts of competitive behavior. In a dozen states, agents are prohibited from discounting their prices even if they perform less than the usual amount of services for their customers. In eight states, real estate agents are not permitted to perform fewer services than the local realty association specifies, even if the customer does not want those services. These crimps on competition make life both comfortable and profitable for real estate agents, but it's not such a good deal for home buyers and sellers. In the United States, the average real estate agent's commission is 5.1 percent of the sale price of the home; the average commission in other countries is 3.6 percent. Thus, by keeping the competition out, real estate agents in America are able to charge about one-third more for their services.

SOME HAIRY COMPETITION

Sometimes the government gets involved in some unlikely markets in its efforts to prevent the ravages of competition from taking their toll. Consider hair braiding. Some African Americans like to have their hair straightened in beauty shops, a procedure that requires a touch-up every four weeks, for an average monthly cost (excluding cutting and styling) of about $100. An alternative is to get one's hair braided at a braiding salon. There are now about ten thousand of these salons across the country. Braids need maintenance only once every ten weeks, cutting the cost to $50 per month. The same low cost and convenience that make braiding salons attractive to consumers also make them threatening to the conventional beauty shops that straighten hair, especially in fashion-conscious California. Claiming that they are seeking to protect consumers, agents of the California Barbering and Cosmetology Board regularly raid the salons of unlicensed hair braiders. Not surprisingly, the hair braiders think the state is actually trying to protect state-licensed cosmetologists at beauty shops, who must spend $6,000 for sixteen hundred hours of training to get their licenses. Indeed, one of the braiders, Ali Rasheed, argues that the marketplace is better than state licensing boards at protecting consumers. "It's simple," he says. "If I mess up your hair, you don't come back. You spread the word. And very quickly I'd be out of business." Perhaps so, but it looks like the state of California doesn't want to give consumers that option.

GOVERNMENTS DON'T LIKE COMPETITION EITHER

Back in New York, there is an example of the fact that the government likes to protect itself from competition, too. New York City is well known for its massive public transit system, comprising both subways and bus lines. What is not so well known is that mass transit in New York City started off as private enterprise. The first horsecars and elevated trains in the city were developed by private companies. Moreover, even though New York's first subway was partly financed by a loan from the city, it was otherwise a private operation, operated profitably at a fare of a nickel (the equivalent of less than a dollar today).

New York's politicians refused to allow fares to rise during the inflation of World War I, yielding financial losses for the private transit companies. Promising to show the private sector how to run a transit system efficiently while simultaneously offering to protect the public from the "dictatorship" of the transit firms, the city took over the subway, merged it with the bus line, and promptly started raising fares. Despite fare increases double the inflation rate, however, costs have risen even faster, so that today, even though the basic fare is $2.25, the city *loses* about as much on each passenger because fares don't cover costs.

Enter the jitneys, privately owned vans that operate along regular routes, like buses, but charge as little as $1 a passenger and make detours for pickups and drop-offs on request. Actually, we should have said "attempted entry" by the jitneys because the New York City Council—at the insistence of the public transit system—has denied operating permits to almost all jitney operators who have applied. The council says it is only seeking to prevent the vans from causing accidents and traffic problems, but even fully insured drivers who have met federal requirements for operating interstate van services are routinely denied permits. Thus, most of the hundreds of jitneys operating in New York City are doing so illegally. Even the few jitneys that have managed to get licensed are forbidden from operating along public bus routes—in the name of public safety, of course.

Transportation economists such as Daniel Klein have argued that public transit systems could once more be profitable—instead of losing an average of 50 cents on the dollar—if the jitneys were given a chance. "Government has demonstrated that it has no more business producing transit than producing cornflakes. It should concentrate instead on establishing new rules to foster competition," says Klein. Unfortunately for the jitneys and their customers, however, that competition would come at the expense of New York's public transit system. Thus, for the foreseeable future, it seems the jitneys will have to compete only by breaking the laws because, like most competitors, the New York City mass transit system just hates competition.

DISCUSSION QUESTIONS

1. Consider two different ways of beating your competition. One way is to offer your customers lower prices and better service. The other is to get a law passed that raises your competitors' costs—for example, by imposing special operating requirements on them. Can you see any difference between these two methods, assuming that both succeed in keeping your competition out?

2. Although governments at all levels sometimes act to prevent some individuals from competing with others, the federal government is probably the most active in this role, state governments are less active, and local governments are the least active. Can you explain this pattern?

3. Is there any difference between prohibiting entry by a group of firms and levying a special tax on those firms?

4. Manicurists and pedicurists are required to be licensed in both California and Florida. In California, people practicing these occupations must take 600 hours of classroom training; in Florida, they must take only 240 hours of classroom training. *Ceteris paribus* (that is, holding other factors constant), in which state would you expect pedicures and manicures to be more expensive? Explain. How could you use per capita consumption of pedicures and manicures in the two states to help you decide whether the classroom training requirement was chiefly designed to improve the quality of pedicures and manicures or to keep the competition out?

5. Although New York City's mass transit system is the largest in the country, it is not the only one that is heavily subsidized by taxpayers—in fact, as far as we know, *all* mass transit systems are heavily subsidized by taxpayers. Suggest at least one economic and one political reason why these systems are heavily subsidized.

6. Labor unions are a device for limiting competition, in this case competition among workers. The union bargains on behalf of all members, presumably resulting in a higher wage for workers and higher costs for employers. Use this fact, combined with the fact that international trade has played an increasing role in the American economy over the last fifty years, to explain the observation that union membership has declined as a share of private sector employment over this period in the United States. Your explanation should be consistent with the fact that union membership has *not* declined as a share of *public* sector employment over this period.

PART FIVE

Political Economy

Introduction

The chief focus of economics has always been on explaining the behavior of the private sector. Yet dating back at least to the publication of Adam Smith's *Wealth of Nations* in 1776, economists have never missed an opportunity to apply their theories to additional realms of behavior. For the past fifty years or so, much of this effort has been devoted to developing theories that explain the actions of governments, as well as the consequences of those actions. This undertaking is often referred to as the study of **political economy,** for it often involves a mixture of politics and economics. As the selections in Part Five hint, economists do not yet have a unified theory of government. Nevertheless, they are making progress and are sometimes able to offer surprising insights.

HEALTH CARE REFORM

Our first foray into the realm of political economy in Chapter 19 is a revealing look at health care. We examine the 2010 decision by Congress and President Obama to turn our entire health care system on end, in the name of "reform." Here we shall learn that the problem with the health care system was not what the politicians claimed it to be. We will also see that the proposed solution will not do what is claimed for it, but it will do plenty of things that are going to make most Americans very unhappy. But by the time all of this unfolds, it may be impossible politically to reverse the process. So our forecast is that, down the road, Americans are going to look back at 2010 as a very unpleasant turning point in the history of health care in our country.

THE PENSION CRISIS

Promises are easy to make and difficult to fulfill. Nowhere is this old saying truer than in politics, and when the promises offer benefits now and don't entail most of the costs until later, we have the recipe for a policy disaster. As we see in Chapter 20, this is exactly what is brewing in state and local governments all over America. These governments have made promises of generous pensions to government employees and, for decades, have been racking up financial obligations implied by these promises. Well, now that the baby boomer generation is starting to retire, the promises are coming home to roost. The result is a series of financial crises spreading across cities, counties, and states all over America. No one yet knows how the crises will be resolved, but of one fact we can be sure: The resolution will be painful for everyone involved.

MORTGAGE MELTDOWN

We next turn to an examination of another crucial sector of the American economy—housing—in Chapter 21. Between 1995 and 2010, the U.S. housing market went on the wildest ride in its history: House prices soared and then swiftly crashed. Similarly, home ownership and construction first rose dramatically and then even more quickly sank precipitously. The result, by 2010, was chaos in credit markets and misery and hardship for millions of Americans. Although many people were initially mystified by this series of events, it turns out that the principal culprit was none other than our own Congress. Operating under a banner promoting "affordable housing," Congress implemented policies that caused mortgage lenders to dramatically reduce the financial standards expected of home buyers who wished to obtain a mortgage. These lower standards enabled many more people to qualify for mortgages, increasing the demand for housing and thus leading to the housing boom of 1995–2005. But these same lower standards meant that people in weaker financial shape were heavily represented among home buyers—which played a central role in the housing crash and mortgage meltdown of 2006–2010. The congressional objective of "affordable housing" was temporarily achieved, but at a long-term cost that will be heavily borne by many of the same people who were supposed to be helped. Once again, we see that in politics as elsewhere, there is no free lunch.

RAISING LESS CORN AND MORE HELL

Shifting our attention to rural America, it is fair to say that farmers have exploited the nuances of political economy as well as anyone in this nation, a point we elaborate on in Chapter 22. More than seventy years ago, American farmers convinced the federal government to guarantee that farmers receive prices for their crops well above the **equilibrium prices** and that taxpayers and consumers of food should bear the costs of making these high prices stick. Ever since, consumers have faced higher prices for many crops because of various **target prices** and **price-support programs,** and taxpayers have faced higher tax bills as well. Indeed, the average American household pays about $500 per year in higher food prices and higher taxes due to federal programs benefiting "farmers"—even though most of this money actually ends up in the pockets of shareholders in giant agribusiness corporations. Moreover, as the experience of New Zealand reveals, government farm programs are *not* necessary to protect the vitality or **productivity** of the farm sector. Thirty years ago, New Zealand brought a halt to all of its efforts to protect farmers from **competition.** The result was innovation, cost cutting, and aggressive international marketing by New Zealand farmers, who are now stronger and more productive than ever before.

THE GRAYING OF AMERICA

For thirty years, the nation struggled with the baby boom generation as it graduated from bassinets to BMWs. For the next thirty years, we will have to grapple with the problems that arise as the boomers progress from corporate boardrooms to nursing homes. As we note in Chapter 23, the United States is aging at the fastest rate in its history. As the nation ages, two major problems in political economy are emerging. First, there is the matter of paying the Social Security and Medicare bills of the rapidly growing elderly portion of the population. Second, as increasing numbers of people retire, there will be fewer workers capable of bearing the growing tax burden. America must learn new ways of harnessing the productive capabilities of the elderly and accept that as much as we may wish otherwise, the elderly may largely have to fend for themselves.

CHAPTER 19

Health Care Reform

The trite but true saying "Nothing is more important than your health" should be replaced these days with another: "Nothing is more important than who pays for health insurance and health care." The most massive change in our nation's health care insurance and delivery systems occurred in 2010. The stakes are big. Americans spend 17 percent of total national annual income on health care—we are, indeed, the world's health-care spending champions.

HOW ABOUT THE UNINSURED?

So what about all those people who are said to be shut off from this health care system because they lack health insurance? The typical claim is that 15 percent of Americans lack coverage—but like many numbers you hear in political debates, this one needs to be taken with a grain (or perhaps a shaker) of salt. Of the forty-five million people said to lack health coverage in America, about eighteen million are aged 18–34, a group for which health expenditures are far lower than average. About twelve million are fully eligible for publicly provided (and paid-for) health insurance, but choose not to take it. And among all of the uninsured, fully half are uninsured only part of each year. The bottom line is that only about 3 percent of Americans are likely to have a significant demand for health insurance and yet be unable to get insurance on a persistent basis. For these individuals, the lack of insurance is an onerous, often terrifying, fact of life. But it is important to keep in mind that the number of people in this group is a far cry from the numbers that are normally bandied about.

Rising Health Care Costs in America

Fifty years ago, spending on health care in this country was not even 6 percent of national income. Today it is 17 percent, about equally divided between public spending and private spending. And there is no doubt that even as we speak, health care costs have been rising in America. There are at least four reasons why health care costs have gone up so much:

1. **An aging population**—The top 5 percent of health care users incur more than 50 percent of all health care costs. Senior citizens (all of them covered by Medicare) make up most of the top users. It is not surprising, therefore, that as our population ages, we will be spending more on health care. Currently, about 13 percent of U.S. residents are over sixty-five. By 2035, this proportion will have risen to 22 percent. Given that the elderly consume in excess of four times as much per capita health care services as the rest of the population, the demand for such services is certain to go up with our aging population.

   Of course, populations in Western Europe, Canada, Japan, and other industrialized nations are rising as well. But there the elderly have not played as big a role in pushing up health care costs as in America. The reason is simple. In those other nations, which have national health insurance systems, the elderly are sharply limited in the amount of health care they are allowed to utilize. This is much different from the U.S. Medicare system, which effectively lets senior citizens choose to have whatever health care services they wish.

2. **More expensive technologies**—Each advance in medical technology brings with it more expensive equipment and prescription drugs. A magnetic resonance imaging (MRI) scanner costs at least $2 million. A positron emission tomography (PET) scanner costs over $4 million. Each time these machines are used, the fees range to as high as $2,000 per procedure. New drugs for cancer can easily cost $250,000 for one course of treatment. Innovation in medicine has played a key role in improving the quality of health care in America, and neither innovation nor spending on it is about to stop. Therefore, we can expect increasing expenditures in medicine just because of advances in equipment and drugs.

3. **When someone else pays**—Between the government (through **Medicare** and **Medicaid**) and insurance companies, more than

80 percent of health care spending is paid for by someone else—a **third party**. Less than 20 percent is paid directly by individuals. This was not always the situation. In 1930, third parties paid only about 4 percent of health care expenditures.

When someone else pays for medical services, we encounter the problem of **moral hazard:** When third parties pay for medical care, a larger quantity is demanded. You may think that people do not react to the price of medical services, but they do. When Medicare went into effect in 1965, the volume of federal government–reimbursed medical services increased by more than 65 percent above what was anticipated when the program was made into law. And when senior citizens received new coverage for prescription medicines in 2003, their spending on prescriptions ended up being *double* the forecast.

Consider an example: If you have a health insurance policy that pays everything, then you have little incentive to reduce your medical care purchases. Why not see a doctor about every sniffle "just in case"? If, in contrast, you have to pay the first $1,000 out of your pocket before an insurance company (or the government) will start paying for your medical care expenses, you will react differently. You will engage, at a minimum, in more wellness activities and you will be less inclined to seek medical care for minor problems. Physicians in hospitals face a type of moral hazard problem, too. If they are reimbursed for every procedure by an insurance company or by the government, they will tend to ask for more tests and procedures "just in case." That means we pay more for medical care.

4. **Obesity**—The Centers for Disease Control and Prevention (CDC) have estimated that almost one-third of Americans are obese. Certainly, this problem is not new, but fifty years ago, obesity was a rarity. The CDC estimates that about 10 percent of total U.S. medical expenditures are attributable to obesity. About half of these expenditures are being paid for by Medicare and Medicaid. Many expenditures for obese people relate to obesity-caused type 2 diabetes—a disease that is rising at a record rate in the United States. As obesity rises, spending on medical care will follow. (For the causes of increased obesity, see Chapter 3.)

HEALTH CARE REFORM TO THE RESCUE?

A bitterly fought battle over health care reform occurred in the U.S. Congress until new health care legislation was signed into law by

President Obama in 2010. After briefly reviewing the key aspects of the several thousand pages of the new law on this matter, you will see that not all of the promised results can actually come to fruition, especially the promise that "spiraling health care costs will come down."

Here is a brief point-by-point summary of the federal government's new national health care program:

1. **Health care regulations**—Health insurance companies must cover everyone who applies, including those with preexisting medical problems. (As explained below, this new rule will weigh heavily and expensively on young people.)

2. **Individual mandate**—Just about everyone living in the United States must either purchase health care coverage or pay a fine up to $750 per year for an individual or $2,250 per year per family (twenty-one states have challenged this mandate in federal court).

3. **Employer mandate**—Firms with more than fifty employees must offer health insurance coverage or pay an annual fine of up to $750 per employee who obtains federal subsidies for such coverage.

4. **Health care insurance subsidies**—A variety of subsidies and tax credits will be provided to lower-income people and smaller firms.

5. **Higher taxes**—A special tax rate of 3.8 percent will apply to nearly all income earnings above $200,000 for individuals and $250,000 for a married couple.

The Moral Hazard Problem Will Worsen

You have already been introduced to the moral hazard problem that arises when third parties pay for medical care. Health care reform will worsen moral hazard. Once the national health care program fully goes into effect, tens of millions of U.S. residents are going to be paying a smaller percentage of their health care expenses themselves than they did previously. Consequently, the direct price paid by them for health care services will fall. As a result, the quantity demanded of health care services will rise. Also, because health insurers will be required to cover this expanded consumption of medical services, total expenditures on health care will increase even faster.

Finally, the moral hazard problem will become worse because more U.S. residents will face reduced incentives to make decisions that promote better health. As people have more health problems as a consequence of this increase in moral hazard, the demand for health care will increase. And as you know, when demand rises, so too will prices and expenditures.

WHY YOUNG PEOPLE WILL PAY MORE

The new law means that soon everyone must buy health insurance. The law also states that insurance companies must give full coverage to those with preexisting illnesses, but without charging them a higher rate. What does that mean? Simply that healthy young people—who will be required to buy insurance policies—will not pay a low price that reflects the low risk of them getting sick. One analysis conducted for the *Associated Press* estimates that beginning in 2014, young adults seeking coverage in the individual health insurance market will pay almost 20 percent more for the same coverage that they could buy today. To see why this is likely to be a modest impact of the new rules, consider this fact: Typically, insurance companies have charged six or seven times as much to older customers as to younger ones in those states that had no restrictions. The new federal law limits this ratio to three to one. That means that a sixty-year-old can be charged only three times as much as a twenty-five-year-old. So, who gets stuck? Young adults will, in the form of higher premiums.

WON'T EXTRA PREVENTIVE CARE CUT HEALTH CARE SPENDING?

Supporters of health care reform argue that it will encourage a lot more preventive care, thereby reducing overall health care spending. Stanford University Medical Professor Abraham Verghese argues that spending more on preventive care will actually drive costs *up*, not down. First of all, everyone knows what illness-prevention strategies we can do as individuals—lose weight, eat better, exercise more, smoke less, and wear a seatbelt while driving a car. These are cheap, save lives, and cut health care costs.

All other preventive strategies end up costing the economy more. Increased medical screening leads to discovering more potential medical problems and therefore more expenses in the form of additional screening tests and medications. Professor Verghese uses the following example. A test that discovers high cholesterol in a person who is feeling fine is really the discovery of a risk factor and not a disease. Elevated cholesterol levels mean that you have a greater chance of having a heart attack. You could reduce your cholesterol levels through weight loss, better diet, and lots of exercise. Or, you can take a pill every day in the form of a drug called a statin. That pill will reduce your cholesterol levels. Using a statin in the general population costs about $150,000 for every *year* of life it saves in men and costs even more in women. Sorry, no savings to be found here.

There Are Indeed No Free Lunches

From the onset, the health care reform debate was couched in absurd contradictions, at least for those who understand **limited resources** versus unlimited wants, **budget constraints**, and supply and demand. No legislation that promises to subsidize tens of millions of U.S. residents who currently have no health care insurance can possibly lead to lower overall medical care expenditures. That does not mean that such legislation is wrong—that's a value judgment and not a conclusion arising from economic analysis. Nevertheless, it is past time that everyone who takes place in the discussion of health care and its reform acknowledges one simple fact. Throughout all recorded history, when any good or service becomes cheaper to the person who uses that good or service, quantity demanded will rise, no matter what the political arguments are to the contrary.

Discussion Questions

1. Is it correct to apply standard economic analysis to something as important as medical care? Why or why not?

2. What are some of the ways in which government could force individuals to undertake their own illness-preventing activities?

3. If the government attempts to reduce health care expenditures by lowering the fees that physicians can charge for certain procedures, what might be the result in the short run? In the long run?

4. Why don't most current health care insurance plans cover preexisting illnesses? Who benefits from this current general rule? When health care reform legislation abolishes this rule, who will be hurt?

5. Currently, most U.S. residents cannot buy health care insurance coverage from a company based in another state. The new legislation leaves this restriction in place. Who benefits from this situation? Who loses?

6. What is special about health care that justifies so much government intervention? In other words, what problems would arise if the health care sector were completely unregulated and unsubsidized?

CHAPTER **20**

The Pension Crisis

It is never too early to think of your future. We refer not to your future classes or what you will do when you graduate. Nor do we speak of your future family, should you choose to have one. And not your self-imposed plan to stay healthy in the future. Rather, you might want to start thinking about how big your pension will be when you retire. That may seem a long way off, but for some—those who go to work for some cities and for some states—your pension might start in just twenty years.

CALIFORNIA ISN'T CALLED THE "GOLDEN" STATE FOR NOTHING

Today, in the face of one of its most serious fiscal crises ever, California taxpayers are footing the bill for former police officers, firefighters, and prison guards who can retire at age fifty with a pension that equals 90 percent of their final year's salary. There are more than fifteen thousand government retirees in California who receive pensions that exceed $100,000 per year (and this does not count payments from federal taxpayers through the Social Security system).

Consider the odd case of Gary Clift. He spent 26 years in the California Department of Corrections & Rehabilitation. Then he retired. He now collects 78 percent of the $112,000 salary he earned in his last year of work. He also gets full health care coverage for life, which adds a tidy sum to his retirement package. Ironically, Clift spent his last two years at work analyzing legislation that would raise the state's expenditures on retirement benefits. He got nowhere when he raised a red flag about increasing pension costs. As he said, "It's just taxpayers' money, so nobody cares."

Before we go any further with the relationship between government pension payments and California's fiscal problems, let's first look at the concept of retirement and pensions.

To Retire, Normally You Have to Save

If we look back in time far enough, the concept of retirement did not exist. Individuals worked until they were physically unable to continue, and died soon thereafter. That was back when just about everyone in the world was poor. Those who could not work were often cared for by family members in large households. Not surprisingly, in very poor countries today, having lots of kids continues to be a form of retirement security—in fact, they may be the only thing standing between a retiree and starvation.

Through **economic growth**, individuals in many nations have been able to **save** in order to create **wealth** that can be used later on. If you do not **consume** everything that you earn, you can put aside funds to purchase houses and to make investments. Hence, when you choose to give up gainful employment, you have a stock of wealth that you can draw down during your remaining years.

If you work for a large company or a government, your retirement benefits will likely come from a pension plan run by your employer. Hopefully (for you), your employer will put aside funds in investments that will yield enough income to provide you with your promised pension. If the actual **rates of return** on these investments turn out to be as predicted by the pension plan, then there will be enough funding for all employees who retire to receive their promised pensions. If this condition is satisfied, we say that the employer (company or government) has a **fully funded pension liability**. Whenever employers do not set aside enough funds to cover future pensions, we say that they have **unfunded liabilities**. Now let's go back to the state of California to see how it has become the king of unfunded liabilities.

The Golden State Turns Red

The term "red ink" usually refers to losses being suffered by a private company or to current year **budget deficits** incurred by a government entity. In recent years, California's red ink of this variety has been in the neighborhood of $10–$20 billion per year. But current California budget deficits are peanuts compared to its unfunded liabilities, mainly due to contractually guaranteed future pensions for its employees.

In the last dozen years, California state revenues—mainly from taxes—increased about 25 percent. Pension costs for that state's public employees, in contrast, increased by about 2,000 percent. No, that is not a typo. Recall our example of Gary Clift above. When he retired from the Department of Corrections & Rehabilitation, he was eligible to apply for a disability "bonus" that would have added many thousands of dollars to his pension every year. Gary had this option not because was disabled, but because the state of California says that working for the Department of Corrections is stressful—and so an employee *might* become disabled. Gary didn't put in for the disability bonus, but he was the only manager at the prison where he worked that did not.

California's problem is more widespread than simply the prisons, however. In the 1960s, about 5 percent of retiring California state workers received so-called public safety pensions. That meant the individuals had been working in a "dangerous" job. Today, about 35 percent of retiring state workers obtain this "public safety" retirement bonus, which was intended originally just for firefighters and police officers. In addition, California is the only state that uses the last year of an employee's salary to determine her or his long-term pension benefits, rather than averaging over the salaries of the last several years of work. Because pay usually rises over time, California's method generates extra pension benefits— and extra liabilities for taxpayers.

But there is more. Every year for decades, the legislature in Sacramento has improved public pension benefits. Consider just one of those passed in 1999. It was supposed to cost the state about $650 million per year by 2010. It actually cost $3.1 billion in 2010 and $3.5 billion in 2011.

Okay, so how bad can it be—a few billion here and a few billion there? Well, some studies have estimated that California has a $500 billion unfunded pension liability problem. And this problem cannot go away by itself because the courts have consistently upheld government employee pension benefits as untouchable contracts, except in a few rare cases in which a local government declares bankruptcy. In one recent year alone, over $3 billion of California state spending was diverted to pension costs from other programs. The diversion of state spending to fund pensions seems certain to do nothing but rise in the future.

A CLOSER LOOK AT THE "GARDEN STATE"

New Jersey, the self-described "garden state," is starting to look wilted. It, too, has been running billions of dollars of pension red ink per year. By the latest estimates, the New Jersey employee pension fund is well over $30 billion in the hole. What does that mean for a typical four-member household in New Jersey? Each is on the hook for about $16,000 in tax liabilities, just to make up this underfunding.

How did New Jersey get in this mess? Well, as in California, a big part of the problem started back in the 1990s. The stock market was booming, producing high rates of return on state investments. Under the assumption that these abnormally high returns were the new reality, state legislatures enhanced retirement benefits. Two stock market crashes later, the hoped-for returns haven't materialized, but the promised pensions are still there.

THE TOTAL PICTURE

Throughout the United States, only four states—Florida, New York, Washington, and Wisconsin—have fully funded pension systems. The remaining states are facing different degrees of fiscal disaster. Illinois and Kansas, for example, have enough assets on hand to pay for only 50–60 percent of their pension liabilities.

The PEW Center on the States did an exhaustive study just prior to the 2008 financial meltdown, and concluded that the fifty states had a $1 *trillion* pension funding gap. The states combined had contractually promised $3.35 trillion in pension, health, and other retirement benefits but only had $2.35 trillion on hand to pay for them. In all likelihood this $1 trillion gap is much greater today because of stock market losses since 2008, and the fact that most states still have unrealistic assumptions about future rates of return. (And, by the way, cities are also in deep trouble. One conservative estimate puts the funding gap for them at nearly $600 billion.)

THE PRIVATE SECTOR HAS PROBLEMS, TOO

Don't think that government decision makers at the state and local level have been the only ones to create unfunded pension liabilities. In the private sector, large corporations have found themselves with growing pension funding problems. One major company that has long loved to hide future pension liabilities is General Motors. In an effort to report better earnings, that company routinely used aggressive accounting practices and made pension contributions that were just a fraction of what it really needed to make. Eventually, though, GM's actual pension promises became due. When the company tried to pay for these costs by hiking the price of the cars it manufactured, those cars quickly became uncompetitive. Consumers started buying other brands that were cheaper for the same quality. The result was GM bankruptcy and a federal takeover. Taxpayers own a high percentage of shares in "Government Motors," as it is now sometimes called. Hence, taxpayers are now on the hook for future pension liabilities of the company.

GM is not alone. Over 75 percent of the largest five hundred corporations in the United States have unfunded pension fund obligations. It is perhaps no surprise that many of these companies have lobbied Congress to let them off the hook from meeting their legal obligations to more fully fund their pension plans.

Bankruptcies on the Horizon?

Returning our examination to the public sector, even though you may not be expecting to retire for decades, your economic well-being is already changing because of retirement commitments that cities and states have already made. In order to fulfill those unfunded pension liabilities, city and state governments are cutting back on essential services—education, police and prisons, and firefighters. You might think that we should not or "cannot" let essential government services be cut back just to pay pension benefits. Right now that is reality, however, all across the country.

Is there a way to reduce unfunded pension liabilities? Yes, but it is ugly. Just ask the residents of Vallejo, California. In 2008, eighteen police personnel and firefighters unexpectedly retired early. That city of 120,000 was immediately obligated to pay out several million dollars for their first year of retirement. This is a city that was already forking over $220 million for pensions and health care. Vallejo City government filed for **bankruptcy**.

Under so-called Chapter 9 of our **Bankruptcy Code**, municipal governments can propose their own reorganization plans and void union contracts without having to sell off their assets, such as buildings and investments. The public pension obligations of Vallejo were lumped together with all the rest of its obligations. Everyone from private accounting firms to public pensioners who were owed money had to take a "haircut"—accept less than 100 cents on the dollar owed. So now we see at least one way that cities, indeed, even states, can get out of the jam in which they find themselves. Declaring bankruptcy can allow them to renegotiate future pension benefits to put them more in line with future funding possibilities.

Right now, some cities are defaulting on the loans that they took out in past years. In a recent year, $3 billion in city debt was not paid when it came due. As we have already seen, that is a trivial amount compared to total unfunded pension liabilities. When more municipal governments choose to go bankrupt, the rate of municipal bond defaults will increase accordingly. This process will be painful and costly for retirees and bondholders alike. But the simple fact is this: State and local governments have been making promises they cannot realistically keep. Something must give and that means one of three things must happen. State and local spending on other programs must be slashed, taxes have to be hiked dramatically, or pensions need to be cut. Eventually, the easy political promises of the past must collide with the hard economic reality of the future.

WHY ISN'T THE FEDERAL GOVERNMENT IN THE SAME FIX?

As you might have noticed, there has been little discussion of the federal government's retirement system to which all of us contribute— **Social Security**. The reason is that Social Security is a **pay-as-you-go system**. The federal government has *not* taken your Social Security "contributions" and invested them in some special account. Indeed, there is no "account" earning interest now so that it will be there with your name on it when you choose to retire in your sixties. While you may have heard about something called a Social Security trust fund, that fund is just on paper. It's a myth, and a huge liability itself, about which you will learn more in Chapter 23.

DISCUSSION QUESTIONS

1. If there is no government- or company-provided pension system, how can an individual create a financially safe retirement?

2. Why would a state or local government ever commit more resources for future pension benefits than it could possibly have resources to pay?

3. Many state and local governments have been using an assumed 8 percent rate of return figure when calculating future funding of promised pension benefits. Why do you suppose they used this rather than an assumption of 2 percent, or even 0 percent?

4. Why can't state and local governments simply continue to borrow funds through the bond market to cover not only shortfalls in current tax revenues but also shortfalls in future available funding to pay contractual pension benefits?

5. The grim economic climate since 2008 has caused many workers to defer their retirements. How will this affect large employers in state and local governments?

6. In the private sector, one in five workers have been promised lifetime pensions. In the public sector, four in five workers have lifetime pensions. Why does the private sector offer so few lifetime pensions compared to the public sector?

CHAPTER 21

Mortgage Meltdown

Between 1995 and 2010, the U.S. housing market went on the wildest ride in its history. Over the years 1995–2005, median real (inflation-adjusted) house prices soared 60 percent nationwide and then crashed, falling 40 percent in just four years. Over the same period, the proportion of Americans who owned homes, normally a variable that changes quite slowly, leapt from 64 percent to 69 percent and then quickly dropped back to 66 percent. Meanwhile, the number of new houses built each year soared from 1.4 million to 2.2 million and then plummeted to below 500,000 per year.

THE HOUSING MARKET COLLAPSES

But what really got people's attention—and created huge pressures on financial markets here and abroad—was the fact that just as quickly as people had snapped up houses during the boom years of 1995–2005, they simply *abandoned* their houses beginning in 2006, refusing to make any more payments on their mortgages. In a typical year, about 0.3 percent of homeowners (fewer than one out of three hundred) stop making mortgage payments each year and thus have their houses go into **foreclosure**, a process in which the borrower must give up ownership in a home because of a failure to meet payment obligations. The foreclosure rate doubled to 0.6 percent in 2006, doubled again in 2007, and rose yet again in 2008. In some hard-hit states, such as Nevada, foreclosures exploded to more than *ten times* the normal nationwide rate.

Across the country, people were literally walking away from their homes, leaving them in the hands of banks and other lenders. These lenders then took huge financial losses when forced to sell the abandoned properties in a market in which house prices were already falling.

The result was further downward pressure on prices, which gave more owners the incentive to walk away from their homes, which raised foreclosures, and so forth. Within just a few years, the housing market was more depressed than it had been any time since, well, the Great Depression of the 1930s.

THE ROLE OF CONGRESS

What happened? To answer this, we need to examine why, over this fifteen-year period, the housing market first exploded and then imploded, causing financial chaos on a worldwide scale. Although numerous factors played a role, the principal culprit was none other than our own Congress. Operating under a banner promoting "affordable housing," Congress first amended key mortgage-lending legislation and then put considerable implicit and explicit pressure on government-sponsored mortgage agencies to make more loans to potential home buyers. These actions encouraged mortgage lenders to dramatically reduce the financial standards expected of home buyers who wished to obtain mortgages. These lower standards enabled many more people to obtain mortgage funding, increasing the demand for housing and leading to the housing boom of 1995–2005. But these same lower standards meant that people in weaker financial shape were heavily represented among home buyers, which in turn played a central role in the housing crash and mortgage meltdown of 2006–2010. To see how this evolved, we are going to have to do some digging in the history books.

A BRIEF HISTORY OF MORTGAGE LEGISLATION

Prior to World War II, most home mortgages were of short duration, such as one or two years (as opposed to fifteen to thirty years, which is common now). During the Great Depression, many risk-weary lenders refused to renew mortgages when they came due. The state of the economy was such that most borrowers were unable to pay the balance immediately, and so their homes were foreclosed. In response, the U.S. government in 1934 created the Federal Housing Administration (FHA) to guarantee some home mortgages from default and in 1938 created the Federal National Mortgage Association (FNMA, known as Fannie Mae) to purchase mortgages from the FHA, enabling the latter to guarantee still more mortgages. In 1968, Congress authorized Fannie Mae to buy mortgages from virtually all lenders, and in 1970, Congress created Freddie Mac (the Federal Home Mortgage Loan Corporation) to offer competition to Fannie Mae. Both Fannie Mae and Freddie Mac are referred to as "government-sponsored enterprises" (GSEs); both are technically independent of the federal government, but both are subject to congressional oversight and, it turns out, to political pressure to do what Congress wants them to do.

The next key congressional action came in 1977 when the Community Reinvestment Act (CRA) was passed, a law that required banks to lend in all neighborhoods of the geographic areas where they operated, even areas where risks were likely to be much higher than the banks would normally undertake. In 1995, the CRA was amended so that banks were, in effect, *compelled* to ignore their lending standards when making loans in low-income and minority neighborhoods or else face the wrath of government regulators. Not long thereafter, Congress began putting considerable pressure on Fannie Mae and Freddie Mac to buy up the low-quality mortgages being made under the CRA, in the hopes that this would encourage lenders to make still more low-quality loans. And indeed it did. The banks soon recognized that with the two GSEs standing ready to take the worst of their mortgages off their hands, they could earn hefty fees for originating the mortgages and then dump the risks of default off onto Fannie Mae and Freddie Mac. At this point, many potential lenders, including banks, savings and loans, and mortgage brokers, concluded that if Fannie Mae and Freddie Mac were happy to buy up risky mortgages at the drop of a hat, so to speak, then it was OK to hold on to some of the risky mortgages they were making. After all, these mortgages (called subprime mortgages) fattened profits with their above-average interest rates, and if the market turned sour, the GSEs would presumably stand ready to take them off lenders' hands.

REGULATORY PRESSURE

Thus, we see that it was regulatory and legislative pressure from the federal government (spearheaded by Congress) that pushed mortgage lenders to cut their lending standards in truly remarkable ways. For example, lenders have historically insisted on down payments ranging from 5 to 20 percent on home loans. This gives borrowers an incentive to keep making monthly payments (or else they lose their down payment on foreclosure), and it provides a cushion for the lender (to ensure it gets all its money back on foreclosure). Under pressure from federal regulators, however, lenders were induced to cut required down payments and even to make so-called piggyback loans, giving borrowers a *second* mortgage on top of the first whose sole function was to provide cash for the down payment. In effect, down payments were driven to zero or close thereto.

But there was more. Federal regulators pushed banks to:

- Ignore mortgage applicants' credit histories if they were less than stellar
- Forgo confirmation of applicants' current or past employment or income levels
- Permit applicants to have lower than normal income-to-loan ratios
- Count as part of income such sources as unemployment insurance and welfare payments, despite the temporary nature of such payments.

Banks that had never before offered loans under such conditions soon made them routinely, pushed by the requirements of the CRA and pulled by the willingness of Fannie Mae and Freddie Mac to acquire the loans as soon as the ink was dry. And because the GSEs were so active in making the market for loans, many lenders felt comfortable in making and holding on to such loans, even buying more loans from other lenders.

Congress's avowed intention in this process was to "help promote affordable housing," especially for low-income and minority individuals. Congress claimed to be particularly interested in making home owner-ship possible for people who had been renters all their lives. And indeed, low-income and minority individuals were for the first time able to own their homes—at least for a while. But once banks became comfortable with making and disposing of high-risk loans, they quickly became ame-nable to making such loans to anyone who showed up, first-time buyer or not. And if the loan was to buy a house in a low-income or minor-ity neighborhood, it became that much more attractive, because of the possibility that it would keep the bean-counting regulators happy. Thus, beginning in the late 1990s and accelerating rapidly in 2002 (when the house price trajectory shot up), speculators—people buying a second or third house in the hopes of selling it quickly for a profit—became an in-creasingly important part of the market. Indeed, it is now estimated that one-quarter of all borrowers over this period were making speculative purchases of this sort.

THE ROLE OF ADJUSTABLE-RATE MORTGAGES

Not surprisingly, speculators wanted to make low down payments and to obtain **adjustable-rate mortgages (ARMs)**. The ARMs offered slighter lower initial interest rates and payments (because borrowers absorbed the risk of higher rates in the future). They also gave lenders the flexibility to offer low "teaser" interest rates (and thus ultra low payments) during the first few years of the mortgage. Such mortgages were considerably riskier for borrowers because of the hazard of higher payments later, when the mortgages "popped" (automatically adjusted their interest rates to full long-run levels). But by then, of course, speculators hoped to have sold for a profit and paid off the mortgage. The spread of ARMs, especially those with low teaser rates, was accelerated by people who bought homes hoping to refinance at a low fixed rate later, after rising home prices built equity for them in their houses.

All went well until 2005, when many of the early ARMs began to pop (with payments adjusting upward sharply). Some borrowers found that they were unable to make the higher payments and were thus forced to sell their homes. This slowed the rise in house prices by 2006, making housing less attractive as an investment, which in turn reduced the speculative demand and put further downward pressure on prices. In markets such as Arizona, California, Florida, and Nevada, where speculative activity had been the greatest, house prices started to *fall*, and growing numbers of individuals (especially those who put up low or no down payments) found themselves "upside down," owing more on their mortgages than their houses were worth. By the middle of 2006, the prudent financial course for such people was to stop making payments (especially on ARMs that had popped) and to simply walk away when the lender began foreclosure proceedings.

THE EVIDENCE ON ADJUSTABLE-RATE MORTGAGES

Many accounts of this process in the popular press have claimed that it is exclusively high-risk, subprime mortgages that are at the root of the crisis. This sounds sensible enough, because subprime mortgages have always had relatively high foreclosure rates; indeed, the subprime foreclosure rate has historically been about eight times as high as the rate on prime mortgages (1.6 percent per year versus 0.2 percent per year). Hence, subprime mortgages now, as in normal times, are disproportionately represented among foreclosures. But a closer look at the data also reveals that foreclosures on *both* types of mortgages shot upward in the middle of 2006, with foreclosures on subprime mortgages soon reaching 4 percent and those on prime mortgages hitting 0.5 percent. Thus, it appears that both types of borrowers began to get in trouble at the same time; not just subprime mortgages were affected.

The data also reveal that it is chiefly borrowers who obtained ARMs who have been at the root of the meltdown. Prior to 2006, foreclosures on ARMs and on fixed-rate mortgages were occurring at about the same rate.

But beginning in early 2006, even as the foreclosure rate on fixed-rate mortgages hardly budged, the rate on ARMs exploded: on prime ARMs, the rate leapt by a factor of 5, while the foreclosure rate on subprime ARMs tripled. Moreover, it was on ARMs that foreclosures started up first (at the very beginning of 2006). Forced sales on these homes started the downward pressure on house prices, which gave more owners the incentive to walk away from their homes, which raised foreclosures, and so forth. Soon enough, the entire market had begun to implode.

THE LASTING DAMAGE

By the time you read this, we expect (and hope!) that the housing market will have shown signs of recovery. But we also hope that the lesson of this episode will not be forgotten. The road to the mortgage meltdown of 2006–2010 was paved by our very own U.S. Congress, which sought to subvert the market to achieve its political goals. The methods used are perhaps little different than those Congress usually employs when it hopes to achieve politically popular social objectives. But the very real difference of this episode is the enormous social cost that it has brought on Americans of all races and all income levels. Literally millions of Americans had their hopes of home ownership first artificially raised and then cruelly dashed. The financial losses and emotional stresses inflicted on individuals, the blighted neighborhoods littered with abandoned houses, and the turmoil felt throughout the states most affected are all costs that will imprint the American scene for years to come.

DISCUSSION QUESTIONS

1. It seems likely that members of Congress, even the strongest supporters of the CRA and those who put the most pressure on the GSEs to buy high-risk mortgages, will likely escape being held responsible for any part of the mortgage meltdown. Can you suggest why?

2. Many large lenders, along with Fannie Mae and Freddie Mac, obtained funding for their activities by selling bonds that offered as collateral the mortgages that were made using those funds. These bonds are often referred to as "mortgage-backed securities." Many billions of dollars of these mortgage-backed securities were purchased by citizens and governments of foreign lands. Explain how this fact helped the financial crisis in America spread to other nations.

3. In light of the fact that foreclosure rates have been much higher on ARMs than on fixed-rate mortgages, what do you predict will

happen in the future to the proportion of mortgages that are of each type? Explain.

4. In effect, the CRA and the actions of Fannie Mae and Freddie Mac acted to subsidize home purchases by people who otherwise would not have purchased houses. All subsidies must be financed by taxes, implicit or explicit, on someone. Who is paying the "taxes" in this case? Explain.

5. Suppose you ranked states from highest to lowest based on their foreclosure rates over the years 2006–2010. In what states do you predict that prices rose the most from 1995 to 2005? In what states do you predict that prices fell the most from 2006 to 2010? Explain your reasoning.

6. Would you expect housing price volatility (the combination of rise and fall) over the period 1995–2010 to be greatest in urban housing markets or rural housing markets? Would you expect such volatility to be highest in areas with lots of immigration from other states and emigration to other states, or little immigration and emigration of this type? Explain you reasoning in each case.

CHAPTER 22

Raising Less Corn and More Hell

When politician Mary Lease stumped the Kansas countryside in 1890, she urged the farmers to raise "less corn and more hell," and that is just what they have been doing ever since.

A Brief History of American Farming

The two decades before World War I witnessed unparalleled agricultural prosperity in the United States. This "golden age of American farming" continued through the war as food prices soared. The end of the war, combined with a sharp recession in 1920, brought the golden age to a painful halt. Even the long economic recovery from 1921 to 1929—the Roaring Twenties—did little to help American farmers. European countries were redirecting their resources into agricultural production, and new American **tariffs** on foreign goods severely disrupted international trade. Because food **exports** had been an important source of farmers' incomes, the decline in world trade reduced the **demand** for American agricultural products and cut deeply into food prices and farm income.

The sharply falling food prices of the 1920s led farmers to view their problem as one of overproduction. Numerous cooperative efforts were thus made to restrict production, but virtually all of these efforts failed. Most crops were produced under highly competitive conditions, with large numbers of buyers and sellers dealing in products that were largely undifferentiated. One farmer's corn, for example, was the same as any other farmer's corn. Thus, producers were unable to enforce collective output restrictions and price hikes on a voluntary basis. But what farmers failed to do by voluntary means in the 1920s, they accomplished via government directives in the 1930s. An effective farm **price-support**

program was instituted in 1933, marking the beginning of a policy of farm **subsidies** in the United States that continues today.

The Market for Agricultural Commodities

We can understand the results of price supports and other government farm programs by first examining the market for agricultural commodities in the absence of government intervention. In that competitive market, a large number of farmers supply any given commodity, such as corn. The sum of the quantities that individual farmers supply at various prices generates the **market supply** of a commodity. Each farmer supplies only a small part of the market total. No one farmer, therefore, can influence the price of the product. If one farmer were to raise the price, buyers could easily purchase from someone else at the **market-clearing**, or **equilibrium, price**. And no farmers would sell below the market-clearing price. Thus, every unit of output sold by farmers goes for the same price. The price received for the last (*marginal*) unit sold is exactly the same as that received for all the rest. The farmer will produce corn up to the point that if one more unit were produced, its production cost would be greater than the price received. Notice that at higher prices, farmers can incur higher costs for additional units produced and still make a **profit**. Because all farmers face the same basic production decision, all farmers together will produce more at higher prices. Indeed, no farmer will stop producing until he or she stops making a profit on additional units. That is, each farmer will end up selling corn at the market-clearing price, which will equal the costs of production plus a normal profit.[1]

Price Supports

Now, how has the price-support program worked? Under such a program, the government has to decide what constitutes a "fair price." Initially, this decision was linked to the prices farmers received during "good" years—such as during agriculture's golden age. Eventually, the government-established price was determined through intense negotiations between members of Congress from farm states and those from nonfarm states. The key point here is that except for the years of World War II, the "fair" price decreed by the government has generally been well above the equilibrium price that would have prevailed in the

---

1 For society as a whole, normal profit is actually a **cost** of production because it is required to keep the farmer growing corn instead of changing to an alternative occupation.

absence of price supports. This has encouraged farmers to produce more, which ordinarily would simply push prices back down.

How has the government made its price "stick"? There have been two methods. For the first several decades of farm programs, it agreed to buy the crops, such as corn, at a price, called the **support price**, which was high enough to keep farmers happy but not so high as to enrage too many taxpayers. As a practical matter, these purchases have been disguised as "loans" from a government agency—loans that never need to be repaid. The government then stored the crops it purchased, sold them on the world market (as opposed to the domestic market) at prices well below the U.S. support price, or simply gave them away to foreign nations under the Food for Peace program. In each instance, the result was substantial costs for taxpayers and substantial gains for farmers. Under the price-support system, the American taxpayers routinely spent more than $10 billion *each year* for the benefit of corn farmers alone. Smaller but still substantial subsidies were garnered by the producers of wheat, peanuts, soybeans, sorghum, rice, and cotton, to name but a few.

RESPONSES TO PRICE SUPPORTS

In an effort to keep the size of the **surpluses** down, the government has often restricted the number of acres that farmers may cultivate. Under these various **acreage-restriction programs**, farmers wishing to participate in certain government subsidy programs have been required to keep a certain amount of land out of production. About eighty million acres, an area the size of New Mexico, have at one time or another been covered by the agreements. Enticed by high support prices, farmers have found ingenious ways to evade acreage restrictions. For example, soybeans and sorghum are both excellent substitutes for corn as a source of livestock feed. So farmers agreed to cut their corn acreage and then planted soybeans or sorghum on the same land. This action increased the corn surplus and forced the government to extend acreage restrictions and price supports to soybeans and sorghum. Similarly, faced with limitations on the amount of land they could cultivate, farmers responded by cultivating the smaller remaining parcels of land far more intensively. They used more fertilizers and pesticides, introduced more sophisticated methods of planting and irrigation, and applied technological advances in farm machinery at every opportunity. As a result, agricultural output per man-hour is now *twelve times* what it was sixty years ago.

There were a couple of problems with the original price-support system. First, because it kept crop prices high, it kept consumers' food bills high as well. People were spending an extra $10 billion or more on food each year. Another problem with the price-support system was that the surplus crops piled up year after year in government warehouses. Not only was storing the surpluses expensive, but it also eventually became politically embarrassing. For example, at one point, the federal government had enough wheat in its storage bins to make seven loaves of bread for every man, woman, and child *in the world.*

TARGET PRICES

In the early 1980s, the federal government switched to a second system, in which it set a **target price** that was guaranteed to farmers but let the price paid by consumers adjust to whatever lower level it took to get consumers to buy all of the crops. Then the government simply sent a check to farmers for the difference between the target price and the **market price**. This brought consumers' food bills down and eliminated government storage of surplus crops, but it also meant that the cost to taxpayers—up to $25 billion per year—was painfully clear in the huge checks being written to farmers.

The original price-support program hid its subsidies by making it appear as though the crop surpluses were the result of American farmers' simply being "too productive" for their own good. With the direct payments made under the target-price system, however, it became apparent that the government was taking cash out of taxpayers' pockets with one hand and giving it to farmers with the other. Moreover, the target-price system, like our other agricultural programs, geared the size of the subsidies to the amount of output produced by the recipients. Thus, small farmers received trivial amounts, while giant farms—agribusinesses—collected enormous subsidies. The owners of many huge cotton farms and rice farms, for example, received payments totaling more than $1 million apiece.

This fact illustrates who actually benefits from federal farm programs. Although these programs have traditionally been promoted as a way to guarantee decent earnings for low-income farmers, most of the benefits have in fact gone to the owners of very large farms, and the larger the farm, the bigger the benefit. In addition, *all* of the benefits from price supports ultimately accrue to *landowners* on whose land price-supported crops are grown.

MORE POLICY TINKERING

In 1996, Congress made what turned out to be a futile attempt to reduce agricultural subsidies, enacting the seven-year Freedom to Farm Act. The reforms were supposed to increase farmer flexibility and remove market distortions by moving away from price-support payments for wheat, corn, and cotton. In their place, farmers would receive "transition payments." The taxpayer was supposed to save billions of dollars.

It was not to be. Beginning in 1998, Congress passed large farm "supplemental bills" each year, each costing billions of dollars per year that go directly from your paycheck to the bank accounts of the largest agribusiness corporations in America. Then, in 2002, Congress passed what was then the most expensive farm bill in the history of the United States, with an advertised price tag of over $191 billion for a ten-year period. President Bush said, when he signed the bill, "This nation has got to eat." He further said, "Our farmers and ranchers are the most efficient producers in the world. ... We are really good at it."

Congress got even better at subsidizing farmers in 2008 when, despite a veto by President Bush, it passed the Food, Security, and Bioenergy Act—with an advertised ten-year cost of more than $300 billion. The new legislation gave the growers of many crops a choice of federal subsidy programs. Depending on the crop, they can select a mix of what amount to target-price or support-price programs, or they can choose a program offering guaranteed revenues. If crop prices are high, farmers get to sell at those prices, but if prices are low, they get a check that increases their earnings to the guaranteed level.

THE REALITY OF FARM SUBSIDIES

One of the claims often used to promote farm subsidies is that farming earns its practitioners relatively low incomes. In fact, farmers' household incomes have been averaging 20 percent *above* household incomes for nonfarm families over the past decade, and given the size of the subsidies, it is not hard to see why. In one recent year, when farm profits were $72 billion, the federal government handed out $25 billion in subsidies to farmers, almost 50 percent more than it spent on welfare payments for poor families. Millionaires such as Ted Turner and David Rockefeller receive hundreds of thousands of dollars per year in taxpayer-financed agricultural subsidies. When we add the billions in direct subsidies to the billions in higher food prices that result from the farm program, we find that the average American household will pay more than $5,000 in higher food prices and taxes under the latest farm bill. And still, two-thirds of all farm subsidies will go to the top 10 percent of farms, most of which earn over $250,000 annually. Thus, large agribusinesses continue to be the chief beneficiaries of our generous agricultural policy.

Farmers can now receive payments for *not* growing crops they used to grow. In fact, if they sell their land to someone else, the right to receive these payments goes with the land. So in many cases, even if the land is subsequently carved up into lots on which people build homes, the happy homeowners are eligible for these "direct payments," made because years ago the land was used to grow, say, rice. The price tag in one recent year: $1.3 billion. Farmers also receive payments to compensate them for losses they don't actually incur. To see how this works, let's suppose the government's target price for corn is $4.00 per bushel and that a farmer manages to sell his crop for $5.00 per bushel during a period of the year when prices were a bit higher than usual. If at any time during the year the price per bushel fell below $4.00, say, to $3.40, the farmer can claim a "deficiency payment" from the government. In this case, the farmer would be eligible for 60 cents per bushel ($4.00 – $3.40) for every bushel produced, even though the corn actually sold for $5.00.

FARM POLICY IN OTHER NATIONS

Perhaps we should not complain too much about farm programs in the United States, for at least we don't have Japanese farm programs. In Japan, a combination of subsidies for domestic farmers and tariffs on imported food has pushed farm incomes to a level roughly *double* the average income in the country as a whole. The subsidies and tariffs also have driven up the price of an ordinary melon to $100 (yes, one hundred dollars). Even the Europeans seem to find lavishing largesse on farmers irresistible. In recent years, Americans have been shelling out about $40 billion per year for farm subsidies. The European Union (EU) has been spending more than $130 billion per year on farm subsidies. To be sure, the EU is about 50 percent more populous than the United States, but even adjusting for this, the huge spending there means that the average EU citizen is spending twice as much subsidizing farmers as we spend here.

Politicians from the farming states argue that we cannot abandon our farmers because the United States would end up with too many bankrupt farms and not enough food. But there is evidence from at least one country that such a scenario is simply not correct. In 1984, New Zealand's government ended all farm subsidies of every kind, going completely "cold turkey" without any sort of transition to the new era of free markets for food. Agricultural subsidies in New Zealand had accounted for more than 30 percent of the value of agricultural production, even higher than what has been observed in the United States. The elimination of subsidies in New Zealand occurred rapidly, and there were no extended phaseouts for any crops. Despite this, there was no outbreak of farm bankruptcies. Indeed, only 1 percent of farms have gone out of business in New Zealand since 1984. Instead, the farmers responded by improving their techniques, cutting costs, and aggressively marketing their products in export markets.

The results have been dramatic. The value of farm output in New Zealand has increased by more than 40 percent (in constant-dollar terms) since the subsidy phaseout. The share of New Zealand's total annual output attributed to farming has increased from 14 percent to 17 percent. Land **productivity** has increased at about 6 percent per year. Indeed, according to the Federated Farmers of New Zealand, the country's experience thoroughly debunked the myth that the farming sector cannot prosper without government subsidies.

Are any members of the U.S. Congress listening?

DISCUSSION QUESTIONS

1. American corn farmers receive billions of dollars in taxpayer subsidies each year. These subsidies allow them to sell their grain at prices below what it costs to produce it, particularly for export markets. How do U.S. corn subsidies hurt Mexican farmers?

2. If it is so obvious that farm subsidies hurt consumers, why do such subsidies continue to be voted in by Congress? (*Hint:* See the discussion of **rational ignorance** in Chapter 26.)

3. What groups would be the major beneficiaries if farm subsidies in the United States were eliminated?

4. Why do you suppose that farmers, rather than economists, receive subsidies from the federal government? (*Hint:* If you are tempted to answer that there are more farmers than economists, ask yourself, what would happen to the number of self-proclaimed economists if the federal government started offering subsidies to economists?)

5. What are the likely environmental impacts of our farm programs? Explain.

6. Under the federal Duck Stamp program wildfowl hunters pay a fee to the federal government each year, the proceeds from which are used to purchase land for wildfowl habitat. Do you think farmers support or oppose the Duck Stamp program? Explain.

CHAPTER 23

The Graying of America

America is aging. The 78 million baby boomers who pushed the Beatles and the Rolling Stones into stardom are beginning to retire. In less than twenty years, roughly 20 percent of all Americans will be sixty-five or older. Just as the post–World War II baby boom presented both obstacles and opportunities, so does the graying of America. Let's see why.

THE ORIGINS OF THE "SENIOR BOOM"

Two principal forces are behind America's "senior boom." First, we're living longer. Average life expectancy in 1900 was forty-seven years; today, it is seventy-eight and is likely to reach eighty within the next decade. Second, the birthrate is near record-low levels. Today's mothers are having far fewer children than their mothers or grandmothers had. In short, the old are living longer, and the ranks of the young are growing too slowly to offset that fact. Together, these forces are pushing up the proportion of the population over age sixty-five; indeed, the number of seniors is growing at twice the rate of the rest of the population. In 1970, the **median age** in the United States—the age that divides the older half of the population from the younger half—was twenty-eight; it is now thirty-eight and rising. Compounding these factors, the average age at retirement is low by historical standards. The result is more retirees relying on fewer workers to help ensure that their senior years are also golden years.

THE COSTS OF THE ELDERLY

Why should a person who is, say, college age be concerned with the age of the rest of the population? Well, old people are expensive. In fact, people over sixty-five now consume over one-third of the federal government's budget. Social Security payments to retirees are the biggest item, now running over $700 billion per year. Medicare, which pays hospital and doctors' bills for the elderly, costs around $500 billion per year and is increasing rapidly. Moreover, fully one-third of the $300 billion annual budget for Medicaid, which helps pay medical bills for the poor of all ages, goes to people over the age of sixty-five.

Under current law, the elderly will consume 40 percent of all federal spending within less than fifteen years: Medicare's share of the gross domestic product (GDP) will double, as will the number of very old—those over eighty-five and most in need of care. Within about twenty-five years, probably *half* of the federal budget will go to the old. In a nutshell, senior citizens are the beneficiaries of an expensive and rapidly growing share of all federal spending. What are they getting for our dollars?

Today's elderly are already more prosperous than any previous generation. Indeed, the annual discretionary income of Americans over sixty-five averages 30 percent higher than the average discretionary income of all other age groups. Each year, inflation-adjusted Social Security benefits paid to new retirees are higher than the first-year benefits paid to people who retired the year before. In addition, for the past forty years, cost-of-living adjustments have protected Social Security benefits from inflation. The impact of Social Security is evident even at the lower end of the income scale: The poverty rate for people over sixty-five is much lower than for the population as a whole. Retired people today collect Social Security benefits that are two to five times what they and their employers contributed in payroll taxes plus interest earned.

Not surprisingly, medical expenses are a major concern for many elderly. Perhaps reflecting that concern, each person under the age of sixty-five in America currently pays an average of more than $2,000 per year in federal taxes to subsidize medical care for the elderly. Indeed, no other country in the world goes to the lengths that America does to preserve life. Some 30 percent of Medicare's budget goes to patients in their last year of life. Coronary bypass operations, costing over $40,000 apiece, are routinely performed on Americans in their sixties and seventies. For those over sixty-five, Medicare picks up the tab. Even heart transplants are now performed on people in their sixties and paid for by Medicare for those over sixty-five. By contrast, the Japanese offer no organ transplants. Britain's National Health Service generally will not provide kidney dialysis for people over fifty-five. Yet Medicare subsidizes dialysis for more than one hundred thousand Americans, half of them over age sixty. The cost: more than $5 billion per year. Overall, the elderly receive Medicare benefits worth five to twenty times the payroll taxes (plus interest) they paid for this program.

THE COSTS ARE PAID BY YOU

The responsibility for the huge and growing bills for Social Security and Medicare falls squarely on current and future workers because both programs are financed by payroll taxes. Thirty years ago, these programs were adequately financed with a payroll levy of less than 10 percent of the typical worker's earnings. Today, the tax rate exceeds 15 percent of median wages and is expected to grow rapidly.

By the year 2020, early baby boomers, born in the late 1940s and early 1950s, will have retired. Late baby boomers, born in the early 1960s, will be nearing retirement. Both groups will leave today's college students, and their children, a staggering bill to pay. For Social Security and Medicare to stay as they are, the payroll tax rate may have to rise to 25 percent of wages over the next decade. And a payroll tax rate of 40 percent is not unlikely by the middle of the twenty-first century.

One way to think of the immense bill facing today's college students and their successors is to consider the number of retirees each worker must support. In 1946, the burden of one Social Security recipient was shared by 42 workers. By 1960, nine workers had to foot the bill for each retiree's Social Security benefits. Today, roughly three workers pick up the tab for each retiree's Social Security and Medicare benefits. By 2030, only two workers will be available to pay the Social Security and Medicare benefits due each recipient. Thus, a working couple will have to support not only themselves and their family but also someone outside the family who is receiving Social Security and Medicare benefits.

POLITICAL ECONOMY IN ACTION

Congress and the executive branch have seemed unwilling to face the pitfalls and promises of an aging America. Although the age of retirement for Social Security purposes is legislatively mandated to rise to sixty-seven, the best that politicians in Washington, DC, appear able to do is appoint commissions to "study" the problems we face. And what changes are our politicians willing to make? We got a sample of this in 2003, with new legislation promising taxpayer-funded prescription drug benefits for senior citizens. Even people in favor of the new program called it the largest expansion in **entitlement programs** in forty years. Before passage of the law, President Bush claimed it was going to cost $35 billion per year, but within a couple of months, that estimate had been hiked to over $50 billion. In fact, the benefits of the program will be less than claimed, and the costs will be even higher, because more than three-quarters of senior citizens had privately funded prescription drug plans *before* the new law took effect. These private plans are already disappearing, leaving seniors with fewer choices and sticking younger taxpayers with a larger tax bill.

By now you may be wondering how we managed to commit ourselves to the huge budgetary burden of health and retirement benefits for senior citizens. There are three elements to the story. First, the cause is worthy: After all, who would want to deny the elderly decent medical care and a comfortable retirement? Second, the benefits of the programs are far more concentrated than the costs. A retired couple, for example, collects more than $25,000 per year in Social Security and consumes another $15,000 in subsidized medical benefits. In contrast, the typical working couple pays only about half of this each year in Social Security and Medicare taxes. Hence, the retired couple has a stronger **incentive** to push for benefits than the working couple has to resist them. And finally, senior citizens vote at a far higher rate than members of any other age group, in no small part because they are retired and thus have fewer obligations on their time. They are thus much more likely to make it clear at the ballot box exactly how important their benefits are to them.

THE FUTURE PATH

It is possible for government to responsibly address the crisis in funding programs for senior citizens. Chile, for example, faced a national pension system with even more severe problems than our Social Security system. Its response was to transform the system into one that is rapidly (and automatically, as time passes) converting itself into a completely private pension system. The result has been security for existing retirees, higher potential benefits for future retirees, and lower taxes for all workers. Americans could do exactly what the Chileans have done—if we chose to do so.

In the meantime, if Social Security and Medicare are kept on their current paths and older workers continue to leave the workforce, the future burden on today's college students is likely to be unbearable. If we are to avoid the social tensions and enormous costs of such an outcome, the willingness and ability of older individuals to retain more of their self-sufficiency must be recognized. To do otherwise is to invite a future in which the golden years are but memories of the past.

DISCUSSION QUESTIONS

1. How do the payroll taxes levied on the earnings of workers affect their decisions about how much leisure they consume?

2. When the government taxes younger people to pay benefits to older people, how does this affect the amount of assistance that younger people might voluntarily choose to offer older people?

3. When the government taxes younger people to pay benefits to older people, how does this affect the size of the bequests that older people are likely to leave to their children or grandchildren when they die?

4. In general, people who are more productive earn higher incomes and thus pay higher taxes. How would a change in the immigration laws that favored more highly educated and skilled individuals affect the future tax burden of today's American college students? Would the admission of better-educated immigrants tend to raise or lower the wages of American college graduates? On balance, would an overhaul of the immigration system benefit or harm today's college students?

5. How would a change in immigration laws that allowed *more* legal immigration affect the budget crisis we face with Social Security and Medicare?

6. How does the promise of guaranteed Social Security and Medicare benefits affect an individual's decision to save during the years before retirement age?

PART SIX

Property Rights and the Environment

Introduction

You saw in Part Four that **monopoly** produces outcomes that differ significantly from the outcomes of **competition** and yields gains from trade that fall short of the competitive ideal. In Part Six, you will see that when **externalities** are present—when there are discrepancies between the **private costs** of action and the **social costs** of action—the competitive outcome differs from the competitive ideal. Typically, the problem in the case of externalities is said to be *market failure,* but the diagnosis might just as well be termed *government failure.* For markets to work efficiently, **property rights** to **scarce goods** must be clearly defined, cheaply enforceable, and fully transferable, and it is generally the government that is believed to have a **comparative advantage** in ensuring that these conditions are satisfied. If the government fails to define, enforce, or make transferable property rights, the market will generally fail to produce socially efficient outcomes, and it becomes a moot point as to who is at fault. The real point is: What might be done to improve things?

SAVE THAT SPECIES

As we see in Chapter 24, the world's ocean fisheries are in decline. Since 1950, nearly 30 percent of all fisheries have collapsed, and in forty years, *all* of the world's fisheries could disappear. The problem is that in almost all of the world's fisheries, the governmentally established rules of fishing are such that to "own" a fish, someone must catch the fish, that is, kill it. Thus, each harvester knows that if he or she doesn't take the fish now, the future benefits (from growth and reproduction) of leaving the fish in the water will be enjoyed by someone else who later catches the larger fish or its offspring. The fishers thus "race to fish," catching the fish before

161

they have a chance to grow more fully and often before they have had a chance to reproduce. This causes declining fish stocks and, eventually, collapse of the fishery. Mounting evidence shows that so-called "catch share" systems can reverse this process. Under such systems of property rights, a **total allowable catch (TAC)** size is determined, based on biological and other scientific criteria. Then members of the fishing community are assigned shares of the TAC. The shares, often called **individual transferable quotas (ITQs),** can be used, sold, or leased to others. The catch shares give fishermen enforceable, transferable **property rights** in the fish, much as they have such property rights in their boats and gear. The fishers then have an incentive to protect and maintain the value of the fishery, just as they do to protect and maintain their other property. Not only does this system dramatically improve both the biological and the economic health of fisheries, but it can also be easily modified for use with *any* species. The message of this chapter is thus that saving a species is easy—as long as property rights to the members of the species are clearly established and cheaply enforceable and transferable.

Greenhouse Economics

We turn from the world's oceans to its atmosphere in Chapter 25. Evidence is growing that human action is responsible for rising concentrations of so-called greenhouse gases in the earth's atmosphere and that left unchecked, this growth may produce costly increases in the average temperature of our planet. Given the nature of the problem—a **negative externality**—private action taken on the individual level will not yield the best outcome for society. Thus, the potential gains from government action, in the form of environmental regulations or taxation, are substantial. The key word here is *potential,* for government action, no matter how well intentioned, does not automatically yield benefits that exceed the **costs.** As we seek solutions to the potential problems associated with greenhouse gases, we must be sure that the consequences of premature action are not worse than those of delaying action until the problem can be examined further. If we forget this message, greenhouse economics may turn into bad economics—and worse policy.

Ethanol Madness

Getting our government to take the actions that simultaneously protect our environment and our wealth is sometimes seemingly impossible. We explore the reasons behind this fact in Chapter 26, where we answer this simple query: If the **biofuel** ethanol doesn't protect the environment or conserve resources, why do we mandate its use as a gasoline additive and subsidize its production? Here we find that the principles of **political economy,** explored in Chapters 19–23, can be used to answer this question, too. It is true (as we emphasized in Chapter 5) that a critical function of government is to provide the institutional structure necessary for the creation and retention of our total wealth, broadly construed. Nevertheless, the essence of much government policymaking has nothing to do with making the economic pie larger. Instead, many government policies are directed at dividing up the pie in new ways, so that one group gets more resources at the expense of some other group. To do this successfully, politicians must be adept at exploiting the **rational ignorance** of voters, concentrating the benefits of policies among a few favored recipients while dispersing the costs of those policies across a large number of disfavored individuals. In the case of ethanol, we see that members of Congress do this in ways that enrich farmers and large ethanol producers at the expense of motorists and taxpayers—and, we should add, at the expense of the environment also.

THE TRASHMAN COMETH

As both population and per capita income rise, consumption rises faster than either, for it responds to the combined impetus of both. With consumption comes the residue of consumption, also known as plain old garbage. Many of us have heard of landfills being closed because of fears of groundwater contamination or of homeless garbage scows wandering the high seas in search of a place to off-load; all of us have been bombarded with public service messages to recycle everything from aluminum cans to newspapers. The United States, it seems, is becoming the garbage capital of the world. This is no doubt true, but it is also true that the United States is the professional football capital of the world—and yet professional football teams seem to have no problem finding cities across the country willing to welcome them with open arms. What is different about garbage? You are probably inclined to answer that football is enjoyable and garbage is not. True enough, but this is not why garbage sometimes piles up faster than anyone seems willing to dispose of it. Garbage becomes a problem only if it is not priced properly—that is, if the consumers and businesses that produce it are not charged enough for its removal and the landfills where it is deposited are not paid enough for its disposal. The message of Chapter 27 is that garbage really is no different from the things we consume in the course of producing it. As long as the trashman is paid, he will come, and as long as we have to pay for his services, his burden will be bearable. We will still have garbage, but we will not have a garbage problem.

CHAPTER 24

Save that Species

Codfish off the New England and eastern Canadian coasts were once so abundant, it was said, that a person could walk across the sea on their backs. The fish grew into six-foot-long, 200-pound giants, and generations of families from coastal communities knew they could count on the fish for a prosperous livelihood. Indeed, the northwestern Atlantic became known as the world's premier cod fishery (a **fishery** is just an area where it is commercially feasible for fish or other aquatic animals to be harvested). Slowly over time, however, nature's bounty began to disappear. Fishing became more difficult, the number of fish caught each year began to diminish, and the average size of the fish shrank. In the recent years, the problems accelerated. Between 1970 and 2000, the catch dropped more than 75 percent, and the typical fish caught these days weighs but twenty pounds. As a result, the Canadians have closed down their cod fishery, and the American fleet is a ghost of its former self.

FISHERY COLLAPSE IS WIDESPREAD

The cod is not alone in its demise. The world's ocean fisheries are in decline. Since 1950, nearly 30 percent of all fisheries have collapsed, and some scientists project that in forty years, *all* of the world's fisheries could disappear. The problem, it is widely agreed, is a failure of humans to manage fisheries in a way that is consistent with both maximum economic benefit and long-term survival of ocean fish stocks. Of course, this wide agreement just begs the real question: Why have humans been able to manage wheat farms and cattle ranches, but failed so miserably in managing fisheries?

The answer starts with the fact that in almost all of the world's fisheries, the governmentally established rules of fishing are such that to "own" a fish, someone must catch the fish, that is, remove it from the water, at which point it typically dies within minutes. This is unlike the rules for cattle, pigs, chickens, or sheep, of course, under which to own an animal one need only put a brand on it, or surround it with a fence, or enclose it in a building. The peculiar rules imposed by governments on most fisheries lead to a peculiar set of incentives.

When the decision is made to harvest any living animal, biological issues are important in accurately gauging the true cost of the harvest. In particular, if harvest does *not* take place, (i) the animal will continue growing, yielding a larger effective harvest in the future, and (ii) it may reproduce, leaving offspring that will also contribute to a larger future yield. In the case of cattle, pigs, and so forth, the harvesters (ranchers and farmers) take both of these facts into account, waiting until growth and reproduction rates have reached the point that it makes sense to harvest the animals now rather than waiting.

But with ocean fish, each harvester knows that if he or she doesn't take the fish now, the future benefits (from growth and reproduction) will be enjoyed by someone else who happens to catch the larger fish or its offspring later on. The fishers respond quite rationally to this incentive. They "race to fish," catching the fish before the fish have a chance to grow more fully and often before they have had a chance to reproduce. This causes declining fish stocks and, eventually, collapse of the fishery.

THE FAILURE OF COMMAND AND CONTROL

Based on a growing body of evidence, however, it is becoming increasingly apparent that a simple change in the way fisheries are managed has the power to stop and even reverse these declines. Traditional management of fisheries by government is referred to as a "command and control" system because in an effort to control the fishers, the government issues a series of commands about allowable behavior. These management systems limit, for example, the number of fishers, the size of boats they may use, the type of fishing gear, and season length, all in an effort to keep total harvests down. Even though such systems historically have held sway around the world, even the best of them suffer from a profound misalignment of **incentives:** the self-interest of the individual harvester is generally inconsistent with actions that would both maximize the value of the fishery and ensure its sustainability. Because individuals don't own any fish until they harvest them, they are motivated to outcompete other harvesters, taking fish that are too small and too young for long-term sustainability. The results are twofold. In the short run, the fishers harvest too many fish, and in the long run, they successfully lobby the government for more lenient rules, adding to the destruction. So far, no government has figured out how to use a command and control system to prevent excessive harvests, reduced stocks, and eventual collapse.

In recent years, the failure of command and control fishery management has become increasingly clear, but the question has been: Is there a viable alternative? Economists have suggested that catch shares assigned to individual harvesters offer such an alternative because property rights systems, of which catch shares are an example, are generally the most effective way to conserve resources.

CATCH SHARE SYSTEMS

Catch share systems combine two features. First, based on biological and other scientific criteria, a **total allowable catch (TAC)** size is determined. Then members of the fishing community (individuals or cooperatives, for example) are assigned shares of the TAC. Typically, the shares are granted to existing fishers in proportion to their historical fishing patterns. The shares, often called **individual transferable quotas (ITQs)**, can then be used, sold, or leased to others. No one is permitted to harvest in excess of the amount specified in the harvester's **quota**. The catch shares give fishermen enforceable, transferable **property rights** to the fish, much as they have such property rights to their boats and gear. These owners of rights then have an incentive to protect and maintain the value of the fishery, just as they do to protect and maintain their other property.

Case studies of the use of catch shares suggest that this system can dramatically improve both the biological and the economic health of fisheries. Alaska, British Columbia, Iceland, and New Zealand all represent locations where catch shares, such as ITQs, are regarded as having succeeded. Recent research covering more than eleven thousand fisheries around the world reveals that catch shares are effective worldwide. In fact, the outcomes for fisheries with and without catch share systems have been studied systematically, accounting for factors (such as ecosystem characteristics and fish species) that might have played a role in the health and viability of the fish stocks. This research approach amounts to conducting a statistically controlled experiment—and the results are striking.

THE POWER OF INCENTIVES

A conventional measure of collapse for a fishery is a decline in catch to a level that is less than 10 percent of the maximum recorded catch for that fishery. By this criterion, an average of more than fifty fisheries have reached collapse each year since 1950, in a worldwide pattern that seems to be pointing toward the demise of all fisheries. But in fisheries where a catch share system is implemented, the process of collapse halts—completely. Moreover, in many of the ITQ fisheries, recovery of fish stocks begins soon after implementation, even as fishermen continue to profitably catch fish.

It is now estimated that had ITQs been implemented in all fisheries beginning in 1970, the incidence of collapse would have been cut by two-thirds. Moreover, instead of watching fisheries collapse today, we would be seeing them getting healthier, even as they were supporting harvesters and nourishing consumers. Most importantly, it appears that the power of ITQs to prevent and even reverse fishery collapse applies to species and ecosystems throughout the world.

CAN WE SAVE THE WHALES, TOO?

Could a catch share system help protect whaling stocks around the world? In principle, the answer is "yes," although three aspects of whales would make the task more difficult. Consider, for example, blue whales, which are believed to migrate thousands of miles each year. A blue whale, which can weigh almost one hundred tons, is difficult to kill even with the most modern equipment. Nevertheless, intensive hunting gradually reduced the stock from somewhere between 300,000 and one million to, at present, somewhere between 3,000 and 4,000. Since 1965, all hunting of the blue whale has been banned by international treaty, although sporadic hunting of blues by some nations, such as Brazil, Chile, and Peru, has continued.

The enormous range of the blue whales means that enforcing any sort of rules regarding their capture—and this includes a catch share system—would likely be quite expensive. It is one thing to enforce catch limits over several thousand square miles. It is quite another to enforce them over millions of square miles. The second difficulty with designing a catch share system for blue whales is that because of the long-standing ban on hunting, and the sharp restrictions on hunting before that, little is known about their population, or whether that population is shrinking or growing. Hence, setting the correct TAC would be extremely difficult.

The final tricky issue of designing a catch share program for whales is that they are a "charismatic" species—that is, people seem to get satisfaction out of simply knowing they are out there swimming around. (We doubt, for example, whether you have ever seen a bumper sticker that says "Save the cod.") Thus, whales are said to have "existence value"—

some people get great satisfaction just out of knowing that they exist, satisfaction that would be irreparably lost if the whales were hunted to extinction. Clearly, although harvesters and biologists might be quite knowledgeable about growth and reproduction rates of all sorts of fish and ocean-going mammals, they are unlikely to know the value that Uncle Fred or Aunt Jane in Peoria place on the survival of the blue whale species. So people worry that a catch share system for whales might yield an unacceptably low stock of whales. As we'll see in a moment, however, the biologists and harvesters or whales might not have to know anything at all about Uncle Fred or Aunt Jane to make sure that there are plenty of whales to keep them happy and the whales healthy.

SERVE THE BISON

Ted Turner, the founder of CNN and the owner of the Atlanta Falcons football team, has fifteen ranches spanning two million acres. Ted also owns fifty thousand head of bison spread out over fourteen of these ranches. Simply put, Ted owns more bison than anyone else in the world. His bison holdings are obviously nowhere near as big as the enormous herds that once dominated the American plains. But they are big enough to ensure genetic diversity among the animals, and also to make it a good bet that bison are not going to become extinct at any time in the foreseeable future.[1] There are no doubt many reasons Ted has so many bison hanging around, but of one of them we can be certain: He turns thousands of head into burgers and steaks every year, both for his own chain of restaurants and for many hundreds more restaurants that serve bison on their menus. And although Ted raises the most bison in America, there are plenty of other bison ranchers out there doing much the same thing and for the same reason, adding thousands more bison to the national total.

So, just acting in their own self-interests, Ted and his fellow ranchers are able to keep bison stocks plenty big enough to ensure the survival of the species, and thus big enough to satisfy the desires of Aunt Jane and Uncle Fred that the bison continue to exist. Moreover, Ted's herds are big enough to *simultaneously* satisfy the existence value demands of a million (or even 7 billion) people around the world, all without any of these demanders putting up a penny of their own money (unless they stop by for a burger, of course).

---

1 Note that we don't claim that this or any system can prevent extinction *forever*. Only about 0.02 percent (about one in five thousand) species that have ever existed are currently extant. There is no evidence to date that any species—*Homo sapiens* included—has any claim on immortality.

In effect, this is exactly what is happening in fisheries around the world where catch share systems are at work. The incentives of the harvesters to keep stocks large enough for profitable fishing are *also* sufficient to protect the fish from any threat of extinction. It thus seems likely that catch share systems have the potential to save the whales, too. Indeed, the consistent ability of catch share systems to enable recovery of fish stocks and of the profits from harvesting illustrates a compelling general message: The clear assignment of enforceable property rights remains the most effective way we know to protect other species from the depredations of *Homo sapiens*.

Discussion Questions

1. Has there ever been a problem with the extinction of dogs, cats, or cattle? Why not?

2. Some people argue that the best way to save rare species is to set up private game reserves to which wealthy hunters can travel. How could this help save endangered species?

3. Is government *ownership* of animals needed to protect species from extinction?

4. In the United States, most fishing streams are public property, with access available to all. In Britain, most fishing streams are privately owned, with access restricted to those who are willing to pay for the right to fish. Anglers agree that over the past thirty years, the quality of fishing in the United States has declined, while the quality of fishing in Britain has risen. Can you suggest why?

5. Aquaculture is the business of raising water-dwelling animals, including fish, mollusks (such as oysters), and shell fish (such as shrimp) in enclosed areas. In the case of fish, this means raising them in large net pens. Do you suppose there is a problem with "overfishing" with aquaculture? What is a key difference between aquaculture animals and wild animals that plays a role in your conclusion?

6. Although much credit is given to buffalo hunters for causing the near extinction of bison, there was another factor at work. Cattle are easily herded by men on horseback and readily contained by barbed wired fences. Bison simply break through ordinary barbed wire and kill (by goring) horses used in any attempt to herd them. Explain how these characteristics of bison helped seal their fate on the Great Plains.

CHAPTER 25

Greenhouse Economics

The sky may not be falling, but it is getting warmer—maybe. The consequences will not be catastrophic, but they will be costly—maybe. We can reverse the process but should not spend very much to do so right now—maybe. Such is the state of the debate over the greenhouse effect—the apparent tendency of carbon dioxide (CO_2) and other gases to accumulate in the atmosphere, acting like a blanket that traps radiated heat, thereby increasing the earth's temperature. Before turning to the economics of the problem, let's take a brief look at the physical processes involved.

Certain gases in the atmosphere, chiefly water vapor and CO_2, trap heat radiating from the earth's surface. If they did not, the earth's average temperature would be roughly 0°F instead of just over 59°F, and everything would be frozen solid. Human activity helps create some so-called greenhouse gases, including CO_2 (mainly from combustion of fossil fuels) and methane (from landfills and livestock). We have the potential, unmatched in any other species, to profoundly alter our ecosystem.

There seems little doubt that humankind has been producing these gases at a record rate and that they are steadily accumulating in the atmosphere. Airborne concentrations of CO_2, for example, are increasing at the rate of about 0.5 percent per year. Over the past fifty years, the amount of CO_2 in the atmosphere has risen a total of about 25 percent. Laboratory analysis of glacial ice dating back at least 160,000 years indicates that global temperatures and CO_2 levels in the atmosphere do, in fact, tend to move together, suggesting that the impact of today's rising CO_2 levels may be higher global temperatures in the future. Indeed, the National Academy of Sciences (NAS) has suggested that by the middle of the twenty-first century, greenhouse gases could be double the levels they were in 1860 and that global temperatures could rise by 2–9°F.[1] The possible consequences of such a temperature increase include:

- A rise in the average sea level, inundating coastal areas, including much of Florida
- The spread of algal blooms capable of deoxygenating major bodies of water, such as Chesapeake Bay
- The conversion of much of the Midwestern wheat and corn belt into a hot, arid dust bowl

THE RESPONSE TO NEGATIVE EXTERNALITIES

When an individual drives a car or heats a house, greenhouse gases are produced. In economic terms, this creates a classic **negative externality.** Most of the **costs** (in this case, those arising from global warming) are borne by individuals *other than* the one making the decision about how many miles to drive. Because the driver enjoys all the benefits of the activity but suffers only a part of the cost, that individual engages in more than the economically efficient amount of the activity. In this sense, the problem of greenhouse gases parallels the problem that occurs when someone smokes a cigarette in an enclosed space or litters the countryside with fast food wrappers. If we are to get individuals to reduce production of greenhouse gases to the efficient rate, we must somehow induce them to act *as though* they bear all the costs of their actions. The two most widely accepted means of doing this are government regulation and taxation, both of which have been proposed to deal with greenhouse gases.

The 1988 Toronto Conference on the Changing Atmosphere, attended by representatives from forty-eight nations, favored the regulation route. The conference recommended a mandatory cut in CO_2 emissions by 2005 to 80 percent of their 1988 level—a move that would have required a major reduction in worldwide economic output. The 1997 Kyoto conference on climate change, attended by representatives from 160 nations, made more specific but also more modest proposals. Overall, attendees agreed that by 2012, thirty-eight

---

1 This may not sound like much, but it does not take much to alter the world as we know it. The global average temperature at the height of the last ice age eighteen thousand years ago—when Canada and most of Europe were covered with ice—was 51°F, a mere 8°F or so cooler than today.

developed nations should cut greenhouse emissions by 5 percent relative to 1990 levels.[2] Developing nations, including China and India (the two most populous nations in the world), would be exempt from emissions cuts. On the taxation front, one prominent U.S. politician has proposed a tax of $100 per ton on the carbon emitted by fuels. It is estimated that such a tax would raise the price of coal by $70 per ton and elevate the price of oil by $8 per barrel. These proposals, and others like them, clearly have the potential to reduce the buildup of greenhouse gases but only at substantial costs. It thus makes some sense to ask: What are we likely to get for our money?

SOME FACTS OF LIFE

Perhaps surprisingly, the answer to this question is not obvious. Consider the raw facts of the matter. On average over the past century, greenhouse gases have been rising, and so has the average global temperature. Yet most of the temperature rise occurred before 1940, whereas most of the increase in greenhouse gases occurred after 1940. In fact, global average temperatures fell about 0.5°F between 1940 and 1970. This cooling actually led a number of prominent scientists during the 1970s to forecast a coming ice age!

Between 1975 and 2000, the upward march of global temperatures resumed, accompanied by rising concentrations of greenhouse gases. At the same time, however, sunspot and other solar activity rose considerably, and the sun became brighter than in a thousand years. Then temperatures started falling, accompanied by diminished solar activity. Many scientists believe that the sun has thus contributed to the earth's temperature fluctuations. Debate remains, however, over how big this contribution has been.

Let us suppose for the moment that barring a significant reduction in greenhouse gas emissions, global warming is under way and that more is on the way. What can we expect? It appears that the answer is a "good news, bad news" story.

GOOD NEWS, BAD NEWS

The bad news is this: The likely rise in sea level by one to three feet will inundate significant portions of our existing coastline. The expected decline in precipitation in key regions will necessitate more widespread use of irrigation. The higher average temperatures will compel more widespread

---

2 This agreement has not been adhered to. In fact, emissions among this group of nations are *higher* than they were in 1990.

use of air conditioning, along with the associated higher consumption of energy to power it. The blazing heat in southern latitudes may make these areas too uncomfortable for all but the most heat-loving souls.

The good news is that the technology for coping with changes such as these is well known and the costs of coping are surprisingly small (on a scale measured in hundreds of billions of dollars, of course). Moreover, many of the impacts that loom large at the individual level will represent much smaller costs at a societal level. For example, although higher average temperatures could prove disastrous for farmers in southern climes, the extra warmth could be an enormous windfall farther north, where year-round farming might become feasible. Similarly, the loss of shoreline due to rising sea levels would partly just be a migration of coastline inland—current beachfront property owners would suffer, but their inland neighbors would gain.[3]

None of these changes are free, of course, and there remain significant uncertainties about how global warming might affect species other than *Homo sapiens*. It is estimated, for example, that temperate forests can "migrate" only at a rate of about sixty miles per century, not fast enough to match the speed at which warming is expected to occur. Similarly, the anticipated rise in the sea level could wipe out between 30 and 70 percent of today's coastal wetlands. Whether new wetlands would develop along our new coastline and what might happen to species that occupy existing wetlands are questions that have not yet been resolved.

Yet the very uncertainties that surround the possible warming of the planet suggest that policy prescriptions of the sort that have been proposed—such as the cut in worldwide CO_2 emissions agreed to at Kyoto—may be too much, too soon. Caution seems particularly wise because the exclusion of China, India, and other developing nations from any emissions cuts could result in huge costs for developed nations but little or no reduction in worldwide greenhouse gases. Some sense of the damage that can be wrought by ignoring such counsel and rushing into a politically popular response to a complex environmental issue is well illustrated by another atmospheric problem: smog.

Gasoline and Smog

Gasoline is a major source of the hydrocarbons in urban air, but its contribution to smog plummeted because cars now run much cleaner than their predecessors. In the 1970s, cars spewed about

---

3 There would be a net loss of land area and thus a net economic loss. Nevertheless, the net loss of land would be chiefly in the form of less valuable inland property.

nine grams of hydrocarbons per mile. Emissions controls brought this down to about 1.5 grams per mile by 1995. The cost of this reduction is estimated to be approximately $1,000 for each ton of hydrocarbon emissions prevented—a number that many experts believe to be well below the benefits of the cleaner air that resulted. Despite the improvements in air quality, smog is still a problem in many major cities. Additional federal regulations aimed primarily at the nine smoggiest urban areas, including New York, Chicago, and Los Angeles, went into effect in 1995. Meeting these standards meant that gasoline had to be reformulated at a cost of about 6 cents per gallon. This brought the cost of removing each additional ton of hydrocarbons to about $10,000—ten times the per-ton cost of removing the first 95 percent from urban air.

Over the past fifteen years, new Environmental Protection Agency (EPA) rules for reformulated gasoline (RFG) have added even more to the cost of gasoline and have had other (presumably unintended) adverse consequences. For example, initially, the RFG standards could be met only with the addition to gasoline of ethanol or methyl tertiary butyl ether (MTBE). Because ethanol was considerably more expensive than MTBE, refiners used MTBE. But after a few years, it appeared that leakage of MTBE from storage tanks was contaminating groundwater and that the substance was highly carcinogenic. Numerous states banned its use on the grounds that whatever it did to improve air quality, its adverse effects elsewhere were likely far more damaging. (The EPA has since allowed refiners more flexibility in meeting the RFG standards.)

Overall, EPA rules on RFG have led to a "patchwork quilt" of regulations across the country: Some dirty-air locations must use one type of gas, while others, with cleaner air, can use different gas. The presence of multiple EPA standards across the country has left supplies of gasoline vulnerable to disruption because fuel often cannot be transshipped from one area to another to meet temporary **shortages.** This fact has contributed substantially to large spikes in the price of gasoline in major Midwestern cities, such as Milwaukee and Chicago, every time there has been even a minor supply disruption.

Overall, the costs of EPA-mandated gasoline reformulation are huge, even though the EPA has never shown that RFG is necessary to meet its air quality standards. The potential benefits of RFG appear to be small compared to the costs, yet we are stuck with this EPA mandate because few politicians want to be accused of being in favor of smog.

The Take Away

There is no doubt that atmospheric concentrations of greenhouse gases are rising and that human actions are playing a role. It is probable that as a result, the global average temperature is rising. If temperatures rise significantly, the costs will be large, but the consequences are likely to be manageable. Given the nature of the problem, private action, taken on the individual level, will not yield the optimal outcome for society. Thus, the potential gains from government action, in the form of environmental regulations or taxation, may be substantial. But the key word here is *potential* because government action, no matter how well intentioned, does not automatically yield benefits that exceed the costs. As we seek solutions to the potential problems associated with greenhouse gases, we must be sure that the consequences of action are not worse than those of first examining the problem further. If we forget this message, greenhouse economics may turn into bad economics—and worse policy.

Discussion Questions

1. Why will voluntary actions, undertaken at the individual level, be unlikely to bring about significant reductions in greenhouse gases such as CO_2?

2. Does the fact that the CO_2 produced in one nation results in adverse effects on other nations have any bearing on the likelihood that CO_2 emissions will be reduced to the optimal level? Would the problem be easier to solve if all the costs and benefits were concentrated within a single country? Within a single elevator or office?

3. The policy approach to greenhouse gases will almost certainly involve limits on emissions rather than taxes on emissions. Can you suggest why limits rather than taxes are likely to be used?

4. It costs about $100,000 per acre to create wetlands. How reasonable is this number as an estimate of what wetlands are worth?

5. Suppose the United States decides to discourage CO_2 emissions by imposing a tax on CO_2 emissions. How large should the tax be?

6. Human-caused (anthropogenic) emissions of CO_2 are only about 3 percent of *total* CO_2 emissions each year. (Oceans are the biggest emitters.) Why is so much attention directed at anthropogenic emissions of CO_2?

CHAPTER 26

Ethanol Madness

Henry Ford built his first automobile in 1896 to run on pure ethanol. If Congress has its way, the cars of the future will be built the same way. But what made good economic sense in the late nineteenth century doesn't necessarily make economic sense in the early twenty-first century—although it does make for good politics. Indeed, the ethanol story is a classic illustration of how good politics routinely trumps good economics to yield bad policies.

ETHANOL MANDATES AND SUBSIDIES

Ethanol is made in the Midwest just like moonshine whiskey is made in Appalachia. Corn and water are mixed into a mash, enzymes turn starch to sugar, yeast is added, and heat ferments the brew. Once this is distilled, the liquid portion is ethanol and the solids are used as a high-protein animal food. The high-proof ethanol is combustible but yields far less energy per gallon than gasoline does. Despite this inefficiency, federal law requires that ethanol be added to gasoline, in increasing amounts through 2022. This requirement is supposed to conserve resources and improve the environment. It does neither. Instead, it lines the pockets of American corn farmers and ethanol makers and incidentally enriches some Brazilian sugarcane farmers along the way.

Federal law has both encouraged and subsidized ethanol as a so-called alternative fuel for more than thirty years. But it was not until 2005 that ethanol really achieved national prominence. The use mandates of the Energy Policy Act, combined with surging gas prices and an existing 51-cent-per-gallon federal ethanol subsidy, created a boom in ethanol production. Soon ethanol refineries were springing up all over the Midwest, and imports of ethanol from Brazil reached record-high levels.

THE SUPPOSED VIRTUES OF ETHANOL

Three factors are typically used to justify federal use mandates and subsidies for ethanol. First, it is claimed that adding ethanol to gasoline reduces air pollution and so yields environmental benefits. That may have been true fifteen or twenty years ago, but even the Environmental Protection Agency (EPA) acknowledges that ethanol offers no environmental advantages over other modern methods of making reformulated gasoline. Hence, neither the congressional mandate to add ethanol nor the 51-cent-per-gallon subsidy for its use as a fuel additive can be justified on environmental grounds.

A second argument advanced on behalf of ethanol is that it is "renewable," in that fields on which corn is grown to produce ethanol this year can be replanted with more corn next year. This is true enough, but we are in little danger of running out of "nonrenewable" crude oil any time in the next century. Indeed, proven reserves of oil are at record-high levels. Perhaps more to the point, the production of ethanol uses so much fossil fuel and other resources that under most circumstances, its production actually *wastes* resources overall compared to gasoline. In part, this is because ethanol is about 25 percent less efficient than gasoline as a source of energy. But it is also because the corn used to make ethanol in the United States has a high **opportunity cost.** If it were not being used to make fuel, it would be used to feed humans and livestock. Moreover, because ethanol production is most efficiently conducted on a relatively small scale, it must be transported by truck or rail, which is far more costly than the pipelines used for gasoline.

The third supposed advantage of ethanol is that its use reduces our dependence on imports of oil. In principle, this argument is correct, but its impact is tiny, and the likely consequences are not what you might expect. Total consumption of all **biofuels** in the United States amounts to less than 3 percent of gasoline usage. To replace the oil we import from the Persian Gulf with corn-based ethanol, at least *50 percent* of the nation's total farmland would have to be devoted to corn for fuel. Moreover, any cuts in oil imports will likely *not* come from Persian Gulf sources. Canada and Mexico are two of the three biggest suppliers of crude oil to the United States, and both countries send almost 100 percent of their exports to the U.S. market.

THE POLITICAL ECONOMY OF ENVIRONMENTAL POLICY

All of this raises an interesting question. If ethanol doesn't protect the environment, conserve resources, or have any compelling foreign policy advantages, why do we mandate its use and subsidize its production? The answer lies at the heart of **political economy,** the use of economics to study the causes and consequences of political decision making. It is true that a critical component of what the government does (such as providing for national defense and law enforcement) provides an institutional structure necessary for the creation and retention of our total wealth. Nevertheless, the essence of much government policymaking, especially in the environmental arena these days, has nothing to do with making the size of the economic pie larger than it otherwise would be. Instead, many government policies are directed at dividing up the pie in new ways so that one group gets more resources at the expense of some other group. To do this successfully, politicians must be adept at concentrating the benefits of policies among a few favored recipients while dispersing the costs of those policies across a large number of disfavored individuals.

At first blush, such an approach sounds completely at odds with the essence of democracy. After all, under the principle of "one person, one vote," it seems that benefits should be widely spread (to gain votes from many grateful beneficiaries) and costs should be concentrated (so that only the votes of a few disfavored constituents are lost). The concept of **rational ignorance** explains what is really going on. It is costly for individuals to keep track of exactly how the decisions of their elected representatives affect them. When the consequences of political decisions are large enough to outweigh the **monitoring costs,** voters swiftly and surely express their pleasure or displeasure, both in the voting booth and in their campaign contributions. But when the consequences to each of them individually are small relative to the monitoring costs, people don't bother to keep track of them—they remain "rationally ignorant."

ETHANOL WINNERS AND LOSERS

In the case of ethanol, about one-fifth of all ethanol for fuel is made by one company, Archer Daniels Midland (ADM). Clearly, even small changes in the price of ethanol are important to ADM. Because both federal use mandates and the federal ethanol subsidy increase the profitability of making ethanol, ADM has strong incentives to ensure that members of Congress are aware of the benefits (to ADM) of such policies. Similarly, corn farmers derive most of their income from sales of corn. Federal ethanol policies increase the demand for corn and thus increase its price. Because the resulting benefits are highly concentrated on corn farmers, each has a strong incentive to ensure that his or her members of Congress understand the benefits (to the farmer) of such policies.

Contrast this with the typical taxpayer or consumer of gasoline. It is true that the $3 billion or so spent on ethanol subsidies each year must come out of taxpayers' pockets. Nevertheless, this amount is spread thinly across tens of millions of federal taxpayers. Similarly, although the mandated use of ethanol in gasoline is estimated to raise the cost of gas by about 8 cents per gallon, this amounts to no more than $50 per year for the typical driver. Neither taxpayer nor motorist is likely to spend much time complaining to his or her senator.

Thus, it is that farmers and ethanol producers are willing to lobby hard for use mandates and subsidies at the same time that taxpayers and drivers put up little effective resistance to having their pockets picked. It may make for bad economics and lousy environmental policy, but it is classic politics.

DISCUSSION QUESTIONS

1. Brazilian ethanol producers (who make ethanol from sugarcane) have lower production costs than U.S. producers. Indeed, even though it costs 16 cents per gallon to transport ethanol from Brazil to the United States, which also imposes an **import tariff** of nearly 60 cents per gallon on Brazilian ethanol, the United States still imports millions of gallons of ethanol per year from Brazil. If Congress really cares about protecting the environment and reducing our reliance on foreign crude oil, why do you suppose we have a large import tariff on ethanol?

2. If imports of Brazilian ethanol begin to rise sharply in the future, what do you predict will happen to the size of the import tariff levied on this good?

3. Why do you suppose the federal government gives special treatment to owners of fertile farmland rather than, say, automobile mechanics?

4. Use the theory of rational ignorance to explain why the ethanol subsidy is only 51 cents per gallon rather than, say, $5 per gallon.

5. The EPA has approved the use of up to 15 percent ethanol in fuel blends. Cars built before 2007 are at risk of considerable engine damage if they run on such "E15" fuel. Who will foot the bill for such damages, if they occur?

6. Why are foreign producers of products so often the subject of special taxes such as the tax on imported ethanol?

CHAPTER 27

The Trashman Cometh

Is garbage really different? To answer this question, let us consider a simple hypothetical situation. Suppose a city agreed to provide its residents with all the food they wished to consume, prepared in the manner they specified, and delivered to their homes for a flat, monthly fee that was independent of what or how much they ate. What are the likely consequences of this city food-delivery service? Most likely, people in the city would begin to eat more because the size of their food bill would be independent of the amount they ate. They would also be more likely to consume lobster and filet mignon rather than fish sticks and hamburger because, again, the cost to them would be independent of their menu selections. Soon the city's food budget would be astronomical, and either the monthly fee or taxes would have to be increased. People from other communities might even begin moving (or at least making extended visits) to the city just to partake of this wonderful service. Within a short time, the city would face a food crisis as it sought to cope with providing an ever-increasing amount of food from a city budget that could no longer handle the financial burden.

If this story sounds silly to you, just change "food delivery" to "garbage pickup." What we have just described is the way most cities in the country have historically operated their municipal garbage-collection services. The result during the 1990s was the appearance of a garbage crisis, with overflowing landfills, homeless garbage barges, and drinking-water wells said to be polluted with the runoff from trash heaps. This seeming crisis—to the extent it existed—was fundamentally no different from the food crisis just described. The problem was not that almost nobody wants garbage or that garbage can have adverse environmental effects or even that we had too much garbage. The problem lay in that (i) we often do not put a price on garbage in the way we put prices on the goods that generate the garbage and (ii) a strange assortment of participants used a few smelly facts to make things seem worse than they were.

AMERICA'S TRASH

First things first. America produces plenty of garbage each year—about 250 million tons of household and commercial solid waste that has to be burned, buried, or recycled. (That works out to sixteen hundred pounds per person.) About 31 percent of this is paper. Yard waste (such as grass trimmings) accounts for another 13 percent. Plastic accounts for about 20 percent of the volume of material that has to be disposed of, but because plastic is relatively light, it makes up only about 12 percent of the weight. More than eighty million tons of this trash is recycled.

Landfills are the final resting place for most of our garbage, although incineration is also widely used in some areas, particularly in the Northeast, where land values are high. Both methods began falling out of favor with people who lived near these facilities (or might eventually), as "not in my backyard" attitudes spread across the land. Federal, state, and local regulations also made it increasingly difficult to establish new waste disposal facilities or even to keep old ones operating. The cost to open a modern 100-acre landfill rose to an estimated $70 million or more, and the permit process needed to open a new disposal facility soared to seven years in some states. Meanwhile, environmental concerns forced the closure of many landfills throughout the country and prevented others from ever beginning operations. By the early 1990s, all but five states were exporting at least some of their garbage to other states. Today, most of the garbage from some densely populated states in the Northeast ends up in other people's backyards: New Jersey ships garbage to six other states, and New York keeps landfill operators busy in nine states. Across the country, some Americans have wondered where all of the garbage is going to go.

A CRISIS THAT WASN'T

Although the failure of America's cities to price garbage appropriately led to an inefficient amount of the stuff, much of the appearance of a garbage crisis has been misleading. Rubbish first hit the headlines in 1987 when a garbage barge named *Mobro,* headed south with New York City trash, couldn't find a home for its load. As it turns out, the barge operator wanted to change his disposal contract after he sailed.

When he tried to conduct negotiations over the radio while under way, operators of likely landfills (mistakenly) suspected he might be carrying toxic waste rather than routine trash. When adverse publicity forced the barge back to New York with its load, many people thought it was a lack of landfill space, rather than poor planning by the barge operator, that was the cause. This notion was reinforced by an odd combination of environmental groups, waste management firms, and the Environmental Protection Agency (EPA).

The Environmental Defense Fund wanted to start a major campaign to push recycling, and the *Mobro* episode gave things the necessary push. As one official for the organization noted, "An advertising firm couldn't have designed a better vehicle than a garbage barge." Meanwhile, a number of farsighted waste management companies had begun loading up on landfill space, taking advantage of new technologies that increased the efficient minimum size of a disposal facility. Looking to get firm contracts for filling this space, the trade group for the disposal industry started pushing the notion that America was running out of dump space. State and local officials who relied on the group's data quickly bought into the new landfills, paying premium prices to do so. The EPA, meanwhile, was studying the garbage problem but without accounting for the fact that its own regulations were causing the efficient scale of landfills to quadruple in size. Thus, the EPA merely counted landfills around the country and reported that they were shrinking in number. This was true enough, but what the EPA failed to report was that because landfills were getting bigger much faster than they were closing down, total disposal capacity was *growing* rapidly, not shrinking.

RECYCLING

For a while, it seemed that recycling was going to take care of what appeared to be a worsening trash problem. In 1987, for example, old newspapers were selling for as much as $100 per ton (in 2011 dollars), and many municipalities felt that the answer to their financial woes and garbage troubles was at hand. Yet as more communities began putting mandatory recycling laws into effect, the prices for recycled trash began to plummet. Over the next five years, 3,500 communities in more than half the states had some form of mandatory curbside recycling. The resulting increase in the supply of used newsprint meant that communities soon had to pay to have the stuff carted away. For glass, the story is much the same. The market value of the used material is routinely below the cost of collecting and sorting it. Numerous states have acted to increase the demand for old newsprint by requiring locally published newspapers to have a minimum content of recycled newsprint. Because of these mandates, the recycling rate for newsprint has doubled over the past twenty years, but the current rate of 70 percent is thought by many experts to be about the practical maximum.

Recycling raises significant issues that were often ignored during the early rush to embrace the concept. For example, the production of 100 tons of deinked fiber from old newsprint produces about 40 tons of sludge that must be disposed of somehow. Although the total volume of material is reduced, the concentrated form of what is left can make it more costly to dispose of properly. Similarly, recycling paper is unlikely to save trees because most virgin newsprint is made from trees planted expressly for that purpose and harvested as a crop. If recycling increases, many of these trees simply will not be planted. In a study done for Resources for the Future, A. Clark Wiseman concluded, "The likely effect of [newsprint recycling] appears to be smaller, rather than larger, forest inventory." Moreover, most virgin newsprint is made in Canada, using clean hydroelectric power. Makers of newsprint in the United States (the primary customers for the recycled stuff) often use higher-polluting energy such as coal. Thus, one potential side effect of recycling is the switch from hydroelectric power to fossil fuels.

PRODUCT BANS

Some analysts have argued that we should simply ban certain products. For example, Styrofoam cups have gotten a bad name because they take up more space in landfills than paper hot-drink cups and because Styrofoam remains in the landfill forever. Yet according to a widely cited study by Martin B. Hocking of the University of Victoria in British Columbia, Canada, the manufacture of a paper cup consumes 36 times as much electricity and generates 580 times as much wastewater as the manufacture of a Styrofoam cup. Moreover, as paper degrades underground, it releases methane, a greenhouse gas that may contribute to global climate change. In a similar vein, consider disposable diapers, which have been trashed by their opponents because a week's worth generates 22.2 pounds of post-use waste, whereas a week's worth of reusable diapers generates only 4 ounces. Because disposable diapers already amount to 2 percent of the nation's solid waste, the edge clearly seems to go to reusable cloth diapers. Yet the use of reusable rather than disposable diapers consumes more than three times as many British thermal units of energy and generates ten times as much water pollution. It would seem that the trade-offs that are present when we talk about "goods" are just as prevalent when we discuss "bads" such as garbage.

GOVERNMENT REGULATION

It also appears that more government regulation of the garbage business is likely to make things worse rather than better, as may be illustrated by the tale of two states, New Jersey and Pennsylvania. A number of years ago, to stop what was described as price gouging by organized crime, New Jersey decided to regulate waste hauling and disposal as a public utility. Once the politicians got involved in the trash business, however, politics very nearly destroyed it. According to Paul Kleindorfer of the University of Pennsylvania, political opposition to passing garbage-disposal costs along to consumers effectively ended investment in landfills. In 1972, there were 331 landfills operating in New Jersey. By 1991, the number had fallen to fifty, because the state-regulated fees payable to landfill operators simply didn't cover the rising costs of operation. More than half of the state's municipal solid waste is now exported to neighboring Pennsylvania, in part because only 13 landfills remain open in New Jersey.

Pennsylvania's situation provides a sharp contrast. The state does not regulate the deals that communities make with landfill and incinerator operators. The market takes care of matters instead. For example, despite the state's hands-off policy, tipping fees (the charges for disposing of garbage in landfills) are below the national average in Pennsylvania, effectively limited by competition between disposal facilities. The market seems to be providing the right **incentives;** in one recent year, there were thirty-one pending applications to open landfills in Pennsylvania but only two in New Jersey, despite the fact that New Jersey residents are paying the highest disposal rates in the country to ship garbage as far away as Ohio and Georgia.

THE MARKET SOLUTION

Ultimately, two issues must be solved when it comes to trash. First, what do we do with it once we have it? Second, how do we reduce the amount of it that we have? As hinted at by the Pennsylvania story and illustrated further by developments elsewhere in the country, the market mechanism can answer both questions. The fact of the matter is that in many areas of the country, population densities are high and land is expensive. Hence, a large amount of trash is produced, and it is expensive to dispose of locally. In contrast, there are some areas of the country where there are relatively few people around to produce garbage, where land for disposal facilities is cheap, and where wide open spaces minimize any potential air-pollution hazards associated with incinerators.

The sensible thing to do, it would seem, is to have the states that produce most of the trash ship it to states where it can be most efficiently disposed of—for a price, of course. This is already being done to an extent, but residents of potential recipient states are (not surprisingly) concerned, lest they end up being the garbage capitals of the nation. Yet Wisconsin, which imports more than a million tons of garbage each year, is demonstrating that it is possible to get rid of the trash without trashing the neighborhood. Landfill operators in Wisconsin are now required to send water table monitoring reports to neighbors and to maintain the landfills for forty years after closure. Operators have also guaranteed the value of neighboring homes to gain the permission of nearby residents and in some cases have purchased homes to quiet neighbors' objections. These features all add to the cost of operating landfills, but as long as prospective customers are willing to pay the price and neighboring residents are satisfied with their protections—and so far these conditions appear to have been met—it would seem tough to argue with the outcome.

Some people might still argue that it does not seem right for one community to be able to dump its trash elsewhere. Yet the flip side is this: Is it right to prevent communities from accepting trash if that is what they want? Consider Gilliam County, Oregon (population 1,645), which wanted Seattle's garbage so badly that it fought Oregon statelegislators' attempts to tax out-of-state trash coming into Oregon. Seattle's decision to use the Gilliam County landfill generated $1 million per year for the little community—some 25 percent of its annual budget and enough to finance the operations of the county's largest school.

GARBAGE BY THE BAG

Faced with the prospect of paying to dispose of its garbage, Seattle had to confront the problem of reducing the amount of trash its residents were generating. Its solution was to charge householders according to the amount they put out. Seattle began charging $16.55 per month (now $26.40) for weekly pick up of a thirty-two-gallon can. Yard waste that has been separated for composting costs $6.50 per month, and paper, glass, and metal separated for recycling are hauled away at no charge. In the first year that per-can charges were imposed, the total tonnage that had to be buried fell by 22 percent. Voluntary recycling rose from 24 percent of waste to 36 percent—a rate almost triple the national average at the time. The "Seattle stomp" (used to fit more trash into a can) became a regular source of exercise, and the city had trouble exporting enough garbage to fulfill its contract with Gilliam County.

The Seattle experience is paralleled by a similar program in Charlottesville, Virginia. A few years ago, this university town of forty thousand began charging 80 cents per thirty-two-gallon bag or can of residential garbage collected at the curb. The results of the city's new policy suggest that people respond to garbage prices just as they do to all other prices: When an activity becomes more expensive, people engage in less of it. In fact, after controlling for other factors, the introduction of this unit-pricing plan induced people to reduce the volume of garbage presented for collection by 37 percent.

Where did all of the garbage go? Well, some of it didn't go anywhere because many residents began practicing their own version of the Seattle stomp, compacting garbage into fewer bags. Even so, the total weight of Charlottesville's residential garbage dropped by 14 percent in response to unit pricing. Not all of this represented a reduction in garbage production because some residents resorted to "midnight dumping"—tossing their trash into commercial Dumpsters or their neighbors' cans late at night. This sort of behavior is much like the rise in gasoline thefts that occurred in the 1970s when gas prices jumped to the equivalent of over $3 per gallon. But just as locking gas caps ended most gas thefts, there may be a simple way to prevent most midnight dumping. Economists who have studied the Charlottesville program in detail suggest that property taxes or monthly fees could be used to cover the cost of one bag per household each week, with a price per bag applied only to additional bags. According to these estimates, a one-bag allowance would stop all midnight dumping by most one-person households and stop almost half the dumping by a hypothetical three-person household. Moreover, such a scheme would retain most of the environmental benefits of the garbage-pricing program.

The message beginning to emerge across the country, then, is that garbage is no different from the things we consume in the course of producing it. As long as the trashman is paid, he will come, and as long as we must pay for his services, his burden will be bearable.

Discussion Questions

1. How do deposits on bottles and cans affect the incentives of individuals to recycle these products?

2. Why do many communities mandate recycling? Is it possible to induce people to recycle more without requiring that all residents recycle?

3. How do hefty per-can garbage pickup fees influence the decisions people make about what goods they will consume?

4. A community planning on charging a fee for trash pickup might structure the fee in any of several ways. It might, for example, charge a fixed amount per can, an amount per pound of garbage, or a flat fee per month without regard to amount of garbage. How would each of these affect the amount and type of garbage produced? Which system would lead to an increase in the use of trash compactors? Which would lead to the most garbage?

5. How does interstate trade in trash differ from interstate trade in other products?

6. The population concentrations of most counties in the United States tend to be located in the middle of the each county. Where do you think most landfills are located within each county?

PART SEVEN

Globalization and Economic Prosperity

Introduction

Many of the key public issues of our day transcend national borders or affect the entirety of our $16 trillion economy. The rapid developments in information processing, communications, and transportation over the past thirty years are gradually knitting the economies of the world closer together. Political developments, most notably the demise of the Iron Curtain and the dissolution of the Soviet Union, have contributed to this growing **globalization** of world economies, as have reductions in long-standing barriers to international trade. Moreover, over the past decade or so, awareness has been growing that the economic vitality of individual markets is importantly affected by decisions made in Washington, DC.

GLOBALIZATION AND THE WEALTH OF AMERICA

The passage of the North American Free Trade Agreement (NAFTA) and the creation of the **World Trade Organization (WTO)** have substantially reduced the barriers to trade between the United States and most of the rest of the world. If we take advantage of these lower **trade barriers,** we have the opportunity to make ourselves far better off by specializing in activities in which we have a **comparative advantage** and then trading the fruits of our efforts with other nations. Yet voluntary exchange also often redistributes wealth, in addition to creating it, so there will always be some individuals who oppose free trade. There are many smoke screens behind which the self-interested opposition to globalization is hidden, as we see in Chapter 28. Nevertheless, although **protectionism**—the creation of trade barriers such as **tariffs**

189

and **quotas**—often sounds sensible, it is in fact a surefire way to reduce rather than enhance our wealth. If we ignore the value of free trade, we do so only at our peril.

THE $750,000 STEELWORKER

To illustrate the tremendous damage that can result when protectionism gains the upper hand, Chapter 29 examines what happens when tariffs and quotas are imposed in an effort to "save" U.S. jobs from foreign **competition.** The facts are that in the long run, it is almost impossible to protect U.S. workers from globalization, and efforts to do so not only reduce Americans' overall living standards but also end up costing the jobs of other Americans. The moral is that competition is just as beneficial on the international scene as it is on the domestic front.

THE LION, THE DRAGON, AND THE FUTURE

For decades, Americans have worried about competition from cheap labor in China. As you will see in Chapter 30, China has been adopting capitalist **institutions** over the past thirty years and has reaped the rewards, most notably in the form of a rapidly rising standard of living for its people. But accompanying this has been the emergence of China as a major player in world markets. Indeed, China is now America's number two trading partner (after Canada) and may even have risen to number one by the time you read this. The growing volume of trade between the United States and China has created enormous wealth for people in both nations, albeit not without costly adjustments for some individuals. India, too, is becoming an important player in world markets, although its relatively late entry into global competition makes it less significant than China—for the moment. When discussing trade with any nation, however, the crucial fact to keep in mind is that international trade is fundamentally no different from interstate trade or interpersonal trade: As long as it is voluntary, the result is a higher standard of living for all participants.

CHAPTER 28

Globalization and the Wealth of America

The past two decades have been a time of great change for international trade and **globalization.** The North American Free Trade Agreement (NAFTA), for example, substantially reduced the **trade barriers** among citizens of Canada, the United States, and Mexico. On a global scale, the Uruguay Round of the General Agreement on Tariffs and Trade (GATT) was ratified by 117 nations, including the United States. Under the terms of this agreement, GATT was replaced by the **World Trade Organization (WTO),** whose membership now numbers over 150, and **tariffs** were cut worldwide. Agricultural **subsidies** were reduced, patent protections were extended, and the WTO established a set of arbitration boards to settle international disputes over trade issues.

Many economists believe that both NAFTA and the agreements reached during the Uruguay Round were victories not only for free trade and globalization but also for the citizens of the participating nations. Nevertheless, many noneconomists, particularly politicians, opposed these agreements, so it is important that we understand what is beneficial about NAFTA, the Uruguay Round, and free trade in general.

GAINS FROM TRADE

Voluntary trade creates new wealth. In voluntary trade, both parties in an exchange gain. They give up something of lesser value in return for something of greater value. In this sense, exchanges are always unequal. But it is this unequal nature of exchange that is the source of the increased **productivity** and higher wealth that occurs whenever trade takes place. When we engage in exchange, what we give up is worth less than what we get—for if this were not true, we would not have traded. And what is true for us is also true for our trading partner, meaning that both partners end up better off.

Free trade encourages individuals to use their abilities in the most productive manner possible and to exchange the fruits of their efforts. The **gains from trade** lie in one of the most fundamental ideas in economics: A nation gains from doing what it can do best *relative to other nations,* that is, by specializing in endeavors in which it has a **comparative advantage.** Trade encourages individuals and nations to discover ways to specialize so that they can become more productive and enjoy higher incomes. Increased productivity and the subsequent increase in economic growth are exactly what the signatories of the Uruguay Round and NAFTA sought—and are obtaining—by reducing trade barriers.

GLOBALIZATION AND THE OPPOSITION TO IT

Globalization differs from free trade chiefly in the degree of integration across nations. For example, although there is free trade in wine, the wines produced in Australia, California, and France are each created wholly within the geopolitical borders indicated by their labels. Moreover, each remains a distinct economic entity, in that significant relative price changes between, say, French and California wines are observed. In contrast, the market for automobiles has become truly "global." If you purchase a "Japanese" automobile in the United States, assembly of the vehicle may have taken place in Japan, the United States, or even Mexico, and the components of the car may have come from a half-dozen or more different nations. And if you call for customer support for your car, the person answering the phone may be at a call center located in any of a variety of English-speaking nations. Globalization thus means that trade between nations becomes as seamless as trade between states, provinces, or cities within a given nation. Despite the enormous gains from exchange, globalization is routinely opposed by some people. Many excuses are offered for this opposition, but they all basically come down to one issue: When our borders are fully open to trade with other nations, some individuals and businesses in our nation face more competition. As you saw in Chapter 18, most firms and workers hate competition, and who can blame them? After all, if a firm can keep the competition out, **profits** are sure to rise. And if workers can prevent competition from other sources, they can enjoy higher wages and greater selection among jobs. So the real source of most opposition to globalization is that the opponents to trade dislike the competition that comes with it. There is nothing immoral or unethical about this—but there is nothing altruistic or noble about it, either. It is self-interest, pure and simple.

One aspect of globalization that looms large in the minds of its opponents is the unremitting competitive vigilance that it requires. When world markets are completely integrated, one's competitors may emerge at any time from any place—often from corners of the world that one may least expect. And because competitors may only need to create a Web site to get started and can have their products delivered the next day by air freight, that competition can emerge devastatingly quickly. Thus, when operating in a global economy, firms and their employees must contend with a level of uncertainty that is simply not present when trade patterns are less integrated. Note that this highly competitive atmosphere ultimately benefits all of us, but that doesn't make it any less unnerving for those who must endure its pressures, day after day. Competition is tough, and global competition is toughest of all.

BEGGAR-THY-NEIGHBOR

Because of this, opposition to globalization is nothing new. One of the most famous examples of such opposition led to passage of the Smoot–Hawley Tariff of 1930. This major federal statute was a classic example of **protectionism**—an effort to protect a subset of American producers at the expense of consumers and other producers. It included tariff schedules for more than twenty thousand products, raising taxes on affected imports by an average of 52 percent.

The Smoot–Hawley Tariff encouraged beggar-thy-neighbor policies by the rest of the world. Such policies represent an attempt to improve (a portion of) one's domestic economy at the expense of foreign countries' economies. In this case, tariffs were imposed to discourage **imports** so that domestic import-competing industries would benefit. The beggar-thy-neighbor policy at the heart of Smoot–Hawley was soon adopted by the United Kingdom, France, the Netherlands, and Switzerland. The result was a halt to globalization and a massive reduction in international trade that almost certainly worsened the worldwide depression of the 1930s.

Opponents of globalization sometimes claim that beggar-thy-neighbor policies benefit the United States by protecting import-competing industries. In general, this claim is not correct. It is true that some Americans benefit from such policies, but two large groups of Americans lose. First, there are the purchasers of imports and import-competing goods. They suffer from higher prices and reduced selection of goods and suppliers caused by tariffs and import **quotas.** Second, the decline in imports caused by protectionism also causes a decline in **exports,** thereby harming firms and employees in these industries. This follows directly from one of the most fundamental propositions in international trade: *In the long run, imports are paid for by exports.* This proposition simply states that when one country buys goods and services from the rest of the world (imports), the rest of the world eventually wants goods from that country (exports) in exchange. Given this fundamental proposition, a corollary becomes obvious: *Any restriction on imports leads to a reduction in exports.* Thus, any business for import-competing industries gained as a result of tariffs or quotas means at least as much business lost for exporting industries.

DUMPING

Opponents of globalization raise a variety of objections in their efforts to restrict international trade. For example, it is sometimes said that foreign companies engage in dumping, that is, selling their goods in America below cost. The first question to ask is: below *whose* cost? Clearly, if the foreign firm is selling in America, it must be offering the good for sale at a price that is at or below the cost of American firms, or else it could not induce Americans to buy it. But the ability of individuals or firms to get goods at lower cost is one of the *benefits* of free trade, not one of its negatives.

What about claims that import sales are taking place at prices below the foreign company's costs? This amounts to arguing that the owners of the foreign company are voluntarily giving some of their wealth to us, namely, the difference between their costs and the lower price they charge us. It is possible, though unlikely, that they might wish to do this as a way of getting us to try a product that we would not otherwise purchase. But if so, why would we want to refuse this gift? As a nation, we are richer if we accept it. Moreover, it is a gift that will be offered for only a short while, for there is no point in selling below one's cost unless one hopes soon to raise price profitably above cost!

LABOR AND ENVIRONMENTAL STANDARDS

Another argument sometimes raised against globalization is that the goods are produced abroad using unfair labor practices (such as the use of child labor) or using production processes that do not meet American environmental standards. Such charges are sometimes correct. But we must remember two things. First, although we may find the use of child labor (or perhaps sixty-hour work weeks with no overtime pay) objectionable, such practices were once common in the United States. They used to be prevalent in America for the same reason they are now practiced abroad. The people involved were (or are) too poor to do otherwise. Some families in developing nations cannot survive unless all members of the family contribute. As unfortunate as this is, if we insist on imposing our attitudes—shaped in part by our great wealth—on peoples whose wealth is far lower than ours, we run the risk of making them worse off even as we think we are helping them.

Similar considerations apply to environmental standards.[1] It is well established that individuals' and nations' willingness to pay for environmental quality is very much shaped by their wealth. Environmental quality is a **luxury good.** That is, people who are rich (such as Americans) want to consume much more of it per capita than people who are poor. Insisting that other nations meet environmental standards that we find acceptable is much like insisting that they wear the clothes we wear, use the modes of transportation we prefer, and consume the foods we like. The few people who manage to comply will indeed be living in the style to which we are accustomed, but most people will simply be impoverished by the attempt.

Our point is not that foreign labor or environmental standards are, or should be, irrelevant to Americans. Our point is that achieving high standards of either is costly, and trade restrictions are unlikely to be the most efficient or most effective way to achieve them. Just as important, labor standards and environmental standards are all too often raised as smoke screens to hide the real motive—keeping the competition out.

The Political Economy of Trade Barriers

If it is true that globalization is beneficial and that restrictions on trade are generally harmful, we must surely raise the question, how does legislation such as the Smoot–Hawley Tariff (or any other such restriction) ever get passed? As Mark Twain noted many years ago, the reason the free traders win the arguments and the protectionists win the votes is simple. Foreign competition often clearly affects a narrow and specific import-competing industry such as textiles, shoes, or automobiles, and thus trade restrictions benefit a narrow, well-defined group of economic agents. For example, restrictions on imports of Japanese automobiles in the 1980s chiefly benefited the Big Three automakers in this country—General Motors,

---

1 There is one important exception to this argument. In the case of foreign air or water pollution generated near enough to our borders (for example, with Mexico or Canada) to cause harm to Americans, good public policy presumably dictates that we seek to treat such pollution as though it were being generated inside our borders.

Ford, and Chrysler. Similarly, long-standing quotas on the imports of sugar benefit a handful of large American sugar producers. And when tariffs of up to 30 percent were slapped on many steel imports in 2002, an even smaller number of American steelmakers and their employees benefited. Because of the concentrated benefits that accrue when Congress votes in favor of trade restrictions, sufficient lobbying and campaign funds can be raised in those industries to convince members of Congress to impose those restrictions.

The eventual reduction in exports that must follow is normally spread in small doses throughout all export industries. Thus, no specific group of workers, managers, or shareholders in export industries will feel that it should contribute money to convince Congress to reduce barriers to globalization. Furthermore, although consumers of imports and import-competing goods lose due to trade restrictions, they too are typically a diffuse group of individuals, none of whom will be individually affected much because of any single import restriction. It is the simultaneous existence of concentrated benefits and diffuse costs that led to Mark Twain's conclusion that the protectionists would often win the votes. (Concentrated benefits and dispersed costs are at the heart of Chapters 22 and 26 in explaining some U.S. domestic policies.)

Of course, the protectionists don't win all the votes—after all, roughly one-sixth of the U.S. economy is based on international trade. Despite the opposition to globalization that comes from many quarters, its benefits to the economy as a whole are so great that it is unthinkable that we might do away with international trade altogether. Thus, when we think about developments such as NAFTA and the WTO, it is clear that both economic theory and empirical evidence indicate that Americans will be better off after—and because of—globalization.

DISCUSSION QUESTIONS

1. During the late 1980s and early 1990s, American automobile manufacturers greatly increased the quality of the cars they produced relative to the quality of the cars produced in other nations. What effect do you think this had on American imports of Japanese cars, Japanese imports of American cars, and American exports of goods and services other than automobiles?

2. Over the past twenty years, some Japanese automakers have opened plants in the United States so that they could produce (and sell) "Japanese" cars here. What effect do you think this had on American

imports of Japanese cars, Japanese imports of American cars, and American exports of goods and services other than automobiles?

3. For a number of years, Japanese carmakers voluntarily limited the number of cars they exported to the United States. What effect do you think this had on Japanese imports of American cars and on American exports of goods and services other than automobiles?

4. Until recently, American cars exported to Japan had driver controls on the left side (as in the United States), even though the Japanese drive on the left side of the road and so Japanese cars sold in Japan have driver controls on the right side. Suppose the Japanese tried to sell their cars in the United States with the driver controls on the right side. What impact would this likely have on their sales in this country? Do you think the unwillingness of American carmakers to put the driver controls on the correct side for exports to Japan had any effect on their sales of cars in that country?

5. The U.S. government subsidizes the export of U.S.-manufactured commercial aircraft. What effect do you think this policy has on American imports of foreign goods and American exports of products other than commercial aircraft? Explain.

6. Who bears the costs and enjoys the benefits of the subsidies mentioned in the previous question?

CHAPTER 29

The $750,000 Steelworker

In even-numbered years, particularly years evenly divisible by 4, politicians are apt to give speeches about the need to protect U.S. jobs from the evils of **globalization.** We are thus encouraged to buy American. If further encouragement is needed, we are told that if we do not voluntarily reduce the amount of imported goods we purchase, the government will impose (or make more onerous) either **tariffs** (taxes) on imported goods or **quotas** (quantity restrictions) that physically limit **imports.** The objective is to save U.S. jobs.

Unlike black rhinos or blue whales, U.S. jobs are in no danger of becoming extinct. There are an infinite number of potential jobs in the American economy, and there always will be. Some of these jobs are not very pleasant, and many others do not pay very well, but there will always be employment of some sort as long as there is **scarcity.** Thus, when a steelworker making $72,000 per year says that imports of foreign steel should be reduced to save his job, what he really means is this: He wants to be protected from **competition** so he can continue his present employment at the same or higher salary rather than move to a different employment that has less desirable working conditions or pays a lower salary. There is nothing wrong with the steelworker's goal (better working conditions and higher pay), but it has nothing to do with saving jobs.

THE NATURE OF TRADE

In any discussion of the consequences of restrictions on international trade, it is essential to remember two facts. First, *we pay for imports with exports*. It is true that in the short run, we can sell off assets or borrow from abroad if we happen to import more goods and services than we export. But we have only a finite amount of assets to sell, and foreigners do not want to wait forever before we pay our bills. Ultimately, our accounts can be settled only if we provide (export) goods and services to the trading partners from whom we purchase (import) goods and services. Trade, after all, involves quid pro quo (literally, something for something). The second point to remember is that *voluntary trade is mutually beneficial to the trading partners*. If we restrict international trade, we reduce those benefits, both for our trading partners and for ourselves. One way these reduced benefits are manifested is in the form of curtailed employment opportunities for workers. In a nutshell, even though tariffs and quotas enhance job opportunities in import-competing industries, they also cost us jobs in export industries; the net effect seems to be *reduced* employment overall.

What is true for the United States is also true for other countries: They will buy our goods only if they can market theirs because they too have to export goods to pay for their imports. Thus, any U.S. restrictions on imports—via tariffs, quotas, or other means—ultimately cause a reduction in our exports, because other countries will be unable to pay for our goods. Hence, import restrictions must inevitably decrease the size of our export sector. So imposing trade restrictions to save jobs in import-competing industries has the effect of costing jobs in export industries.

PROTECTION FOR AUTOMOBILES

Import restrictions also impose costs on U.S. consumers. By reducing competition from abroad, quotas, tariffs, and other trade restraints push up the prices of foreign goods and enable U.S. producers to hike their own prices. Perhaps the best-documented example of this is the automobile industry.

Due in part to the enhanced quality of imported cars, sales of domestically produced automobiles fell from nine million units in 1978 to an average of six million units per year between 1980 and 1982. **Profits** for U.S. automobile manufacturers plummeted as well, turning into substantial losses for some of them. U.S. automakers and autoworkers' unions demanded protection from import competition. They were joined in their cries by politicians from automobile-producing states. The result was a voluntary agreement by Japanese car companies (the most important competitors of U.S. firms) that restricted U.S. sales of Japanese cars to 1.68 million units per year. This agreement—which amounted to a quota even though it never officially bore that name—began in April 1981 and continued into the 1990s in various forms.

Robert W. Crandall, an economist with the Brookings Institution, has estimated how much this voluntary trade restriction cost U.S. consumers in terms of higher car prices. According to his estimates, the reduced supply of Japanese cars pushed their prices up by $2,000 apiece, measured in 2011 dollars. The higher price of Japanese imports in turn enabled domestic producers to hike their prices an average of $800 per car. The total tab in the first full year of the program was over $8 billion. Crandall also estimated the number of jobs in automobile-related industries that were preserved by the voluntary import restrictions at about 26,000. Dividing $8 billion by twenty-six thousand jobs yields a cost to consumers of about $300,000 *per year* for every job preserved in the automobile industry. U.S. consumers could have saved over $5 billion on their car purchases each year if instead of implicitly agreeing to import restrictions, they had simply given $100,000 to every autoworker whose job was preserved by the voluntary import restraints.

PROTECTION FOR OTHER INDUSTRIES

The same types of calculations have been made for other industries. Tariffs in the apparel industry were increased between 1977 and 1981, preserving the jobs of about 116,000 U.S. apparel workers at a cost of $50,000 per job each year. At about the same time, the producers of Citizens' Band radios also managed to get tariffs raised. Approximately six hundred workers in the industry kept their jobs as a result, at an annual cost to consumers of over $90,000 per job.

The cost of **protectionism** has been even higher in other industries. Jobs preserved in the glassware industry due to trade restrictions cost $200,000 apiece each year. In the maritime industry, the yearly cost of trade protection is $290,000 per job. In the steel industry, the cost of preserving a job has been estimated at an astounding $750,000 per year. If free trade were permitted, each worker moving to employment elsewhere could be given a cash payment of half that amount each year, and consumers would still save a lot of money.

TOTAL EMPLOYMENT FALLS

Even so, this is not the full story. None of these studies estimating the cost to consumers of preserving jobs in import-competing industries have attempted to estimate the ultimate impact of import restrictions on the flow of exports, the number of jobs lost in the export sector, and thus the total number of jobs gained or lost.

When imports to the United States are restricted, our trading partners will necessarily buy less of what we produce. The resulting decline in export sales means fewer jobs in exporting industries. And the total reduction in trade leads to fewer jobs for workers such as stevedores (who load and unload ships) and truck drivers (who carry goods to and from ports). On both counts—the overall cut in trade and the accompanying decline in exports—protectionism leads to job losses that might not be immediately obvious.

Several years ago, Congress tried to pass a domestic-content bill for automobiles. In effect, the legislation would have required that cars sold in the United States have a minimum percentage of their components manufactured and assembled in this country. Proponents of the legislation argued that it would have protected 300,000 jobs in the U.S. automobile manufacturing and auto parts supply industries. Yet the legislation's supporters failed to recognize the negative impact of the bill on trade in general and on U.S. export industries. A U.S. Department of Labor study did recognize these impacts, estimating that the domestic-content legislation would actually cost more jobs in trade-related and export industries than it protected in import-competing businesses. Congress ultimately decided not to impose a domestic-content requirement for cars sold in the United States.

More recently, when President Bush decided in 2002 to impose tariffs of up to 30 percent on steel imports, the adverse effects on the economy were substantial and soon apparent. To take but one example, prior to the tariffs, the Port of New Orleans relied on steel imports for more than 40 percent of its revenues, in part because once steel coming into the port is offloaded, the ships are cleaned and refilled with U.S. grain for export. By reducing imports, the tariffs slashed economic activity at the port and also reduced U.S. grain exports. Businesses and farms all up and down the Mississippi River were adversely affected. More broadly, the higher costs of imported steel produced a decline in employment in U.S. industries that use steel as an input. Indeed, one study estimated that due to the tariffs, about 200,000 people lost their jobs in 2002 in these industries alone—a number that exceeded the total number of people actually employed by the steel manufacturing firms protected by the tariff.

The Impossibility of Real Protection

In principle, trade restrictions are imposed to provide economic help to specific industries and to increase employment in those industries. Ironically, the long-term effects may be just the opposite. Researchers at the **World Trade Organization (WTO)** examined employment in three industries that have been heavily protected throughout the world: textiles, clothing, and iron and steel. Despite stringent trade protection for these industries, employment *declined* during the period of protection, in some cases dramatically. In textiles, employment fell

22 percent in the United States and 46 percent in the European Union. The clothing industry had employment losses ranging from 18 percent in the United States to 56 percent in Sweden. Declines in employment in the iron and steel industry ranged anywhere from 10 percent in Canada to 54 percent in the United States. In short, restrictions on free trade are no guarantee against job losses, even in the industries supposedly being protected.

The evidence seems clear: The cost of protecting jobs in the short run is huge. And in the long run, it appears that jobs cannot be protected, especially if one considers all aspects of protectionism. Free trade is a tough platform on which to run for office. But it is the one that yields the most general benefits if implemented. Of course, this does not mean that politicians will embrace it, and so we end up "saving" jobs at a cost of up to $750,000 each.

DISCUSSION QUESTIONS

1. Who gains and who loses from import restrictions?

2. What motivates politicians to impose trade restrictions?

3. If it would be cheaper to give each steelworker $375,000 per year in cash than impose restrictions on imports of steel, why do we have the import restrictions rather than the cash payments?

4. Most U.S. imports and exports travel through our seaports at some point. How do you predict that members of Congress from coastal states would vote on proposals to restrict international trade? What other information would you want to know when making such a prediction?

5. When you go shopping for a new computer, is your real objective to "import" a computer into your apartment, or is it to "export" cash from your wallet? What does this tell you about the true object of international trade—is it imports or exports?

6. Some U.S. policy is designed to subsidize exports and thus increase employment in export industries. What effect does such policy have on our imports of foreign goods and thus on employment in industries that compete with imports?

CHAPTER 30

The Lion, the Dragon, and the Future

For decades after the Communists' rise to power in 1949, China was best known for poverty and repression, and its aggression came mostly on the military front. But in recent years, *economic* aggression has become the byword. Although both poverty and repression are still the norm, both are changing for the better. China, it seems, is trying to learn from capitalism, even if not converting to it.

THE AWAKENING OF CHINA

China's economic offensive began thirty years ago in its southeastern province of Guangdong. The Chinese leadership decided to use this province as a test case, to see if capitalist **direct foreign investment** could stimulate **economic growth** in a way that could be politically controlled. The experience was deemed a success—economic growth soared amid political stability. What the government learned from the experience helped it smooth the 1997 transition of Hong Kong from British to Chinese control. Most important in terms of China's long-term economic aspirations, many foreign investors came to view the Guangdong experiment as solid evidence that they could invest in China without fear that the Communist government would confiscate their capital. The result: Foreign investment in China soared.

There are two powerful forces that are attracting economic investment to China: **demand** and **supply.** On the demand side, almost 1.4 billion people live there, some 20 percent of the world's population. Although **per capita income** is still low by world standards, it has been increasing by more than 6 percent per year, after adjusting for inflation. At that rate, the standard of living for the Chinese people—and hence their **purchasing power** in world markets—is doubling every decade or so. China is already the world's largest cell-phone market, and China will soon account for 25 percent of the world's purchases of personal computers. Indeed, China now spends over $150 billion per year on information technology and services. By 2030, the Chinese economy will likely have eclipsed the United States' and become the world's largest.

With its huge population, China also offers attractions on the supply side. Highly skilled workers have been plentiful in the Chinese labor market with hundreds of thousands of engineering graduates each year. In many cities, the fact that the Chinese workforce is generally well educated and often English-speaking has helped make the country attractive to foreign employers. Collaborative scientific ventures between Chinese researchers and U.S. firms are becoming increasingly common. A research team at Beijing University played a role in deciphering the genetic makeup of rice, for example. American computer hardware and software firms Intel, IBM, Oracle, and Microsoft have shifted some key components of their research to China in recent years. Indeed, American firms of all types are setting up operations in China. Chinese firms, meanwhile, are proving to be formidable competitors both at home and abroad.

CONCERNS IN OTHER NATIONS

The situation has become critical in Japan, where wages are much higher than in China but whose technological lead over China is gradually eroding. "Are we to become a vassal of the Chinese dynasty again?" asked one Japanese official, clearly concerned that his nation's manufacturing firms were having trouble competing with Chinese firms. Eventually, Japanese firms will adjust to the growing economic presence of China, but the transition may be unpleasant.

Americans are more concerned about the likely impact on the U.S. economy of China's capitalist ambitions. Will the dragon consume American firms and jobs as it grows? The short answer is no. The long answer has two elements. To this point, a key element of China's competitiveness has been the low wages there. Even though American and European firms operating in China choose to pay their workers more than state-owned enterprises pay, this has still yielded considerable savings. As recently as ten years ago, unskilled and semiskilled labor in China cost only 25 percent as much as in Europe. Moreover, in the past, foreign firms have been able to hire engineers for salaries that are only 10–20 percent of the cost of hiring engineers in the West.

Markets in China

Labor markets in China are changing rapidly, however. Between 2000 and 2010, average real wages rose 60 percent, with bigger increases among higher-skilled workers. Many firms were unable to hire as many workers as they would have liked, and most firms had to upgrade their fringe benefits and other on-the-job amenities just to retain existing workers. Wages are still well below American and European levels, but the gap has closed, thereby cutting the competitive advantage of many Chinese firms. The recent worldwide recession has altered labor market conditions in China as it has elsewhere. But it is unlikely to impede China's march to economic superpower status.

Higher wages in China will also translate into higher demand for goods produced by American and European firms. China, like all nations, must in the long run import goods equal in value to those it exports (unless China intends to give its exports away, which so far no one is claiming). This means that just as China has become a potent supplier of many goods and services, it is at the same time becoming a potent demander of still other goods and services.

Thus far, the Chinese demand for goods has not been as visible in American markets because American firms tend to produce goods and services designed for higher-income consumers, and China has relatively few of those. In the meantime, the demand-side influence of the Chinese economy is already showing up, albeit in odd places. To take one example, right now China's most important import from the United States is trash. Ranging from used newspapers to scrap steel, Chinese companies buy billions of dollars' worth of the stuff every year to use as raw materials in the goods they produce. In addition to yielding profits (and employment) in these U.S. export industries, this exportation of U.S. trash reduces the burden on U.S. landfills and, by pushing up the prices of recyclable scrap, encourages more recycling in the United States.

Eventually, of course, we'd like to be sending China more than our rubbish, and that time is coming. As China's economy grows, so will the number of affluent Chinese, and with 1.4 billion potential candidates, that ultimately means *plenty* of consumers for America's high-end goods. Thus, the long-run effects of China's growth will mean a different American economy—we'll be producing and consuming different mixes of goods and services—but America will also be a richer nation. Voluntary exchange creates wealth, and the Chinese dragon is big enough to create a lot of wealth.

THE LION OF INDIA

To China's southwest, another giant is stirring. Around 1990, the lion of India began to throw off the self-imposed shackles of nearly a half century of markets largely closed to international **competition.** The central government, for example, began opening state-owned companies to competition from private-sector rivals. FedEx and United Parcel Service (UPS) have made huge inroads on the Indian postal service, and numerous foreign firms are now competing with the state-owned telephone service, which had long been a complete **monopoly.**

Entry into the Indian market brought familiarity with its workforce, many of whose members are fluent in English. The technical capabilities of graduates of top Indian universities, combined with their English skills and low wages, made them perfect staffers for a proliferation of call centers that have opened throughout India. Tens of thousands of technical and customer relations jobs that used to go to Middle America are now held by the growing middle class in India. It was in many respects this very movement that brought **outsourcing** into the American consciousness.

But India, too, is struggling with growth. The talent pool at the top is thin: Only a dozen or so of India's seventeen thousand universities and colleges can compete with America's best, and the wages of graduates of these top schools are soaring. Moreover, India suffers from overwhelming infrastructure problems: Much of its road system is either overcrowded or in disrepair, and its port facilities are in desperate need of modernization. For the time being, such transportation problems are likely to keep India from becoming a major manufacturing powerhouse. India has also been hampered by its huge and seemingly permanent government bureaucracy. For example, despite the fact that the postal service there has lost more than half of its business to newcomers such as FedEx and UPS, none of the 550,000 postal service employees can be fired.

CAPITALISM VERSUS COMMUNISM

At least India is a democracy, and its legal system, inherited from the British, who ruled there for so long, is in close conformity with the legal systems of most developed nations. Matters are rather different in China. As noted in Chapter 5, political and legal **institutions** are crucial foundations for sustained economic growth. Despite the advances China has made over the past thirty years, its wealth-creating future may be clouded unless it can successfully deal with two fundamental institutional issues.

First, there is the matter of resolving the tension inherent when a Communist dictatorship tries to use capitalism as the engine of economic growth. Capitalism thrives best in an environment of freedom and itself creates an awareness of and appreciation for the benefits of that freedom. Yet freedom is antithetical to the ideological and political tenets of the Communist government of China. Will the government be tempted to confiscate the fruits of capitalist success to support itself? Or will growing pressure for more political freedom force the government to repress the capitalist system to protect itself? Either route would likely bring economic growth in China to a swift halt.

The second potential long-run problem faced by China lies in that nation's cultural attitude toward **intellectual property.** In a land in which imitation is viewed as the sincerest form of flattery, it is routine to use the ideas of others in one's own pursuits. As a result, patent and copyright laws in China are far weaker than in Western nations. Moreover, actions elsewhere considered to be commercial theft (such as software piracy) are largely tolerated in China. If foreign firms find that they cannot protect their economic **assets** in the Chinese market, foreign investment will suffer accordingly, and so will the growing dragon that depends on it so heavily.

DISCUSSION QUESTIONS

1. Currently, AIDS is spreading rapidly in China and India. If the governments of these nations fail to stop the spread of AIDS, what are the likely consequences for future economic growth in China and India?

2. In 1989, a massive protest against political repression in China was halted by the government's massacre of more than 150 individuals at Tiananmen Square in Beijing. What impact do you think that episode had on foreign investment and growth in China during the years immediately thereafter?

3. Most of the advances in institutions in China have come in the cities rather than in the countryside. Indeed, local officials in farming villages actively redistribute wealth among villagers to keep the distribution of income among local farmers roughly equal. Thus, a farmer's success or failure with his crops has little impact on his family's standard of living. Given these facts, where do you think the economic growth in China has occurred over the past thirty years, in the cities or on the farms? Explain.

4. Explain how the following factors will influence India's ability to succeed in a highly competitive, rapidly changing global marketplace: (a) an educational system that is largely state-operated and that emphasizes job security for teachers and professors; (b) a transportation infrastructure that is largely antiquated and in disrepair; and (c) a political system that is adept at protecting favored constituents from competition and handing out favors that have concentrated benefits and widely dispersed costs.

5. How does protection of rights to intellectual property help promote innovation?

6. What are the central threats to future economic growth in China and India?

Glossary

absolute advantage: the ability to produce more of a good, without regard for the costs of forgone output of other goods

acreage-restriction program: a federal government limit on the number of acres that a farmer can plant with a particular crop

adjustable-rate mortgages (ARMs): debt obligations for which houses serve as the collateral and on which the lender may move the interest rate up or down by specified amounts at specified times

adverse selection: a process in which "undesirable" (high-cost or high-risk) participants tend to dominate one side of the market, causing adverse effects for the other side; often results from *asymmetric information*

assets: all tangible and intangible items to which an individual or institution holds a legal claim of ownership

asymmetric information: circumstance in which participants on one side of a market have more information than participants on the other side of the market; often results in *adverse selection*

bank run: the simultaneous attempt by many of a bank's depositors to convert checkable and savings deposits into currency because of a perceived fear for the bank's solvency

biofuels: fuels made from once-living organisms or their by-products

capital stock: the collection of productive assets that can be combined with other inputs, such as labor, to produce goods and services

cartel: a group of independent businesses, often on an international scale, that agree to restrict trade, to their mutual benefit

civil law system: a legal system in which statutes passed by legislatures and executive decrees, rather than judicial decisions based on precedent, form the basis for most legal rules

common law system: a legal system in which judicial decisions based on precedent, rather than executive decrees or statutes passed by legislatures, form the basis for most legal rules

comparative advantage: the ability to produce a good at a lower opportunity cost than others; the principle of comparative advantage implies that individuals, firms, and nations will specialize in producing goods for which they have the lowest opportunity cost compared to other entities

compensating differential: additional pay given to workers employed in particularly hazardous or unpleasant jobs

competition: rivalry among buyers or sellers of outputs or among buyers or sellers of inputs

constant-dollar price: price corrected for changes in the purchasing power of the dollar, taking inflation and deflation into account

constant-quality price: the price of a good adjusted upward or downward to reflect the higher- or lower-than-average quality of that good

consumer price index: a measure of the dollar cost of a typical bundle of consumer goods relative to the cost of that bundle in a base year

cost: the highest-valued (best) forgone alternative; the most valuable option that is sacrificed when a choice is made

demand: the willingness and ability to purchase goods

demand curve: a graphic representation of demand—a negatively sloped line showing the inverse relationship between the price and the quantity demanded

direct foreign investment: resources provided to individuals and firms in a nation by individuals or firms located in other countries, often taking the form of foreign subsidiary or branch operations of a parent company

disposable income: the maximum amount of spending consumers can undertake after they have paid direct taxes, such as income taxes

dynamic analysis: an assessment of the economic impact of a policy that takes into account the induced responses to that policy

Earned Income Tax Credit: a tax policy that offers payments from the government to people who earn relatively low wages

economic good: any good or service that is scarce

economic growth: sustained increases over time in real per capita income

economic profits: profits in excess of competitive profits, which are the minimum necessary to keep resources employed in an industry

elastic demand: characteristic of a demand curve in which a given percentage change in price will result in a larger inverse percentage change in quantity demanded; total revenues and price are inversely related in the elastic portion of the demand curve

elasticity: a measure of the responsiveness of one variable to a change in another variable; it is the ratio of two percentage changes

elasticity of demand: responsiveness of the quantity of a commodity demanded to a change in its price per unit

elasticity of supply: responsiveness of the quantity of a commodity supplied to a change in its price per unit

entitlement program: a government program that guarantees a certain level of benefits to persons who meet the requirements set by law

equilibrium price: price that clears the market when there is no excess quantity demanded or supplied; the price at which the demand curve intersects the supply curve; also called market-clearing price

exports: sales of goods or services to a foreign country

externalities: benefits or costs of an economic activity that spill over to a third party; pollution is a negative spillover or externality

fixed exchange rates: a system of legally fixed prices (rates) at which two or more national currencies trade (exchange) for one another

foreclosure: the legal process by which a borrower in default under a mortgage is deprived of his or her interest in the mortgaged property

free good: any good or service available in larger quantities than desired at a zero price

full cost: the combined measure of all of the things that must be given up to undertake an activity; includes both the money price (other goods that must be sacrificed) and the value of the time that must be sacrificed

gains from trade: the extent to which individuals, firms, or nations benefit by engaging in exchange

globalization: the integration of national economies into an international economy as a result of lower trade barriers and reduced transportation and communication costs

human capital: the accumulated training, education, and knowledge of workers

illiquid: not readily convertible to cash

import tariff: a tax applied specifically to imports of goods or services from another nation

imports: purchases of goods or services from a foreign country

in-kind transfers: grants of goods and services rather than cash to recipients who meet certain criteria; examples include Medicare, Medicaid, subsidized housing, food stamps, and school lunches

incentives: perceived consequences of actions or decisions; they may be positive or negative, monetary or nonmonetary

income elasticity of demand: a measure of the responsiveness of demand to changes in income, calculated as the percentage change in demand for a good divided by the percentage change in consumer income

income mobility: the tendency of individuals to move around in the income distribution over time

inelastic: relatively unresponsive

inelastic demand: characteristic of a demand curve in which a given change in price will result in a less than proportionate inverse change in the quantity demanded; total revenue and price are directly related in the inelastic region of the demand curve

inflation: a rise in the dollar cost of achieving a given level of satisfaction, often measured in terms of the dollar cost of a particular standard bundle of goods

insolvent: in a financial condition in which the value of one's assets is less than the value of one's liabilities

institutions: the basic rules, customs, and practices of society

intellectual property: creative ideas and expressions of the human mind that have commercial value and receive the legal protection of a property right, as through the issuance of a patent, copyright, or trademark

labor force participation rate:the sum of all people who are working or are available for and looking for work, divided by the population; both numerator and denominator are generally restricted to persons aged 16 and above

law of demand: law stating that quantity demanded and price are inversely related—more is bought at a lower price and less at a higher price (other things being equal)

law of supply: law stating that a direct relationship exists between price and quantity supplied (other things being equal)

liabilities: amounts owed; monetary claims against an individual or an institution

luxury good: a good for which the income elasticity of demand is greater than 1, meaning that people spend an increasing proportion of their income on the good as they get richer

marginal analysis: analysis of what happens when small changes take place relative to the status quo

marginal benefits: additional benefits associated with one more unit of a good or action; the change in total benefits due to the addition of one more unit of production

marginal costs: changes in total costs due to a change in one unit of production

market-clearing price: *see* "equilibrium price"

market share: the proportion of total sales in an industry accounted for by a specific firm or group of firms in that industry

market supply: total quantities of a good offered for sale by suppliers at various prices

median age: age that exactly separates the younger half of the population from the older half

minimum wage: the lowest hourly wage that firms may legally pay their workers

models, or theories: simplified representations of the real world used to make predictions or to better understand the real world

monitoring costs: costs that must be incurred to observe the behavior of a politician or other agent to whom responsibilities have been delegated

monopolistic competition: the situation that exists when producers and sellers offer for sale similar products with slight variations in features or quality; although the products are priced above their average minimum cost, competition among firms reduces long-run economic profits to zero

monopoly: a single supplier; a firm that faces a downward-sloping demand curve for its output and therefore can choose the price at which it will sell the good; an example of a price searcher

monopoly power: the ability of a company to charge a price for its product that is in excess of the marginal cost of producing the product

monopsonist: a firm operating as a monopsony

monopsony: a single buyer; a firm that faces an upward-sloping supply curve for its input and therefore can choose the price at which it will buy the good; an example of a price searcher

moral hazard: the tendency of an entity insulated from risk to behave differently than it would behave if it were fully exposed to the risk

natural resource endowments: the collection of naturally occurring minerals (such as oil and iron ore) and living things (such as forests and fish stocks) that can be used to produce goods and services

negative externality: a cost associated with an economic activity that is paid by third parties; pollution is a negative externality because, for example, someone other than the driver of an automobile bears part of the cost of the car's exhaust emissions

negative tax: a payment from the government made to supplement the incomes of people who earn low wages

nominal prices: the costs of goods, expressed in terms of a nation's currency, such as the dollar

nonprice competition: offering additional services or higher product quality to attract business instead of cutting prices to do so

oligopoly: a firm that is one of very few sellers (or buyers) in a market; in such a case, each firm reacts to changes in the prices and quantities of its rivals

opportunity cost: the highest-valued alternative that must be sacrificed to attain something or to satisfy a want

outsourcing: the practice of having workers located in foreign lands perform tasks (typically services) that have traditionally been performed by domestic workers

per capita income: average income per person

perfectly elastic: characterized by an infinite value for the ratio of the percentage change in quantity over the percentage change in price; visually, a perfectly inelastic curve appears horizontal

perfectly inelastic: characterized by a zero value for the ratio of the percentage change in quantity over the percentage change in price; visually, a perfectly inelastic curve appears vertical

physical capital: nonhuman productive resources

political economy: the study of the causes and consequences of political decision making

price discrimination: selling at prices that do not reflect differences in marginal costs; different prices with the same marginal costs, for example, or the same prices with different marginal costs

price elasticity of demand: the percentage change in quantity demanded divided by the percentage change in price; see also "elasticity of demand"

price elasticity of supply: the percentage change in quantity supplied divided by the percentage change in price; see also "elasticity of supply"

price searcher: a firm that must search for the profit-maximizing price because it faces a downward-sloping demand curve (if it is a seller) or an upward-sloping supply curve (if it is a buyer); often used as a synonym for monopoly or monopsony

price-support program: a government program that mandates minimum prices for crops

price taker: any economic agent that takes the market price as given; often used as a synonym for a firm operating in a market characterized by *pure competition*

private costs: costs incurred by the relevant decision maker

product differentiation: distinguishing products by brand name, color, and other minor attributes

productivity: output produced per unit of input

profit: income generated by selling something for a higher price than was paid for it; in production, the income generated is the difference between total revenues received from consumers who purchase the goods and the total cost of producing those goods

property and contract rights: legal rules governing the use and exchange of property and enforceable agreements between people or businesses

property rights: set of rules specifying how a good may be used and exchanged

protectionism: the imposition of rules designed to protect certain individuals or firms from competition, usually competition from imported goods

proven reserves: estimated quantities of oil and gas that geological and engineering data demonstrate with reasonable certainty to be recoverable in future years from known reservoirs under existing economic and operating conditions

purchasing power: ability or means to acquire goods and services

pure competition: a market structure in which participants individually have no influence over market prices; all act as price takers

quota: a limit on the amount of a good or an activity; often used in international trade to limit the amount of some foreign good that may be imported into a country

rate of return: the net benefit, in percentage terms, of engaging in an activity; for example, if the investment of $1.00 yields a gross return of $1.20, the net benefit is $0.20 and the rate of return is $0.20/$1.00 = 20 percent

rational ignorance: a state in which knowledge is incomplete because obtaining perfect information is too costly

real per capita income: gross domestic product (GDP) corrected for inflation and divided by population

real price: a price that is adjusted for inflation and is expressed in terms of some base year

relative prices: the costs of goods, expressed in terms of other goods or in terms of a basic bundle of goods

rent control: a system in which the government tells building owners how much they can charge for rent

resource: any input used in the production of desired goods and services

revealed preferences: the likes and dislikes of consumers, as demonstrated by the choices they make in the marketplace

rule of law: the principle that relations between individuals, businesses, and the government are governed by clearly enumerated rules that apply to everyone in society

scarce: not free; something must be sacrificed to obtain

scarce good: any good that commands a positive price

scarcity: state of nature in which resources are limited even though wants are unlimited; scarcity means that nature does not freely provide as much of everything as people want

shortage: situation in which an excess quantity is demanded or an insufficient quantity is supplied; the difference between the quantity demanded and the quantity supplied at a specific price below the market-clearing price

social cost: the full cost that society bears when a resource-using action occurs; for example, the social cost of driving a car is equal to all private costs plus any additional cost that other members of society bear (such as air pollution and traffic congestion)

solvent: in a financial condition in which the value of one's assets is greater than the value of one's liabilities

static analysis: any assessment of the economic impact of a policy that does not fully take into account the induced responses to that policy

stock: the quantity of something at a particular point in time; an inventory of goods is a stock, as is a bank account at a point in time; stocks are defined independent of time, although they are assessed at a point in time

subsidies: government payments for the production of specific goods, generally designed to raise the profits of the firms receiving the subsidies and often intended to increase the output of the subsidized goods

supply: the willingness and ability to sell goods

supply curve: a graphic representation of supply, which slopes upward (has a positive slope), reflecting the positive relationship between price and quantity supplied

supply schedule: a set of prices and the quantity supplied at each price; a schedule showing the rate of planned production at each relative price for a specified time period

support price: the minimum price that farmers are guaranteed to receive for their crop, as set by the federal government; if the market price falls below the support price, the government purchases enough of the crop to bring the market price up to the support price

surplus: excess quantity supplied or an insufficient quantity demanded; the difference between the quantity supplied and the quantity demanded at a price above the market-clearing price; as applied to the government budget, an excess of tax receipts over expenditures

target price: the minimum price that farmers are guaranteed to receive for their crop, as set by the federal government; if the market price falls below the target price, farmers receive a payment equal to the difference between the two (multiplied by their production of the crop)

tariff: a tax levied on imports

tax credit: an offset against current or future income taxes

tax rate: proportion of the value of the taxed item that is collected in taxes

tax revenue: total dollar value of taxes collected

technological change: a change in the set of feasible production possibilities, typically the result of the productive implementation of new knowledge

trade barriers: any rules having the effect of reducing the amount of international exchange; tariffs and quotas are trade barriers

trade-off: term relating to opportunity cost. In order to get a desired economic good, it is necessary to trade off (give up) some other desired economic good in a situation of scarcity; a trade-off involves making a sacrifice in order to obtain something

transaction costs: costs of conducting exchanges of goods

Type I error: an error of commission, such as might arise when an unsafe drug is mistakenly permitted to be sold

Type II error: an error of omission, such as might arise if a beneficial drug is mistakenly prevented from reaching the market

user fees: charges imposed for the use of a good or service; often applied to the charges applied by governments for the use of government-owned resources, ranging from roads to parks

voucher: a document that authorizes a person to receive a specified dollar amount of services at no charge

white-collar jobs: employment in which workers rely chiefly on their intellect and knowledge rather than their physical skills

World Trade Organization (WTO): an association of more than 145 nations that helps reduce trade barriers among its members and settles international trade disputes among them

zone pricing: setting different retail prices in different geographic areas, depending on the characteristics of customers in those areas; a practice of major oil companies

SELECTED REFERENCES

Chapter 1   Death by Bureaucrat

Kazman, Sam. "Deadly Overcaution: FDA's Drug Approval Process." *Journal of Regulation and Social Cost* 1, no. 1 (1990): 35–54.

Peltzman, Sam. "An Evaluation of Consumer Protection Legislation: The 1962 Drug Amendments." *Journal of Political Economy* 81, no. 1 (1973): 1049–1091.

Walker, Steven. "S.O.S. to the FDA." *Wall Street Journal Online*, August 26, 2003. (http://online.wsj.com/article/SB106185410295150100-search.html)

Chapter 2   The Economics of Oil Spills

Casselman, Ben, and Russel Gold. "BP Decisions Sets Stage for Disaster." *wsj.com*, May 27, 2010.

Committee on Oil in the Sea, National Research Council. *Brief Report from Oil in the Sea III: Inputs, Fates, and Effects*. Washington, D.C.: The National Academic Press, 2002.

Green, Kenneth P., and Steven F. Hayward. "The Dangers of Overreacting to the Deepwater Horizon Disaster." In *Energy and Environment Outlook*. Washington, D.C.: American Enterprise Institute, June 2010.

National Oceanic and Atmospheric Administration (NOAA), Office of Response and Restoration. "Oil Spills in History." (http://response.restoration.NOAA.gov)

"Oil Rig Disasters: Offshore Drilling Accidents." (www.oilrigdisasters.co.uk)

Chapter 3   Supersize It

Kuchler, Fran, and Elise Golan. "Is There a Role for Government in Reducing Overweight and Obesity?" *Choices* (Fall 2004): 41–45.

Loureiro, Mauro. "Obesity: Economic Dimensions of a "Super Size" Problem." *Choices* (Fall 2004): 35–39.

Ogden, Cynthia L., et al. "Prevalence of Overweight and Obesity in the United States, 1999–2004." *Journal of the American Medical Association* 295, no. 13 (April 2006): 1549–1555.

Philpson, Tomas, Carolanne Dai, Lorens Helmshen, and J. N. Variyam. *The Economics of Obesity: A Report of the Workshop Held at USDA's Economic Research Service.* E-FAN-04-004, Economic Research Service. Washington, D.C.: USDA, 2004.

Chapter 4   Flying the Friendly Skies?

Mitchell, Mark L., and Michael T. Maloney. "Crisis in the Cockpit? The Role of Market Forces in Promoting Air Travel Safety." *Journal of Law and Economics* 32, no. 2 (1989): 139–184.

www.airsafe.com. Statistics on airline safety.

www1.faa.gov. Official Web site of the Federal Aviation Administration.

Chapter 5   The Mystery of Wealth

Easterly, William, and Ross Levine. "Tropics, Germs, and Crops: How Endowments Influence Economic Development." *Journal of Monetary Economics* 50, no. 1 (2003): 3–39.

Mahoney, Paul G. "The Common Law and Economic Growth: Hayek Might Be Right." *Journal of Legal Studies* 30, no. 3 (2001): 503–525.

Chapter 6   Sex, Booze, and Drugs

Becker, Gary, Kevin M. Murphy, and Michael Grossman. "The Market for Illegal Goods: The Case of Drugs." *Journal of Political Economy* 114, no. 1 (2006): 38–60.

Benjamin, Daniel K., and Roger LeRoy Miller. *Undoing Drugs: Beyond Legalization.* New York: Basic Books, 1993.

Hardy, Quentin. "Inside Dope." *Forbes*, November 10, 2003, pp. 146–154.

Miron, Jeffrey A., and Jeffrey Zwiebel. "Alcohol Consumption during Prohibition." *American Economic Review* 81, no. 2 (1991): 242–247.

Chapter 7   Kidneys for Sale

Adler, Jerry. "Are Kidneys a Commodity?" *Newsweek*, May 26, 2008.

Harrington, David E., and Edward A. Sayre. "Paying for Bodies, But Not for Organs." *Regulation*, Winter 2006–2007, pp. 14–19.

Meckler, Laura. "A Shortage of Available Kidneys Inspires a Radical Idea: Organ Sales." *Wall Street Journal*, November 16, 2007.

"The Gap between Supply and Demand." *Economist*, October 9, 2008.

Chapter 8   Are We Running Out of Water?

Anderson, Terry, and Pamela S. Snyder. *Water Markets: Priming the Invisible Pump*. Washington, D.C.: Cato Institute, 1997.

Casselman, Ben. "Desperate Sprinklers." *Wall Street Journal*, July 20, 2007.

Libecap, Gary. *Owens Valley Revisited: A Reassessment of the West's First Great Water Transfer*. Stanford, CA: Stanford University Press, 2007.

Santos, Fernanda. "Inch by Inch, Great Lakes Shrink, and Cargo Carriers Face Losses." *New York Times*, October 22, 2007.

Yardley, Jim. "Beneath Booming Cities, China's Future Is Drying Up." *New York Times*, September 28, 2007.

Chapter 9   The (Dis)Incentives of Higher Taxes

Feenberg, Daniel R., and James M. Poterba. "The Alternative Minimum Tax and Effective Marginal Tax Rates." *National Tax Journal* 57, no. 2 (2004): 407–427.

Harberger, Arnold. *Taxation and Welfare*. New York: Little, Brown and Company, 1974.

Mitchell, Daniel J. "What Can the United States Learn from the Nordic Model?" *Cato Institute Policy Analysis*, November 5, 2007.

Chapter 10   Bankrupt Landlords, from Sea to Shining Sea

Downs, Anthony. *Residential Rent Controls: An Evaluation*. Washington, D.C.: Urban Land Institute, 1988.

Glaeser, Edward L., and Erzo F. P. Luttmer. "The Misallocation of Housing under Rent Control." *American Economic Review* 93, no. 4 (2003): 1027–1046.

Chapter 11   (Why) Are Women Paid Less?

Becker, Elizabeth, and Cotton M. Lindsay. "The Limits of the Wage Impact of Discrimination." *Managerial and Decision Economics* 26 (2005): 513–525.

Becker, Gary. *The Economics of Discrimination*. Chicago: University of Chicago Press, 1957.

Heckman, James J. "Detecting Discrimination." *Journal of Economic Perspectives* 12, no. 1 (1998): 101–116.

Chapter 12   The Effects of the Minimum Wage

Baker, Michael, Dwayne Benjamin, and Shuchita Stanger. "The Highs and Lows of the Minimum Wage Effects: A Time-Series Cross-Section Study of the Canadian Law." *Journal of Labor Economics* 17, no. 2 (1999): 318–350.

Card, David, and Alan Krueger. "Minimum Wages and Employment: A Case Study of the Fast-Food Industry in New Jersey and Pennsylvania." *American Economic Review* 84, no. 3 (1994): 772–793.

Neumark, David, and William Wascher. "Minimum Wages and Employment: A Case Study of the Fast-Food Industry in New Jersey and Pennsylvania: Comment." *American Economic Review* 90, no. 5 (2000): 1362–1396.

Rottenberg, Simon (ed.). *The Economics of Legal Minimum Wages.* Washington, D.C.: American Enterprise Institute, 1981.

Chapter 13   Immigration, Superstars, and Poverty

Borjas, George. *Heaven's Door: Immigration Policy and the American Economy.* Princeton, NJ: Princeton University Press, 2001.

Rosen, Sherwin. "The Economics of Superstars." *American Economic Review* 71, no. 5 (1981): 845–858.

U.S. Bureau of the Census. "The Effects of Government Taxes and Transfers on Income and Poverty, 2004." April 27, 2006. (www.census.gov/hhes/www/poverty/effect2004/effect2004.html)

Chapter 14   The Underground World

Barta, Patrick. "The Rise of the Underground Economy." *Wall Street Journal*, March 14–15, 2009, pp. W1–W2.

Caruso, David B. *In NYC, Cash and Connections Can Get You a Kidney.* Associated Press, August 20, 2009.

Embaye, Abel. *Underground Economy Estimates for Non-OECD Countries Using Currency Demand Method.* MPRA Paper no. 20308. January 2010.

Feige, Edgar L. *New Estimates of Overseas U.S. Currency Holdings, the Underground Economy, and the Tax Gap.* MPRA Paper no. 19564. December 2009.

Chapter 15   Patent Trolls and Seed Monopolies

Benjamin, Daniel K., and Roger C. Kormendi. "The Interrelationship between the Markets for New and Used Durable Goods." *Journal of Law and Economics* 17, no. 2 (October 1974): 381–402.

Neuman, William. "Rapid Rise in Seed Prices Draws U.S. Scrutiny." *New York Times*, March 11, 2010.

Pollack, Andrew. "Study Says Overuse Threatens Gains from Modified Crops." *New York Times*, April 15, 2010.

Varchaver, Nicholas. "Who's Afraid of Nathan Myhrvold?" *CNNMoney.com*, June 26, 2006. (Accessed October 31, 2010)

Chapter 16   Contracts, Combinations, and Conspiracies

Kanfer, Steven. *The Last Empire: DeBeers, Diamonds, and the World.* New York: Farrar, Straus & Giroux, 1993.

www.eia.doe.gov. Official Web site of the Energy Information Administration.

Zimbalist, Andrew. *Unpaid Professionals: Commercialism and Conflict in Big-Time College Sports.* Princeton, NJ: Princeton University Press, 2001.

Chapter 17   Coffee, Tea, or Tuition-Free?

Chevalier, Judith, and Austan Goolsbee. "Measuring Prices and Price Competition Online: Amazon.com versus BarnesandNoble.com." *Quantitative Marketing and Economics* 1, no. 2 (2003): 203–222.

Odlyzko, Andrew. *Privacy, Economics, and Price Discrimination on the Internet.* St. Paul: University of Minnesota, Digital Technology Center, 2003.

"They're Watching You." *Economist*, October 18, 2003, p. 77.

Chapter 18   Keeping the Competition Out

Lipton, Eric. "Finding the Intersection of Supply and Demand." *New York Times*, November 23, 2003, p. 31.

www.schallerconsult.com/taxi/topics.htm. Facts on the New York City taxicab and taxi medallion markets.

Chapter 19   Health Care Reform

Cummings, N. A., and W. T. O'Donohue (eds.). *Understanding the Behavioral Healthcare Crisis: The Promise of Integrated Care and Diagnostic Reform.* Routledge Press, 2011.

Esmail, Nadeem. *Waiting Your Turn: Hospital Waiting Lists in Canada*, 19th ed. Vancouver: Fraser Institute, October 2009.

Hill, Brian E. *Stop the Noise: A Physician's Quest to Silence the Politics of Health Care Reform.* Santa Ana, CA: Griggen Publishing Group, 2010.

Mackey, John. "The Whole Foods Alternative to ObamaCare." *Wall Street Journal,* August 29, 2009, Opinion page.

Merion, Noel. *Health Care (Current Controversies).* Cincinnati: Greenhaven Press, 2010.

Tanner, Michael. *Bad Medicine: A Guide to the Real Costs and Consequences of the New Health Care Law.* Cato Institute, 2011.

Chapter 20   The Pension Crisis

Brainard, Keith. *Public Fund Survey Summary of Findings for FY2009.* National Association of State Retirement Administrators, October 2010.

Dugan, Ianthe Jeanne. "Facing Budget Gaps, Cities Sell Parking, Airports, Zoo." *Wall Street Journal,* August 23, 2010.

Fitch, Stephan. "Guilt-Edged Pensions." *Forbes,* February 16, 2009, pp. 79–84.

Malanga, Steve. "How States Hide Their Budget Deficits." *Wall Street Journal,* August 23, 2010.

The PEW Center of the States. *The Trillion Dollar Gap: Unfunded State Retirement Systems and the Roads to Reform.* Washington, D.C.: The PEW Charitable Trust, February 2010.

Chapter 21   Mortgage Meltdown

Liebowitz, Stan J. *Anatomy of a Train Wreck.* The Independent Institute, October 3, 2008.

Lucchetti, Aaron, and Serena Ng. "Credit and Blame: How Rating Firms' Calls Fueled Subprime Mess—Benign View of Loans Helped Create Bonds, Led to More Lending." *Wall Street Journal,* August 15, 2007.

Simon, Ruth. "FirstFed Grapples with Payment-Option Mortgages." *Wall Street Journal,* August 6, 2008.

www.ofheo.gov/HPI.aspx. Web site of the Office of Federal Housing Enterprise Oversight.

www2.standardandpoors.com. Standard & Poor's/Case-Shiller home price indexes.

Chapter 22   Raising Less Corn and More Hell

Becker, Elizabeth. "U.S. Corn Subsidies Said to Damage Mexico: Study Finds Farmers Lose Livelihoods." *New York Times,* August 27, 2003, p. C4.

Edwards, Chris, and Dan DeHaven. *Save the Farms—End the Subsidies.* Washington, D.C.: Cato Institute, 2002.

Fackler, Martin. "Japanese Farmers Losing Clout." *Wall Street Journal,* February 20, 2004, p. A10.

Chapter 23   The Graying of America

Council of Economic Advisers. "Restoring Solvency to Social Security." *Economic Report of the President.* Washington, D.C.: Government Printing Office, 2004, Ch. 6.

Miron, Jeffrey A., and David N. Weil. "The Genesis and Evolution of Social Security." In *The Defining Moment: The Great Depression and the American Economy in the Twentieth Century,* eds. Michael D. Bordo, Claudia Goldin, and Eugene N. White. Chicago: University of Chicago Press, 1998, pp. 297–322.

Chapter 24   Save That Species

Anderson, Terry L., and Peter J. Hill. *The Not So Wild, Wild West: Property Rights on the Frontier.* Stanford: Stanford University Press, 2004.

Coase, Ronald. "The Problem of Social Cost." *Journal of Law and Economics* 3 (1960): 1–44.

Costello, Christopher, Steven D. Gaines, and John Lyman. "Can Catch Shares Prevent Fisheries Collapse?" *Science* 321, no. 5826 (September 2008): 1678–1681.

Grafton, R. Quentin, Dale Squires, and Kevin J. Fox. "Private Property and Economic Efficiency: A Study of A Common-Pool Resource." *Journal of Law & Economics* 43, no. 2 (2000): 679–713.

Lueck, Dean, and Jeffrey A. Michael. "Preemptive Habitat Destruction under the Endangered Species Act." *Journal of Law & Economics* 46, no. 1 (2003): 27–60.

Chapter 25   Greenhouse Economics

Bradsher, Keith. "China's Boom Adds to Global Warming Problem." *New York Times,* October 22, 2003, p. A1.

Castles, Ian, and David Henderson. "The IPCC Emission Scenarios: An Economic–Statistical Critique." *Energy and Environment* 14, nos. 2, 3 (2003): 159–185.

Lomborg, Bjorn. *The Skeptical Environmentalist.* New York: Cambridge University Press, 2001.

Sohngen, Brent, and Robert Mendelsohn. "Valuing the Impact of Large-Scale Ecological Change in a Market: The Effect of Climate Change on U.S. Timber." *American Economic Review* 89, no. 4 (1999): 686–710.

Chapter 26   Ethanol Madness

Barrionuevo, Alexei. "Boom in Ethanol Reshapes Economy of Heartland." *New York Times*, June 25, 2006, p. 1.
Environmental Protection Agency. *Regulatory Announcement: Removal of Reformulated Gasoline Oxygen Content Requirement and Revision of Commingling Prohibition to Address Non-Oxygenated Reformulated Gasoline.* Document no. EPA420-F-06–020. Washington, D.C.: Environmental Protection Agency, February 2006.
Tokgoz, Simla. "Policy and Competitiveness of U.S. and Brazilian Ethanol." *Iowa Ag Review Online*, Spring 2006. (www.card.iastate.edu/iowa_ag_review/spring_06/article3.aspx)
www.eia.doe.gov. Official Web site of the Energy Information Administration.

Chapter 27   The Trashman Cometh

Benjamin, Daniel K. *Recycling Myths Revisited.* no. PS-47. Bozeman, MT: Property and Environment Research Center, 2010.
Fullerton, Don, and Thomas C. Kinnaman. "Household Responses to Pricing Garbage by the Bag." *American Economic Review* 88, no. 2 (1996): 971–984.
Hocking, Martin B. "Paper versus Polystyrene: A Complex Choice." *Science* 251, no. 4993 (February 1991): 504–505.
Hocking, Martin B. "Disposable Cups Have Eco-Merit." *Nature* 369, no. 107 (May 1994): 107.
Rathje, William, and Cullen Murphy. *Rubbish: The Archeology of Garbage.* New York: HarperCollins, 1992.

Chapter 28   Globalization and the Wealth of America

Eichengreen, Barry. "The Political Economy of the Smoot–Hawley Tariff." *Research in Economic History* 12, no. 1 (1989): 1–43.
Federal Reserve Bank of Dallas. *The Fruits of Free Trade.* Annual Report. Dallas, TX: Federal Reserve Bank, 2002.
Irwin, Douglas A. "From Smoot–Hawley to Reciprocal Trade Agreements: Changing the Course of U.S. Trade Policy in the 1930s."

In *The Defining Moment: The Great Depression and the American Economy in the Twentieth Century*, eds. Michael D. Bordo, Claudia Goldin, and Eugene N. White. Chicago: University of Chicago Press, 1998, pp. 325–352.

Chapter 29   The $750,000 Steelworker

Berry, Steven, James Levinsohn, and Ariel Pakes. "Voluntary Export Restraints on Automobiles: Evaluating a Trade Policy." *American Economic Review* 89, no. 3 (1999): 400–430.

Crandall, Robert W. "The Effects of U.S. Trade Protection for Autos and Steel." *Brookings Papers on Economic Activity*, no. 1 (1987): 271–288.

Chapter 30   The Lion, the Dragon, and the Future

Eckholm, Erik, and Joseph Kahn. "China's Power Worries Neighbors." *New York Times*, December 1, 2002, p. 7.

Goodman, Peter S. "China Takes Pivotal Role in High-Tech Production." *International Herald Tribune*, December 5, 2002, p. 2.

Restall, Hugo. "New Property Rights for Chinese Farmers?" *Wall Street Journal Europe*, October 3–5, 2003, p. A7.

INDEX